RAND McNALLY

2025

Road Atlas

Contents

Travel Information

Mountain Retreats 2–7
Travel advice and tips to six of our editor's picks of favorite year-round mountain retreats.

Mileage and Driving Times Map
inside back cover
Distances and driving times between over a hundred North American cities.

Maps

Map legend inside front cover
United States overview map 8–9
U.S. states 10–109
Canada overview map 110–111
Canadian provinces 112–127
Mexico overview map and Puerto Rico 160
U.S. and Canadian cities 128–159

Mountain Retreats editorial contributors
Editorial Director Laura M. Kidder, Mount Hood by Holly Smith Peterson, Park City by Eric Peterson, Taos & The Sangre de Cristos by Eric Peterson, The Ozark Mountains by Gary McKechnie, The Great Smoky Mountains by Gary McKechnie, The Poconos by Dan Schlossberg.

Photo credits
p. 2 ©Thomas Goebal / Getty; p. 3 ©Sean Pavone / Getty; p. 4 (t to b) ©JacobH / Getty, ©Michael DeYoung / Getty; p. 5 ©Bauhaus1000 / Getty; p. 6 ©Ehrlif / Getty ; p. 7©Ali Majdfar / Getty.

©2024 Publishing Holdco, Inc., d/b/a Rand McNally Publishing. All rights reserved. Rand McNally is a trademark of RM Acquisition LLC. All other trademarks appearing in this publication are trademarks of third parties and are the responsibility of their respective owners.

Reproducing or recording maps, tables, text, or any other material that appears in this publication by photocopying, by electronic storage and retrieval, or by any other means is prohibited.

Rand McNally updates this Road Atlas annually, and every effort has been made to provide accurate information. Changes can and do occur, however, and we cannot be legally responsible for any errors, changes, omissions, or any loss, injury, or inconvenience sustained by any person or entity as a result of information or advice contained in this book.

For licensing information and copyright permissions, contact us at permissions@randmcnally.com.

If you have a comment, suggestion, or even a compliment, please contact us at printproducts@randmcnally.com.

randpublishing.com

RAND McNALLY PUBLISHING

State & Province Maps

City Maps

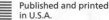 Published and printed in U.S.A.

1 2 3 4 WR 25 24

Mountain Retreats from the Pacific Summits to the Eastern Peaks

Mountains have a special place in the history of America and its travels. After all, we had to scale many a peak to establish the nation and then to expand it.

The six areas featured in this book are filled with travel experiences that tap into the thrills, beauty, and cultural heritage of America's mountain ranges. Whether you want to slide down a slippery slope or simply relax beside the fireplace of a grand lodge, you'll find a mountain retreat that's perfect on your travels across America.

MOUNT HOOD / CASCADE RANGE OREGON

Year-Round Powder Power!
The Mt. Hood region has the Pacific Northwest's best and most beautiful traits. The forbidding volcano itself spikes 11,239 feet skyward, its upper slopes sugared with snowfall year-round and its foothills blanketed with wildflowers in warmer months.

About two-thirds of the way up Mt. Hood, Skibowl is one of the nation's oldest ski resorts and the nation's largest night-skiing facility. Higher still, Timberline Lodge has the country's longest ski season: 10 months a year. In warmer months, you can hike, bike, or horseback ride to waterfalls and hot springs; go kayaking or whitewater rafting; and sample local offerings on farm, vineyard, or brewery tours.

Overnight Highlights
Regardless of the season, a visit to Mt. Hood should include time on the slopes. Not only does **Timberline Lodge & Ski Area** (27500 E. Timberline Rd., 503/272-3410, timberlinelodge.com) have snow year-round, it also has ski and snowboard runs (and lessons) for all levels and a groomed snowshoeing trail.

In winter, **Mt. Hood Meadows** (14040 Hwy. 35, 503/337-2222, skihood.com) has ski and snowboard runs that sprawl across the mountain's sunny, wind-protected, southern face. **Mt. Hood Skibowl** (87000 US 26, Government Camp, 503/272-3206, skibowl. com) welcomes skiers, snowboarders, and tubers to 960 acres of snowfields. Warmer-month adventures include zip-lining, bobsledding, horseback riding, mountain biking, rock climbing, and more.

A drive along the 105-mile **Mt. Hood Scenic Loop** (aka Mount Hood Scenic Byway, fhwa. dot.gov/byways) is an excellent way to get a feel for the region. At the very least, follow the loop 63 miles northwest from Government Camp to the must-see, 620-foot, two-tier Multnomah Falls and its elegantly arched Benson Bridge in the **Columbia River Gorge National Scenic Area** (541/308-1700, fs.usda.gov/crgnsa).

Trillium Lake and Mt. Hood

Getting Oriented
From the gateway city of Portland, it's a captivating 56-mile, 90-minute drive along I-84 and US 26 to Government Camp, the central town on Mt. Hood's slopes. **Sea to Summit Tours & Adventures** (503/286-9333, seatosummit.net) offers shuttle service from Portland International Airport (and other points in the city) to the mountain. **Mt. Hood Express** (503/668-3466, mthoodexpress.com) is a public bus service from the city of Sandy, 28 miles east of Portland, to Government Camp and Timberline Lodge.

Long-Weekend Additions
Mt. Hood Adventure (88220 Government Camp Loop Rd., Government Camp, 503/715-2175, mthoodadventure.com) offers everything from cross-country skiing and snowmobiling outings to kayaking and hiking adventures. Or book a sleigh ride, helicopter tour, or wine-tasting excursion.

Exhibits at the **Mt. Hood Cultural Center & Museum** (88900 Government Camp Loop Rd., Government Camp, 503/272-3301, mthoodmuseum.org) highlight skiing, pioneers, explorers, natural history, and regional art. The four-hour journey on the **Mt. Hood Railroad** (110 Railroad St., Hood River, 541/387-4000, mthoodrr.com) takes you through the Hood River valley, with views of both Mt. Hood and Washington State's Mt. Adams.

Eat & Stay
Blue Ox Bar. Housed in a one-time woodshed, this cozy pub at the Timberline Lodge is the perfect place to wind down with a hand-tossed pizza, light snacks, and microbrews from the Mt. Hood Brewing Co. 27500 E. Timberline Rd., Timberline Lodge, (503) 272-3391, timberlinelodge.com/dining.

Glacier Public House. The menu features hearty European fare (think beef goulash or schnitzel), pasta dishes, and pizza at this fun, friendly Alpine-style gasthaus set in the former Govy Country Store. 88817 E. Government Camp Loop Rd., Government Camp, (971) 275-8512, glacierpublichouse.com.

Mt. Hood Oregon Resort. In addition to a historic golf course, this resort has rooms with contemporary style and amenities, a spa, upscale restaurants, and mountain views. 68010 E. Fairway Ave., Welches, (503) 622-3101, mthood-resort.com.

Timberline Lodge. This 1937 National Historic Landmark, decorated in period style but with modern comforts, is a living museum of photos and memorabilia. It's also a maze of quiet nooks and crannies where you can curl up with a hot chocolate and a book. The slopes here are open ten months of the year. 27500 E. Timberline Rd., Timberline Lodge, (501) 272-3311, timberlinelodge.com.

LOCAL FOOD ALERT!

Marionberries
Known as the "king of the blackberries", marionberries are exclusively grown in Oregon. Developed in the 1940's in Marion County, marionberries ripen in July and are eagerly anticipated by locals and tourists alike. **Apple Valley Country Store** in Hood River offers fresh baked marionberry pies during season, and offers jams, pie fillings, & syrups year-round. applevaleystore.com

Wasatch Wonderland

The sheer amount of winter play land here is staggering: At 7,300 acres, Park City resort is the largest ski area in North America. Then there's chic, steep Deer Valley Resort, one of the most luxurious places in the Rockies to hit the slopes. Backcountry terrain, cross-country ski trails, and an outdoor ice-skating rink are additional draws.

Fans of the Olympics will want to explore the legacy of the 2002 Winter Games at Utah Olympic Park; at Park City resort, site of snowboarding events; and at Deer Valley, which hosted the moguls and slalom events. Come summer, the whole area is a magnet for hikers and mountain bikers. Year-round, Park City proper attracts window shoppers and foodies to its historic Main Street.

The Great Outdoors

In 2015, Vail Resorts acquired Park City Mountain Resort, and the result was **Park City** (1345 Lowell Ave., 435/649-8111, parkcitymountain.com), North America's single-largest ski resort. It's both big and diverse, with a range of terrain for all skill levels among its 300+ trails, 41 lifts, and 8 terrain parks. It's also popular with kids, thanks to attractions such as a mountain coaster and zip-line tours.

Not to be outdone, nearby **Deer Valley Resort** (2250 Deer Valley Dr. S., 435/649-1000, deervalley.com) is a ski-only resort (sorry, no snowboards allowed) known for its creamy groomed runs and luxury lodging and dining. The resort's 2,026 acres feature 42 trails and 21 lifts on 6 mountains.

Advanced and expert skiers can experience as many as six area resorts in a day with the **Ski Utah Interconnect Adventure Tour** (801/534-1907, skiutah.com), offered daily when conditions allow.

Both Park City and Deer Valley resorts have become increasingly popular warm-weather destinations, with lift-served mountain biking, scenic chairlift rides, hiking, horseback riding, and other activities. In addition, the Provo and Weber rivers are blue-ribbon trout streams and beloved by boaters. Head over to **Jans Fly Shop** (1600 Park Ave., 435/649-4949, jans.com) for gear, advice, or a guided fishing trip. **All Seasons Adventures** (435/649-9619, allseasonsadventures.com) offers white-water rafting on the Weber River.

Olympic Legacy

You can relive the 2002 Winter Olympic Games at **Utah Olympic Park** (3419 Olympic Pkwy., 435/658-4200, utaholympiclegacy. org/park). With six jumps, it's still an active Olympic training center for ski jumping and

Getting Oriented

Park City is in northern Utah's Wasatch Range, 33 miles east of Salt Lake City— location of the nearest major airport—via I-80 and UT 224. Downtown centers on Main Street, while the base areas for the town's namesake resort are on Lowell Avenue in Park City proper and on Canyons Resort Drive farther north. Deer Valley Resort's main base village is 1.5 miles southeast of downtown Park City via Deer Valley Drive.

aerials; athletes demonstrate their skills during regular shows. You can try "extreme tubing" on a ski jump, ride a zip line, or bobsled on the actual track used in the 2002 games.

The 389-acre park is also home to the **Alf Engen Ski Museum** (435/658-4240, engenmuseum.org), with interactive exhibits (don't miss the virtual ski jump) on the state's skiing history. The park has two sister facilities: **Utah Olympic Oval** (5662 Cougar Ln., Kearns, 801/968-6825), the speed-skating venue 40 miles west of Park City, and **Soldier Hollow Nordic Center** (2002 Soldier Hollow Ln., Midway, 435/654-2002), the cross-country skiing venue 22 miles south of Park City.

Arts & Culture

Worth an afternoon stroll, Park City's Main Street Historic District features beautifully restored storefronts with eateries and bars, shops and galleries, and museums and theaters—not to mention great mountain views. For cowboy hats, boots, and other duds, mosey over to **Burns Cowboy Shop** (336 Main St., 435/529-7484, burns1876. com). Open since 1965, **Meyer Gallery** (305 Main St., 435/649-8160, meyergallery.com) exhibits and sells primarily contemporary art in a wide range of media.

The **Park City Museum** (528 Main St., 435/649-7457, parkcityhistory.org) delves into the captivating history of a town that saw its fortunes rise and fall with silver before rising again thanks to the skiing and tourism industries.

The historic **Egyptian Theatre** (328 Main St., 855/745-7469, egyptiantheatrecompany. org) stages a mix of drama, comedy, and music productions.

Park City has a full calendar of special events. In January, the **Sundance Film Festival** (435/658-3456, festival.sundance.org), one of the world's top film festivals, takes over just about every venue in town. There's also the **Park City Beethoven Festival** (435/649-5309, beethovenfestivalparkcity.com) from

late June through mid-August and the summer-long **Deer Valley Music Festival** (801/533-6883, deervalleymusicfestival.org), with performances by the Utah Symphony and the Utah Opera at Deer Valley Resort.

Eat & Stay

High West Distillery & Saloon. In a restored garage a block off Main Street, the first distillery to open in Utah in more than a century serves creative entrées that you can pair with handcrafted cocktails made using its signature spirits. 703 Park Ave., (435) 649-8300, highwest.com.

The Mariposa. Open for dinner in ski season only, this inventive eatery perched mid-mountain at Deer Valley Resort is one of the top fine-dining destinations in Utah. The small-plates menu features seafood, pasta, beef, and game dishes. Silver Lake Village, 7600 Royal St., (435) 645-6632, deervalley.com.

Stein Eriksen Lodge. Named for its founder, the late Norwegian skier who won a gold medal in the 1952 Olympics in Oslo, Stein Eriksen Lodge has long epitomized ski-in, ski-out luxury lodging from its mid-mountain location at Deer Valley. 7700 Stein Way, (435) 649-3700, steinlodge.com.

Main Street, Park City

Utah Scones
Thought to have been brought to Utah by Mormon missionaries who worked on Native American reservations, the Utah Scone resembles more a fry bread than traditional scones. At **Park City Roadhouse Grill**, these light, airy concoctions are deep fried and served with powdered sugar and jam. parkcityroadhouse.com

TAOS & THE SANGRE DE CRISTOS NEW MEXICO

Turquoise, Paint & Rock

An intriguing blend of fine arts, riveting history, and mountain scenery, Taos is one of a kind. Taos Plaza, established in the late 1700s by Spanish settlers who arrived in the surrounding valley the century before, is the center of town. Just north of town, the Native American settlement at Taos Pueblo—established about 1,000 years ago—is one of the country's longest continuously inhabited communities.

Surrounded by natural beauty, Taos emerged as an outpost for artists in the early 20th century, when Georgia O'Keeffe and others put it on the creative map. Today, dozens of galleries showcase everything from watercolors to turquoise jewelry to cutting-edge contemporary works. One unmistakable inspiration: the stunning Sangre de Cristo Mountains (Spanish for "blood of Christ"), immediately east of Taos and the southernmost subrange of the Rocky Mountains.

Taos Culture

Historic **Taos Plaza** is a shady park surrounded by adobe storefronts that house galleries and souvenir shops. It's also a good starting point for a walking tour of the Taos Historic District. Three miles north of the plaza, **Taos Pueblo** (120 Veterans Hwy., 575/758-1028, taospueblo.com), a UNESCO World Heritage Site, is one of New Mexico's Eight Northern Indian Pueblos—adobe communities that have been continuously inhabited for more than a millennium.

A pair of excellent museums provides a primer on Taos' legendary arts scene. The **Taos Art Museum** (227 Paseo del Pueblo Norte, 575/758-2690, taosartmuseum.org) focuses on works by members of the Taos Society of Artists who worked in the area from 1898 through the 1930s. The collection at the University of New Mexico's **Harwood Museum of Art** (238 Ledoux St., 575/758-

Taos Pueblo

Getting Oriented

Taos hugs the western side of the Sangre de Cristo Mountains in northern New Mexico. The town is at the intersection of US 64 and NM 68 and 70 miles northeast of Santa Fe via US 84, US 285, and NM 68. Taos Ski Valley is 19 miles northeast of Taos via US 64 and NM 150. Albuquerque International Sunport, 135 miles southwest, is the nearest major airport. Santa Fe Regional Airport is 80 miles south of Taos but has fewer daily flights.

9826, harwoodmuseum.org) includes Native American, Taos Society, and contemporary works.

The Spanish Colonial **Kit Carson Home and Museum** (113 Kit Carson Rd., 575/758-4945, kitcarsonmuseum.org) engages you with exhibits about the legendary frontiersman who lived here from 1843 to 1868.

Mountain Majesty

The standout **Taos Ski Valley** (800/776-1111, skitaos.com) is the state's largest ski area, with about 1,300 acres of skiable terrain and one of North America's highest triple chairlifts on 12,481-foot Kachina Peak.

West of Taos, the 50-mile-long **Rio Grande Gorge** is a dramatic byproduct of the river of the same name. Head to the historic **Rio Grande Gorge Bridge**, about 10 miles northwest of Taos on US 64, to gawk at the 800-foot-deep chasm—or view the gorge by hiking or biking the moderate, 10.3-mile **Rift Valley Loop Trail**, 10 miles southwest of Taos via NM 68 and CR 110.

In the higher country within Carson National Forest, the trails open in late spring. Accessed via a trailhead at Taos Ski Valley, the **Wheeler**

Peak Wilderness (575/758-6200, fs.usda. gov) offers a number of trails, including the strenuous 14.6-mile (round-trip) hike to the summit of New Mexico's highest peak (13,161 feet).

Eat & Stay

Lambert's of Taos. Set in an historic adobe structure, this local institution since 1989 serves up locally sourced, in-season contemporary American cuisine. 123 Bent St., (575) 758-7200, lambertsoftaos.com.

El Monte Sagrado. A spa resort with a secluded location, this luxury getaway (the name is Spanish for "the sacred mountain") is just three blocks from Taos Plaza but a world away in mood, tone, and indulgences. 317 Kit Carson Rd., (575) 758-3502, elmontesagrado.com.

Historic Taos Inn. This 1936 landmark grouping of adobe houses around a central courtyard offers distinctive Southwestern-style accommodations, a lobby bar often dubbed Taos' living room, and a creative eatery called Doc Martin's—named for the county's first physician. 125 Paseo del Pueblo Norte, (855) 963-2180, taosinn.com.

LOCAL FOOD ALERT!

Green Chile Stew
Red or green? In New Mexico, that question only means one thing - how you prefer your chile sauce. A local favorite dish opts for green in green chile stew. At **Doc Martin's** in the historic Taos Inn, pork, vegetables, and loads of Hatch green chiles simmer all day to create a thick, satisfying stew that's a must try. **taosinn.com**

Taos Ski Valley

Show Me a Great Vacation

This scenic region offers a unique mix of Americana that taps into the history and culture of both the Midwest and the South. Covering roughly 50,000 square miles, the Ozark Mountains (aka Ozark Plateau) stretch across southern Missouri and northwestern Arkansas and reach into Oklahoma as well.

Many associate the region with the southwest Missouri town of Branson, where dozens of theaters host concerts and stage shows of every stripe—and at reasonable prices. Nearby Table Rock Lake offers natural entertainment—much of it free. Roughly 50 miles southwest, Eureka Springs, Arkansas, has mineral-rich waters and a historic downtown.

Table Rock Lake

That's Entertainment!

Branson has offered the kind of entertainment generally associated with Nashville or Las Vegas—albeit at more affordable prices—for decades. It all started in the 1950s, when square dances were held in an area cavern. In 1967, the Presley family (no relation to the King) was the first to move its show, Presleys' Country Jubilee, to 76 Country Blvd. in Branson; that show continues in the family's own 1,500-seat theater.

Today, Branson's 45 (give or take) venues fill up with fans of gospel, Motown, light rock, Cajun, bluegrass, and, of course, country music—often performed by big-name talent. Find out what's on through the **Branson Tourism Center** (486 Branson Landing Blvd., Ste. 207, 417/334-4400 or 800/974-0411, bransontourismcenter.com), which also sells tickets and offers show, lodging, and dining packages.

Amid a setting that recalls an 1880s mining town, **Silver Dollar City** (399 Silver Dollar City Pkwy., 417/336-7100, silverdollarcity. com) has more than 40 thrill rides, as well as shows, restaurants, stores, and craftspeople of all sorts. Affiliated with the theme park are

Getting Oriented

Although Ozark peaks rarely top 2,500 feet, the area is marked by rugged hills and woodlands laced with rivers and dotted with rocky outcroppings, caverns, and lakes. Gateway airports include Branson Airport and Springfield-Branson National in Missouri; Clinton National in Little Rock, Arkansas; and Tulsa International in Oklahoma.

Interstate 44 travels east–west through Missouri. Branson is 43 miles south of it along US 65; 76 Country Blvd. serves as the town's main east–west thoroughfare. Several U.S. and/or state routes run from Branson to Table Rock Park, 10 miles southwest, as well as south to Eureka Springs and west to Bentonville.

White Water, a park with watery rides and slides; the **Silver Dollar City Campground**, with campsites, RV sites, cabins, and free shuttle services; and the 270-foot, three-deck Showboat *Branson Belle*, a paddle wheeler with entertaining cruises on Table Rock Lake.

Explore more of Branson's natural side at **Table Rock State Park** (5272 Hwy. 165, 417/334-4704, mostateparks.com), which takes great advantage of an 800-mile shoreline.

History & Art Spring Eternal

Not only does the hilly resort community of Eureka Springs have more than 60 natural cold-water springs, but its Victorian architecture is so well preserved that the entire downtown district is on the National Register of Historic Places. The 90-minute, narrated **Eureka Springs Tram Tours** (137 W. Van Buren St., 479/244-5116, eurekaspringstramtours.com) transport you up and down streets lined with stately buildings.

One of the worst chapters in American history began in the 1830s, when Native Americans were forced to march from their homelands to the Oklahoma Territory; many died along the way. The **Blue Spring Heritage Center** (1537 Hwy. 210, 479/253-9244, bluespringheritage.com) marks a site where the Cherokee people found respite along the infamous Trail of Tears.

Also serene is the circa-1980 **Thorncrown Chapel** (12968 Hwy. 62 W., 479/346-0245, thorncrown.com), a light-filled, glass-and-timber, "Ozark Gothic" structure that soars like the trees surrounding it. The American Institute of Architects named it the nation's fourth-best 20th-century design—behind Frank Lloyd Wright's Fallingwater and New York's Chrysler and Seagram buildings.

West of Eureka Springs en route to Bentonville, the **Pea Ridge National Military Park** (15930 Hwy. 62 E., Garfield, 479/451-8122, nps.gov/peri) marks a 2-day 1862 Civil War battle that resulted in more than 3,000 casualties and a Union victory. The visitors center has a film and exhibits.

Integration with the wooded and watery landscape was key to architect Moshe Safdie's design of the **Crystal Bridges Museum of American Art** (600 Museum Way, Bentonville, 479/418-5700, crystalbridges.org). The views are as compelling as the works by Winslow Homer, Georgia O'Keeffe, Edward Hopper, and others. Admission is free.

Eat & Stay

Branson

Billy Gails Café. Unpretentious meals (massive pancakes are a specialty) in an unpretentious setting (a former filling station) have made this mom-and-pop eatery popular. 5291 Hwy. 265, (417) 338-8883, billygailsrestaurant.com.

Bradford House. A winding staircase and a stately great room with a floor-to-ceiling fireplace are among the stunning features of this Victorian-style B&B situated between downtown and Silver Dollar City. 296 Blue Meadows Dr., (417) 334-4444, staybradfordhouse.com.

Eureka Springs

Grand Taverne. The sage on your pork chop might have come from the chef's balcony herb garden. It's just one part of what makes this dinner spot special. Another is its setting inside the Grand Central Hotel, one of several historic spa hotels. 37 N. Main St., (479) 253-6756, eurekagrandcentral.com.

Crescent Hotel & Spa. History is palpable at the ornate, elegant "Grand Lady of the Ozarks," in operation since 1886. Amenities include a rooftop restaurant, a spa, and ghost tours of what is reputedly America's most haunted hotel. 75 Prospect Ave., (855) 725-5720, crescent-hotel.com.

Chocolate Biscuits and Gravy
For a different take on classic biscuits and gravy, head over to the **Ozark Café** in Jasper, AR, where the gravy is made of chocolate! This smooth, buttery gravy is made with cocoa powder and is popular in the Ozark and Appalachian regions, especially as a Sunday morning treat. ozarkcafe.com

The Country Side of America

The Great Smoky Mountains just might be America's largest time machine. When you visit the national park and the gateway communities that surround it, you feel as though you've traveled back to an earlier, quieter era.

Although you can't fully escape traffic and other signs of today, there's still a welcoming, relaxing sense of the past in Pigeon Forge, Sevierville, Bryson City, Waynesville, and other towns. Even busy Gatlinburg seems dipped in nostalgia, with family-friendly shops where novelties and souvenirs have a decidedly country accent.

Drives in the Country

Several Smoky Mountain roads appeal equally to drivers and motorcyclists—among them, **US 441** (aka Newfound Gap Road) through the national park. Lazy curves, tight switchbacks, and elevations ranging from 1,289 feet in Gatlinburg to 5,048 feet through the Newfound Gap at the Tennessee–North Carolina border make for a scenic and interesting 32-mile drive.

Near the park's north entrance at Gatlinburg, **Little River Road** follows the twisting, turning river before exiting near Townsend farther west. Outside the park's southern entrance near Cherokee, the famed **Blue Ridge Parkway** (blueridgeparkway.org) offers majestic overlooks as it skips across a section of the southern Smokies.

Woods & Waters

Without question, the **Great Smoky Mountains National Park** (nps.gov/grsm, 865/436-1200) is the region's heart and soul. More than 11 million annual visitors enjoy its scenic overlooks, ranger programs, and hikes. Indeed, the park has approximately 800 miles of trails, including a section of the Appalachian Trail.

Several area outfitters can help you ply the waters of the Nantahala, Ocoee, Big Pigeon, and Lower Pigeon rivers. Check out **Wildwater** (866/319-8870, wildwaterrafting.com), or **Nantahala Outdoor Center** (828/785-5082, noc.com). **Rolling River Thunder Company** (800/408-7238 or 706/492-5720, rollingthunderriverco.com) also offers canoeing, kayaking, and tubing.

North Carolina's **Cataloochee Ski Area** (1080 Ski Lodge Rd., Maggie Valley, 828/926-0285, cataloochee.com) is open for skiing and snowboarding from November through March. The peak elevation is 5,400 feet, with a vertical drop of 740 feet.

Getting Oriented

The Smokies, part of the vast Appalachian Mountain system, span nearly 300 square miles along the Tennessee–North Carolina border. The core of the region is Great Smoky Mountains National Park.

Although I-40 runs east–west through the region, twisting two-lane roads trace the area's western edge and scenic US 441 travels southeast from Knoxville through Sevierville, Pigeon Forge, and Gatlinburg in Tennessee.

The most convenient regional airports are Knoxville's McGhee Tyson and Asheville Regional. Hartsfield-Jackson Atlanta International and Charlotte Douglas International are the closest major airports.

Variations on the Theme Park

Country music and down-home flavor are popular in these parts, and **Dollywood** (2700 Dollywood Parks Blvd., Pigeon Forge, 865/428-9488, dollywood.com) delivers both. The theme park, which has more than 40 thrill and water rides, captures the essence of the Smokies with stage shows; Southern restaurants; country stores; and specialty shops.

Ober Gatlinburg Amusement Park and Ski Area (1001 Parkway, 865/436-5423, obergatlinburg.com) has a 120-passenger gondola that carries you on a 2.1-mile ride into the hills for an aerial view of the region. In winter, skiing, snowboarding, and snow tubing provide the thrills.

Small-Town America

In the heart of Gatlinburg, explore the shoulder-to-shoulder gift stores, fudge shops, old-fashioned photo parlors, restaurants, and other attractions lining each side of **Parkway**, the town's main thoroughfare.

Apple Stack Cake

An Appalachian tradition, the Apple Stack Cake was served at special occasions such as Christmas and weddings. Multiple, thin layers of cake baked in a cast iron skillet are stacked with reconstituted dried apple filling and left to absorb for a few days before serving. Enjoy it any time of year, by the slice or a whole cake, at **The Apple Barn Cider Mill & General Store** in Sevierville. **applebarncidermill.com**

For items of a more authentic nature, the Great Smoky Arts & Crafts Community, established around 1937, has a designated **Tennessee Heritage Arts & Crafts Trail** (800/565-7330, gatlinburgcrafts.com) that celebrates the skill of more than 100 locals, whose arts and crafts are rooted in the history of the mountains.

In North Carolina, Waynesville's delightful main street has an outpost of the **Mast General Store** (63 N. Main St., 828/452-2101, mastgeneralstore.com/waynesville), a 1930s-style mercantile packed with nifty country merchandise. Ten minutes west, the **Wheels Through Time Museum** (62 Vintage Ln., Maggie Valley, 828/926-6266, wheelsthroughtime.com) has more than 350 rare American motorcycles and some very cool automobiles.

Scenic drive on the Foothills Parkway

Eat & Stay

The Old Mill Restaurant. True to its name, this restaurant on the Pigeon River actually grinds its own grain for grits, breads, biscuits, and pancakes. The menu features country-fried steak, sugar-cured ham, pot roast, chicken and dumplings, and other comfort foods. 164 Old Mill Ave., Pigeon Forge, TN, (865) 429-3463, old-mill.com.

The Fryemont Inn. The circa-1923 wood-and-stone lodge is listed on the National Register of Historic Places and overlooks both Bryson City and the national park. 245 Fryemont St., Bryson City, NC, (828) 488-2159, fryemontinn.com.

The Lodge at Buckberry Creek. This upscale 44-suite lodge has a rustic-elegant "parkitecture" style with great mountain views. 961 Campbell Lead Rd., Gatlinburg, TN, (866) 305-6343, buckberrylodge.com.

THE POCONOS PENNSYLVANIA

A River Runs Through It

This idyllic region in northeastern Pennsylvania is the perfect antidote to the bustle of Philadelphia and New York, each just two hours away.

"Poconos" is a Native American word meaning "stream between two mountains." That "stream" is the Delaware River, which slices through the Appalachians to form the Delaware Water Gap—itself bounded by Mt. Tammany in New Jersey and Mt. Minsi in Pennsylvania.

Within 2,400 square miles across four counties are hundreds of miles of hiking trails; dozens of golf courses; nine state parks; two national parks; and numerous historic sites, ski areas, sprawling mountain resorts, and quaint inns—enough to please any traveler in any season.

Ties to History

The Poconos region is rich in both history and railroad heritage. The town of Jim Thorpe was the site of one of the nation's first railroads and home to Asa Packer, a railway magnate and founder of Lehigh University. See how the other half lived on a tour of the 1861 **Asa Packer Mansion** (Packer Hill Ave., 570/325-3229, asapackermansion. com), and then take a ride on a vintage train with the **Lehigh Gorge Scenic Railway** (1 Susquehanna St., 570/325-8485, lgsry.com).

A full-scale model of the Stourbridge Lion, America's first commercial steam locomotive (the original is in the Smithsonian), resides in the **Wayne County Historical Museum** (810 Main St., Honesdale, 570/253-3240, waynehistorypa.org). The engine first ran on a 3-mile wooden track laid across a trestle bridge in 1829; today, folks call Honesdale the "birthplace of the American railroad."

Amid the shops and restaurants in small towns such as Hawley, Lackawaxen, Milford, and Stroudsburg, you'll find fascinating local history and charming Victorian architecture. The **Zane Grey Museum** (135 Scenic Dr., Lackawaxen, 570/685-4871, nps.gov/upde), full of the famed novelist's memorabilia, is a striking clapboard-sided farmhouse (circa 1905).

Bushkill Falls

Getting Oriented

Before the Model T was a twinkle in Henry Ford's eye, residents of sweltering cities along the Northeast Corridor hopped trains and headed for the cool Pennsylvania hills. Today, they come by car along I-80 or I-84 from New York and New Jersey and I-476 from Philadelphia.

Part of the Allegheny Plateau, the region has its highest point at 2,133-foot Camelback Mountain. Lehigh Valley (Allentown) is south, Wyoming Valley (coal country) is west, Lake Wallenpaupack is north, and the Delaware Water Gap forms the eastern border.

Gardens and trails surround the imposing 1886 French château–style **Grey Towers National Historic Site** (122 Old Owego Turnpike, Milford, 570/296-9630, greytowers.org), the summer retreat of Gifford Pinchot, first chief of the U.S. Forest Service and twice governor of Pennsylvania.

Examples of exquisite cut glass—including presidential glassware made for Abraham Lincoln and Woodrow Wilson—are on display at the **Dorflinger-Suydam Wildlife Sanctuary and Glass Museum** (55 Suydam Dr., White Mills, 570/253-1185, dorflinger. org), which also has hiking trails, art shows, and outdoor concerts. In Stroudsburg, at the **Monroe County Historical Association Museum** (900 Main St., 570/421-7703, monroehistorical.org), tour the 1795 Georgian-style Stroud Mansion, one-room schoolhouse, and 1882 railroad station.

Action & Adventure

Although the Poconos region attracts more visitors when the weather is warm, ski season is a big draw. **Camelback Mountain** (301 Resort Dr., Tannersville, 570/629-1661, camelbackresort.com) has 39 trails and 42 snowtube lanes, zip lines, the Appalachian Express Mountain Coaster, and a nearby resort with two water parks.

Shawnee Mountain Ski Area (401 Hollow Rd., East Stroudsburg, 570/421-7231, shawneemt.com) has 23 trails, two terrain parks, and a snow-tubing park.

Pocono Raceway (1234 Long Pond Rd., Long Pond, poconoraceway.com, 800/722-3929) hosts summer NASCAR events and other professional competitions. Tour the track (Apr.–Sept.), or test your own skills on the 2.5-mile oval in a NASCAR-style stock car or your own sports car with **Stock Car Racing Experience** (105 Wt Family Blvd., Blakeslee, 570/643-6921, 877stockcar.com).

Nature's Playground

The **Delaware Water Gap National Recreation Area** (1978 River Rd., Bushkill, 570/426-2452, nps.gov/dewa) has more than 100 miles of trails (25 along the Appalachian Trail) to hike or cross-country ski, 30 miles of trails to bike, a scenic drive to explore, and long stretches of river to paddle. There's also a host of ranger-led tours and programs.

Developed in 1927, man-made **Lake Wallenpaupack** (Rte. 6, Hawley, 570/226-3191) is 13 miles long and has 52 miles of shoreline, with many opportunities for swimming, canoeing, boating, and fishing. A winter highlight is the annual ice golf tournament on the frozen lake. And don't miss the "Niagara of Pennsylvania": **Bushkill Falls** (138 Bushkill Falls Trail, Bushkill, 570/588-6682, visitbushkillfalls.com) actually consists of 8 waterfalls along 2 miles of trails, bridges, and walkways.

Eat & Stay

Camelback Resort. Dining choices abound at this amenities-loaded resort with 5 restaurants and 2 bars. In winter, ski, swim, and enjoy a spa treatment. In summer, the resort's Camelbeach Mountain is Pennsylvania's largest outdoor water park. 193 Resort Dr., Tannersville, (855) 515-1283, camelbackresort.com.

Hotel Fauchère. This inn offers extraordinary dining and historical lodging experiences. Louis Fauchère—master chef at Manhattan's Delmonico's Restaurant—opened the inn in 1852. Enjoy brunch in The Delmonico Room, contemporary cuisine in Bar Louis, or alfresco dining on the porch, overlooking the historic main street. 401 Broad St., Milford, (570) 409-1212, hotelfauchere.com.

Skytop Lodge. A 5,500-acre campus of rolling hills and woodlands surrounds this historic (1928) lodge. Numerous activities include golf, tennis, horseback riding, and more. You'll also enjoy two fine-dining restaurants, a tearoom, a deli, and three bars. 1 Skytop Lodge Rd., Skytop, (855) 345-7759, skytop.com.

LOCAL FOOD ALERT!

Scrapple
Resourceful Pennsylvania Dutch settlers used all their pork scraps, added cornmeal and spices, and came up with a savory dish that resembles paté. Head over to **Jubilee Restaurant** in Pocono Pines where they serve it up fried as a side with your favorite breakfast dish. jubileerestaurant.com

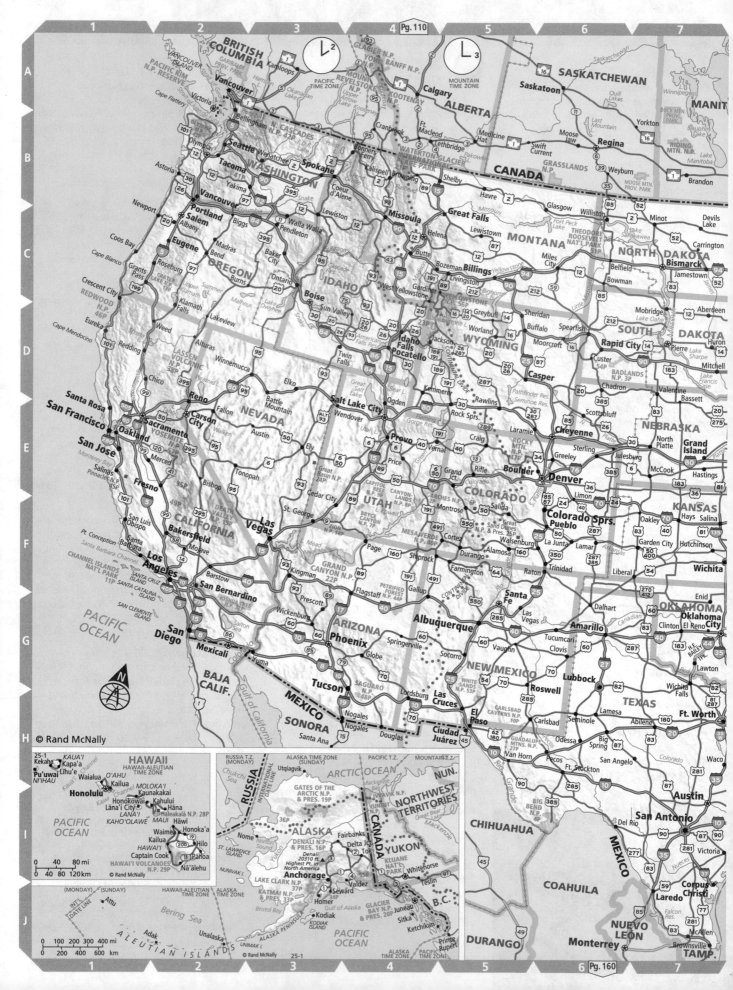

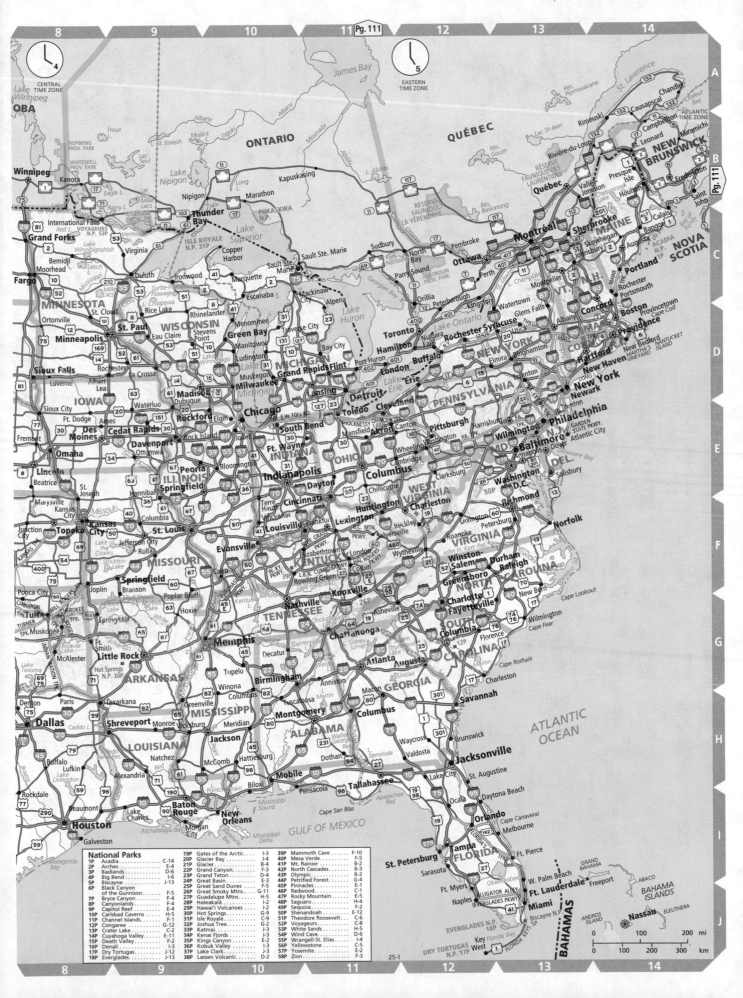

National Parks
1P	Acadia	C-14
2P	Arches	E-4
3P	Badlands	D-6
4P	Big Bend	I-6
5P	Biscayne	J-13
6P	Black Canyon	
	of the Gunnison	F-5
7P	Bryce Canyon	F-4
8P	Canyonlands	E-4
9P	Capitol Reef	F-4
10P	Carlsbad Caverns	H-5
11P	Channel Islands	F-1
12P	Congaree	G-12
13P	Crater Lake	C-2
14P	Cuyahoga Valley	E-11
15P	Death Valley	F-2
16P	Denali	I-3
17P	Dry Tortugas	J-12
18P	Everglades	J-13
19P	Gates of the Arctic	I-3
20P	Glacier Bay	J-4
21P	Glacier	B-4
22P	Grand Canyon	F-3
23P	Grand Teton	D-4
24P	Great Basin	E-3
25P	Great Sand Dunes	F-5
26P	Great Smoky Mtns.	G-11
27P	Guadalupe Mtns.	H-5
28P	Haleakala	I-2
29P	Hawai'i Volcanoes	I-2
30P	Hot Springs	G-9
31P	Isle Royale	C-9
32P	Joshua Tree	G-2
33P	Katmai	J-3
34P	Kenai Fjords	J-3
35P	Kings Canyon	E-2
36P	Kobuk Valley	J-3
37P	Lake Clark	J-3
38P	Lassen Volcanic	D-2
39P	Mammoth Cave	F-10
40P	Mesa Verde	F-5
41P	Mt. Rainier	B-2
42P	North Cascades	B-3
43P	Olympic	B-2
44P	Petrified Forest	G-4
45P	Pinnacles	E-1
46P	Redwood	C-1
47P	Rocky Mountain	E-5
48P	Saguaro	H-4
49P	Sequoia	F-2
50P	Shenandoah	E-12
51P	Theodore Roosevelt	C-6
52P	Voyageurs	C-8
53P	White Sands	H-5
54P	Wind Cave	D-6
55P	Wrangell-St. Elias	I-4
56P	Yellowstone	C-5
57P	Yosemite	E-2
58P	Zion	F-3

25-1

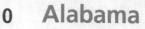
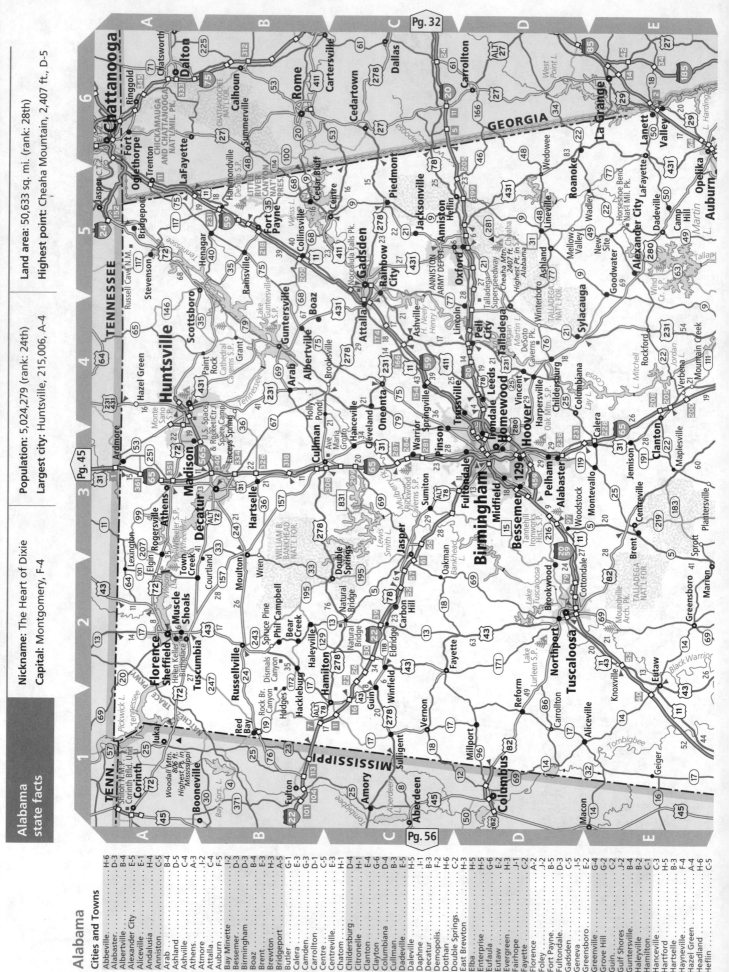

Alabama state facts

Nickname: The Heart of Dixie

Capital: Montgomery, F-4

Population: 5,024,279 (rank: 24th)

Largest city: Huntsville, 215,006, A-4

Land area: 50,633 sq. mi. (rank: 28th)

Highest point: Cheaha Mountain, 2,407 ft., D-5

Alabama

NOTE: Maps are not always in alphabetical order.
See Page 1 for map location in this atlas.

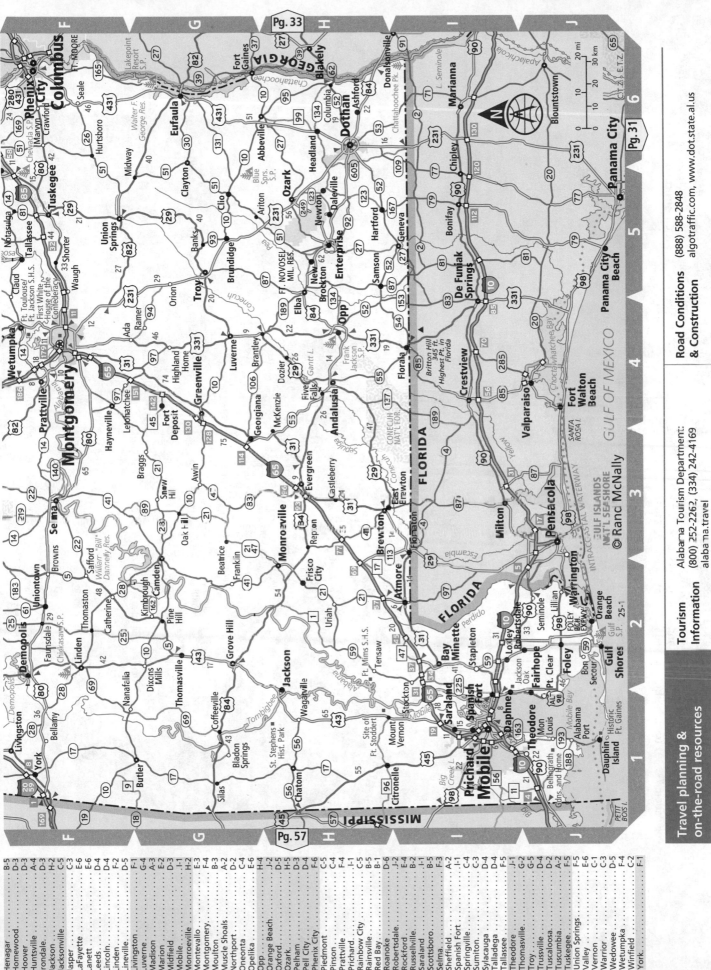

Travel planning & on-the-road resources

| Tourism Information | Alabama Tourism Department: (800) 252-2262, (334) 242-4169 alabama.travel |
| Road Conditions & Construction | (888) 588-2848 algotraffic.com, www.dot.state.al.us |

© Rand McNally

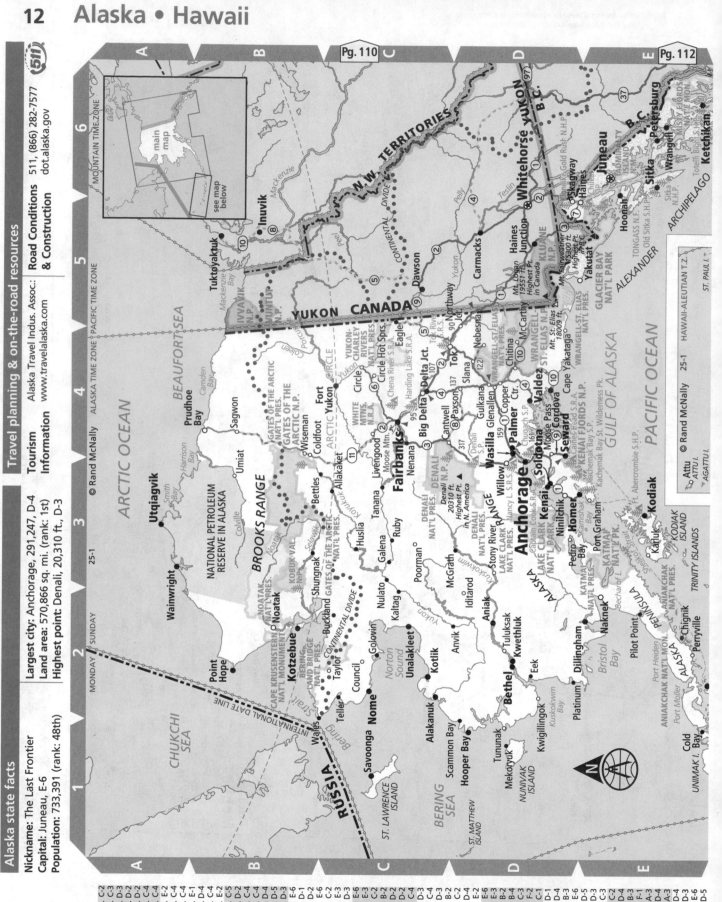

Alaska state facts

Nickname: The Last Frontier
Capital: Juneau, E-6
Population: 733,391 (rank: 48th)

Largest city: Anchorage, 291,247, D-4
Land area: 570,866 sq. mi. (rank: 1st)
Highest point: Denali, 20,310 ft., D-3

Travel planning & on-the-road resources

Tourism	Alaska Travel Indus. Assoc.:	
Information	www.travelalaska.com	
Road Conditions	511, (866) 282-7577	
& Construction	dot.alaska.gov	

Alaska

Cities and Towns

Alakanuk	C-2
Allakaket	C-3
Anchorage	D-3
Aniak	D-2
Bethel	D-2
Big Delta	C-4
Cantwell	C-4
Chignik	E-2
Circle	C-4
Circle Hot Springs	C-4
Cold Bay	E-1
Cordova	D-4
Delta Junction	C-4
Dillingham	E-2
Eagle	C-5
Eek	D-2
Fairbanks	C-4
Fort Yukon	B-4
Glenallen	D-5
Haines	D-6
Homer	E-3
Hoonah	E-6
Hooper Bay	D-1
Iditarod	D-2
Juneau	E-6
Kaltag	C-2
Karluk	E-3
Kenai	D-3
Ketchikan	E-6
Kodiak	E-3
Kotik	D-2
Kotzebue	B-2
Kwethluk	D-2
Kwigillingok	D-2
Livengood	C-3
McGrath	D-3
Nenana	C-4
Ninilchik	D-3
Noatak	B-2
Nome	C-2
Palmer	D-4
Perryville	E-2
Petersburg	E-6
Port Graham	E-3
Point Hope	B-2
Prudhoe Bay	B-4
Ruby	C-3
Sand Point	F-2
Savoonga	C-1
Scammon Bay	D-1
Seward	D-4
Shungnak	B-3
Sitka	E-6
Skagway	D-5
Soldotna	D-3
Tanana	C-3
Taylor	C-2
Tok	C-4
Umiat	B-3
Unalaska	F-1
Utqiagvik	A-3
Valdez	D-4
Wainwright	A-3
Wasilla	D-4
Willow	D-4
Wrangell	E-6
Yakutat	D-5

NOTE: Maps are not always in alphabetical order.
See Page 1 for map location in this atlas.

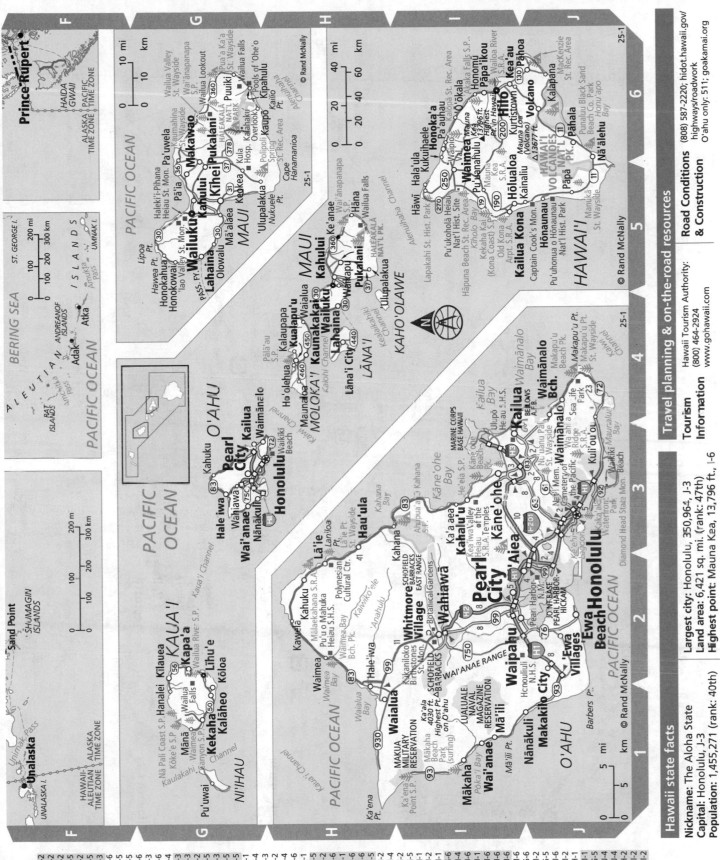

© Rand McNally

Hawaii state facts

Nickname: The Aloha State
Capital: Honolulu, J-3
Population: 1,455,271 (rank: 40th)

Largest city: Honolulu, 350,964, J-3
Land area: 6,421 sq. mi. (rank: 47th)
Highest point: Mauna Kea, 13,796 ft., I-6

Travel planning & on-the-road resources

Tourism Information	Hawaii Tourism Authority: (800) 464-2924 www.gohawaii.com
Road Conditions & Construction	(808) 587-2220; hidot.hawaii.gov/ highways/roadwork O'ahu only: 511; goakamai.org

Hawaii

Cities and Towns

'Aiea J-2
'Ewa Beach J-2
'Ewa Villages J-2
Hale'iwa I-5
Hala'ula H-5
Hāna H-3
Hau'ula I-6
Hilo I-6
Hōlualoa J-5
Hōnaunau J-5
Honoka'a I-6
Honolulu J-3
Honomū I-6
Ho'olehua H-4
Kahalu'u I-3
Kahana I-2
Kahuku I-5
Kahului H-2
Kailua I-3
Kailua Kona J-5
Kainaliu J-5
Kalāheo G-1
Kalaupapa H-4
Kāne'ohe I-3
Kapa'a G-2
Kaunakakai H-4
Kea'au I-6
Kekaha G-1
Kihei H-2
Kīlauea F-1
Kipahulu H-3
Kōloa G-1
Kukuihaele I-6
Kurtistown I-6
Lahaina H-2
Lā'ie I-5
Lāna'i City H-4
Līhu'e G-2
Mā'ili I-1
Makakilo City J-1
Makawao H-2
Maunaloa H-4
Nā'ālehu J-6
Nānākuli J-1
O'ōkala I-6
Pāhala J-6
Pāpa'ikou I-6
Pa'uwela G-2
Pearl City J-2
Pukalani G-5
Volcano J-6
Wahiawā I-2
Wai'anae J-1
Wailuku H-2
Waimānalo I-3
Waimānalo Beach J-4
Waimea G-5
Waipahu J-2
Whitmore Village I-2

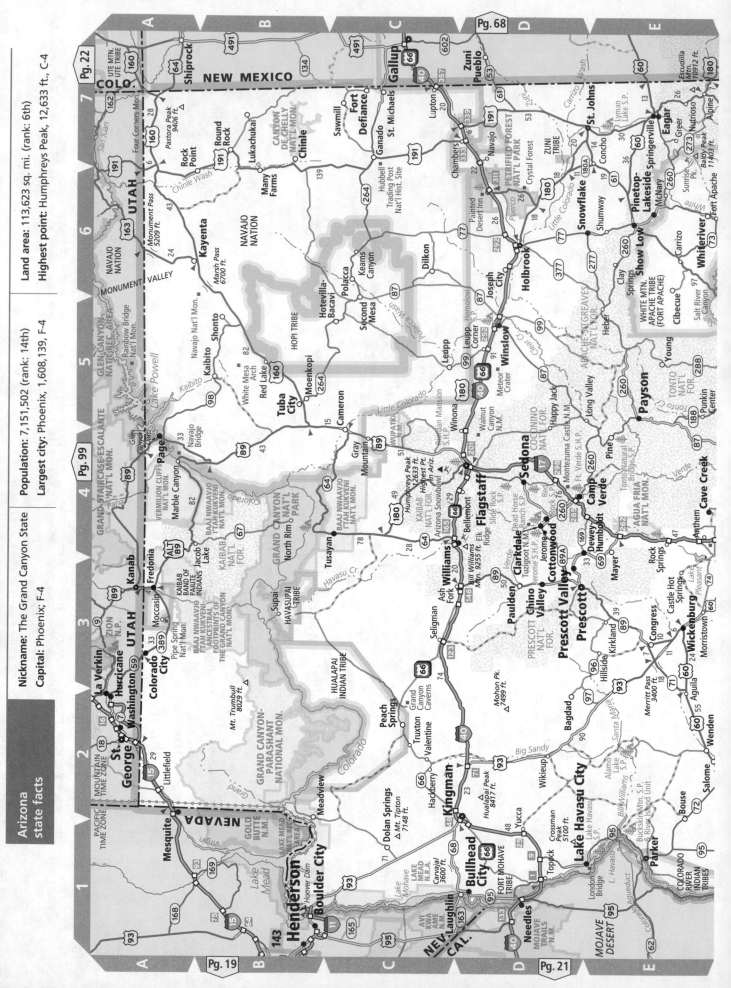

Arizona
state facts

Nickname: The Grand Canyon State

Capital: Phoenix; F-4

Population: 7,151,502 (rank: 14th)

Largest city: Phoenix, 1,608,139, F-4

Land area: 113,623 sq. mi. (rank: 6th)

Highest point: Humphreys Peak, 12,633 ft., C-4

Pg. 22

Pg. 99

Pg. 19

Pg. 21

NOTE: Maps are not always in alphabetical order.
See Page 1 for map location in this atlas.

Arizona 15

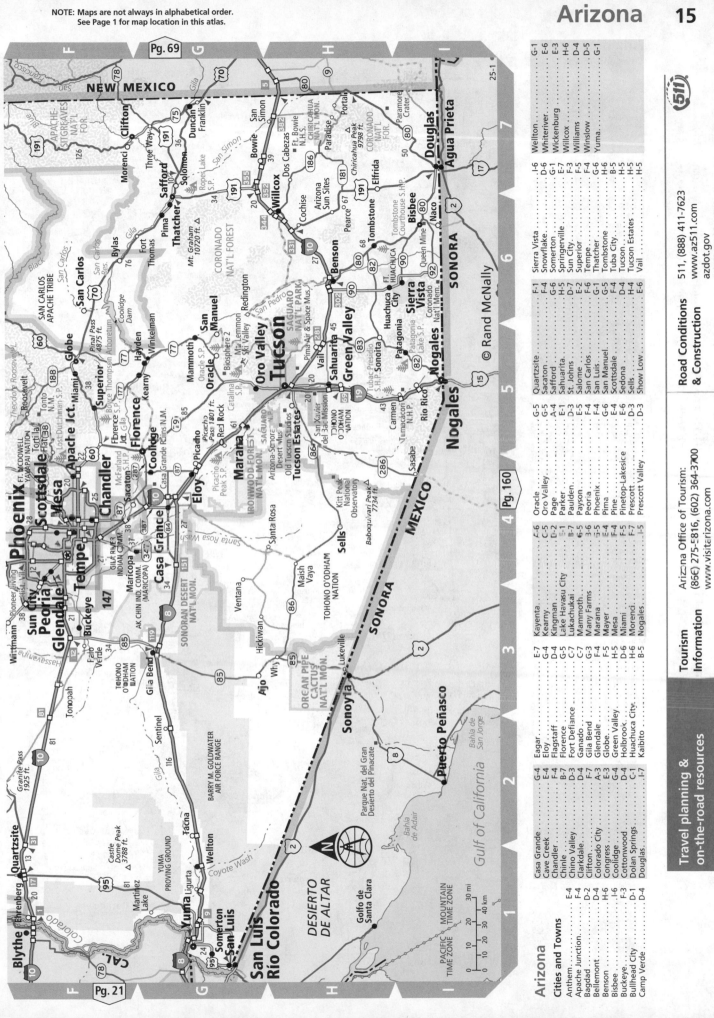

Travel planning & on-the-road resources			
Tourism Information	Arizona Office of Tourism: (866) 275-5816, (602) 364-3700 www.visitarizona.com	**Road Conditions & Construction**	511, (888) 411-7623 www.az511.com azdot.gov

© Rand McNally

Arkansas

Cities and Towns

Land area: 52,024 sq. mi. (rank: 27th)
Highest point: Magazine Mtn., 2753 ft., C-2

Population: 3,011,524 (rank: 33rd)
Largest city: Little Rock, 202,591, D-4

Nickname: The Natural State
Capital: Little Rock, D-4

Arkansas state facts

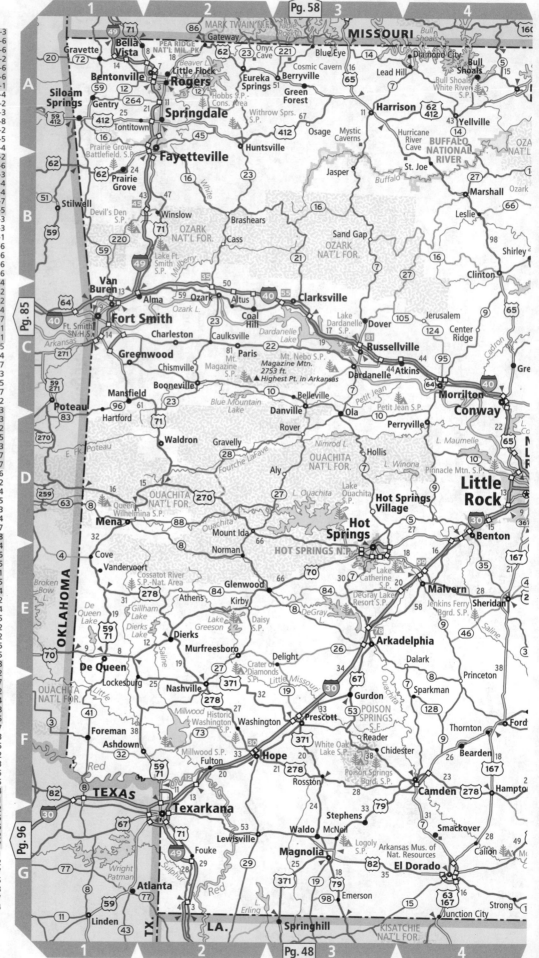

NOTE: Maps are not always in alphabetical order.
See Page 1 for map location in this atlas.

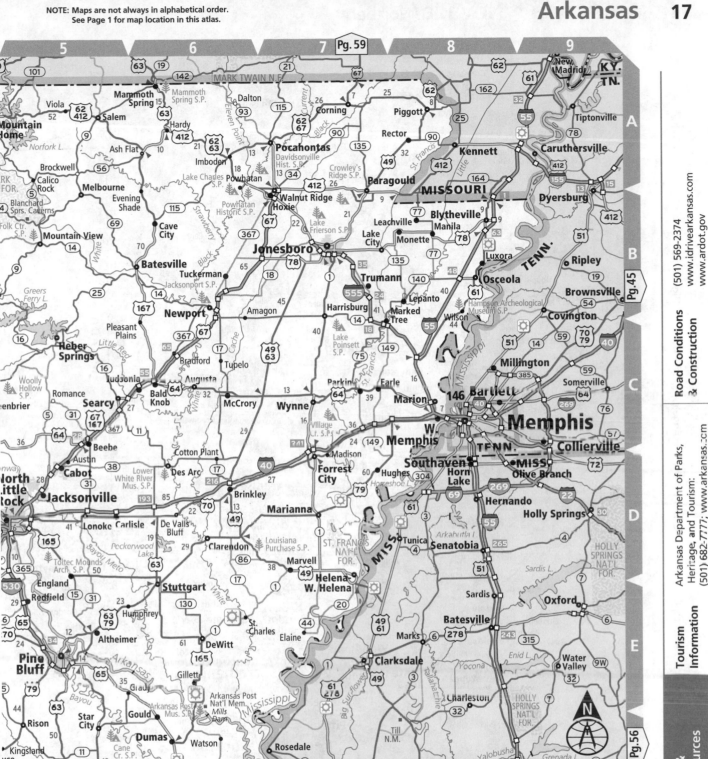

© Rand McNally

Tourism Information

Arkansas Department of Parks, Heritage, and Tourism: (501) 682-7777; www.arkansas.cm

Road Conditions & Construction

(501) 569-2374
www.idrivearkansas.com
www.ardot.gov

Travel planning & on-the-road resources

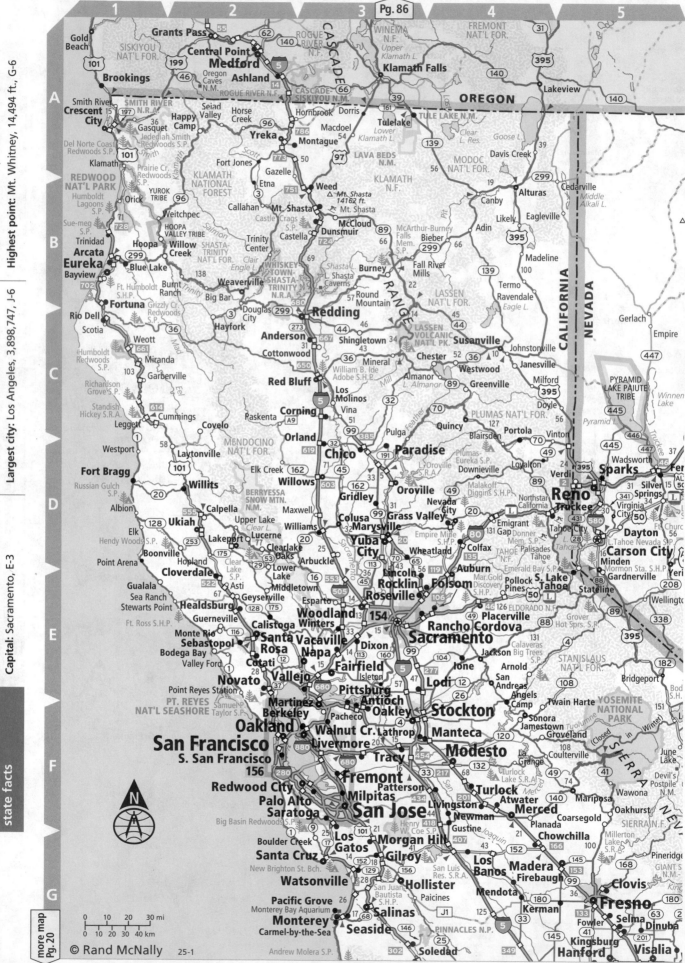

Pg. 86

more map
Pg. 20

California state facts

Nickname: The Golden State

Capital: Sacramento, E-3

Population: 39,538,223 (rank: 1st)

Largest city: Los Angeles, 3,898,747, J-6

Land area: 155,813 sq. mi. (rank: 3rd)

Highest point: Mt. Whitney, 14,494 ft., G-6

© Rand McNally   25-1

NOTE: Maps are not always in alphabetical order.
See Page 1 for map location in this atlas.

California • Nevada/Northern   19

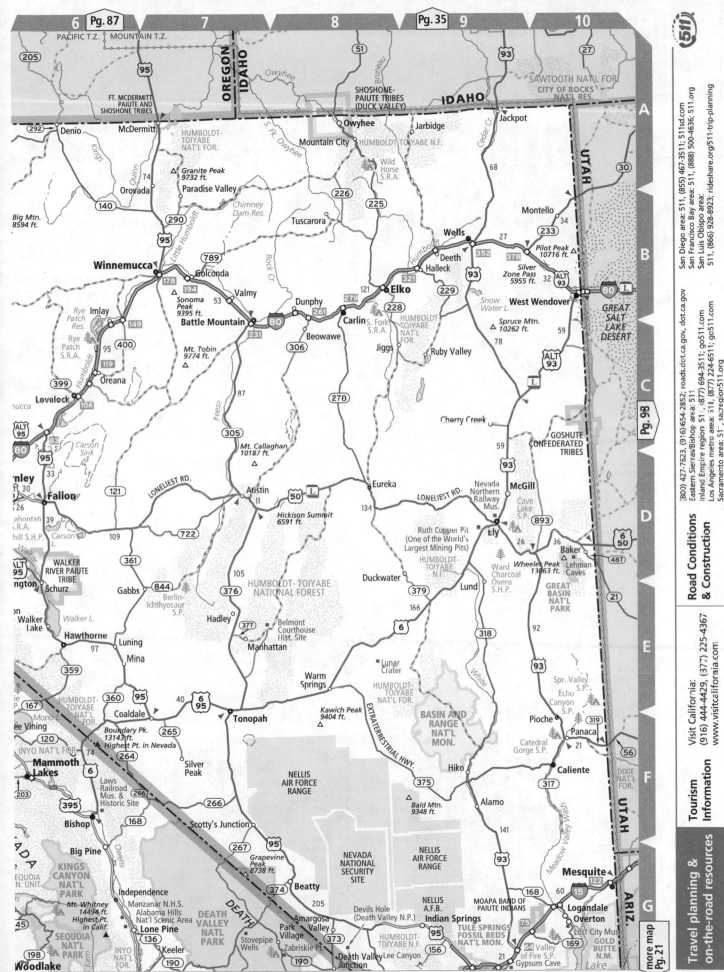

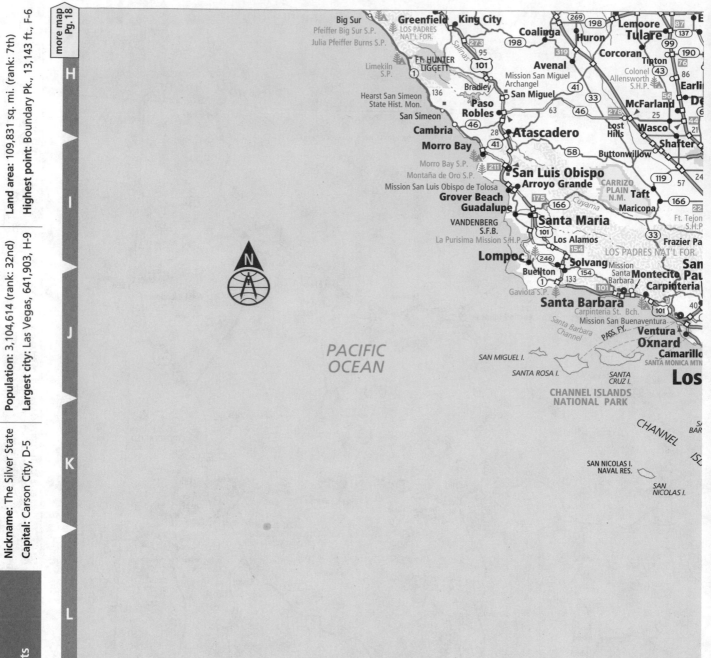

Land area: 109,831 sq. mi. (rank: 7th)

Highest point: Boundary Pk., 13,143 ft., F-6

Population: 3,104,614 (rank: 32nd)

Largest city: Las Vegas, 641,903, H-9

Nickname: The Silver State

Capital: Carson City, D-5

Nevada state facts

more map Pg. 18

PACIFIC OCEAN

0 10 20 30 mi
0 10 20 30 40 km

California

Cities and Towns

NOTE: Maps are not always in alphabetical order.
See Page 1 for map location in this atlas.

California • Nevada/Southern

21

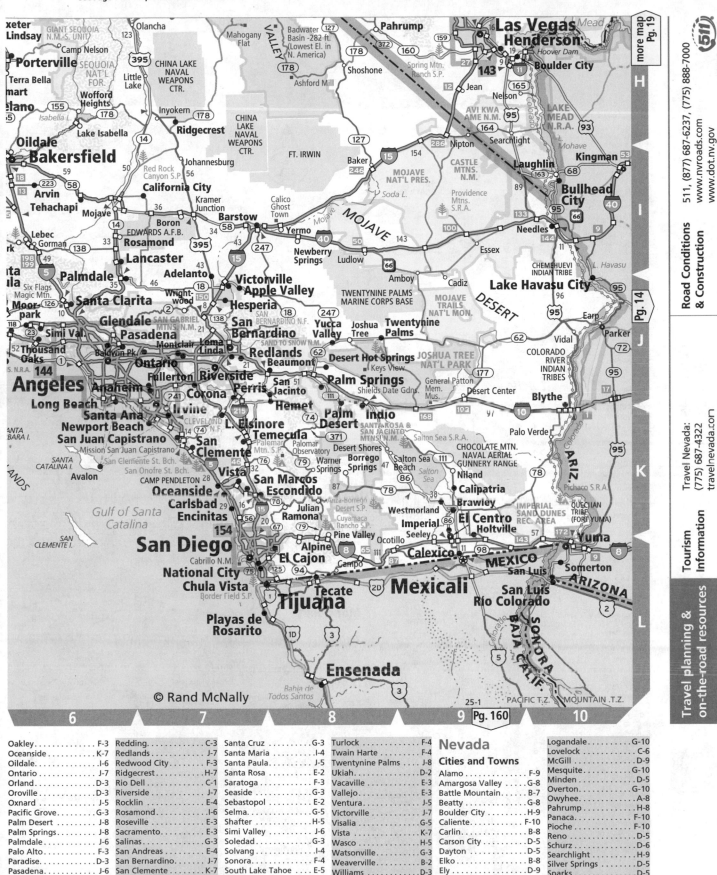

© Rand McNally

511, (877) 687-6237, (775) 888-7000
www.nvroads.com
www.dot.nv.gov

Road Conditions & Construction

Travel Nevada:
(775) 687-4322
travelnevada.com

Tourism Information

Travel planning & on-the-road resources

Colorado

Cities and Towns

Colorado state facts

Land area: 103,610 sq. mi. (rank: 8th)

Highest point: Mt. Elbert, 14,433 ft., D-4

Population: 5,773,714 (rank: 21st)

Largest city: Denver, 715,522, C-6

Nickname: The Centennial State

Capital: Denver, C-6

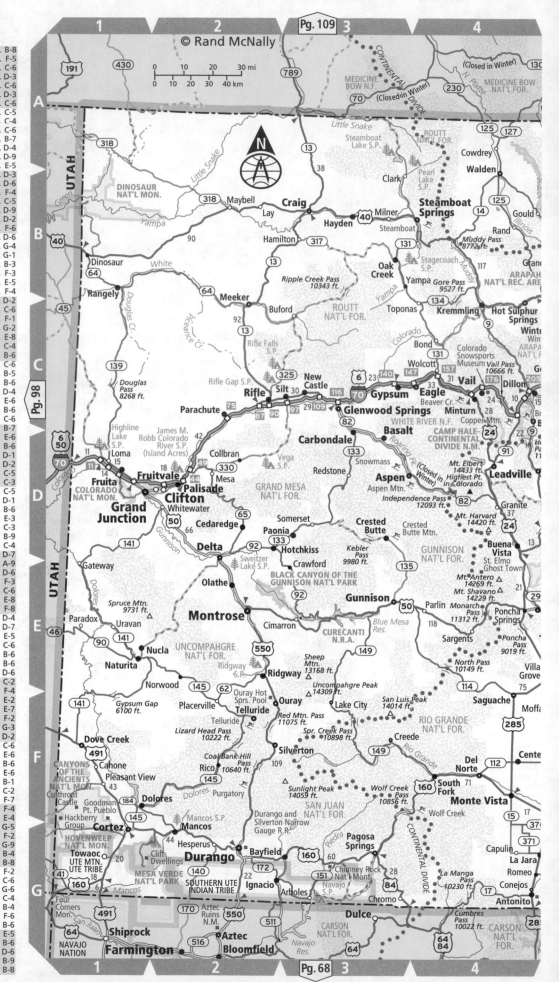

© Rand McNally

NOTE: Maps are not always in alphabetical order.
See Page 1 for map location in this atlas.

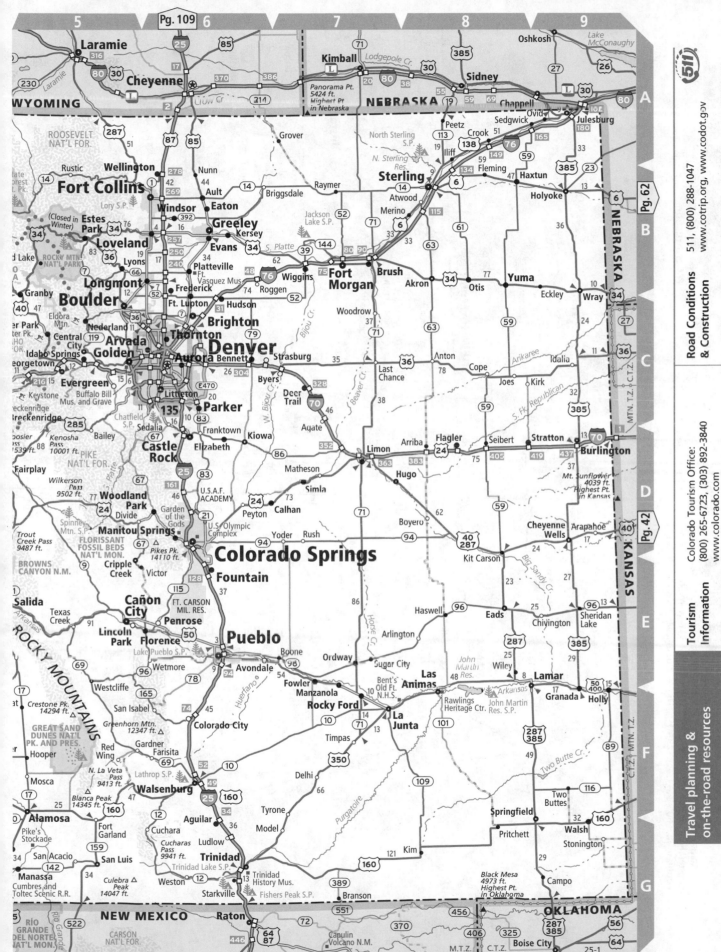

Pg. 109

Pg. 62

Pg. 42

Pg. 68

Pg. 84

Road Conditions & Construction
511, (800) 288-1047
www.cotrip.org, www.codot.gov

Tourism Information
Colorado Tourism Office:
(800) 265-6723, (303) 892-3840
www.colorado.com

Travel planning & on-the-road resources

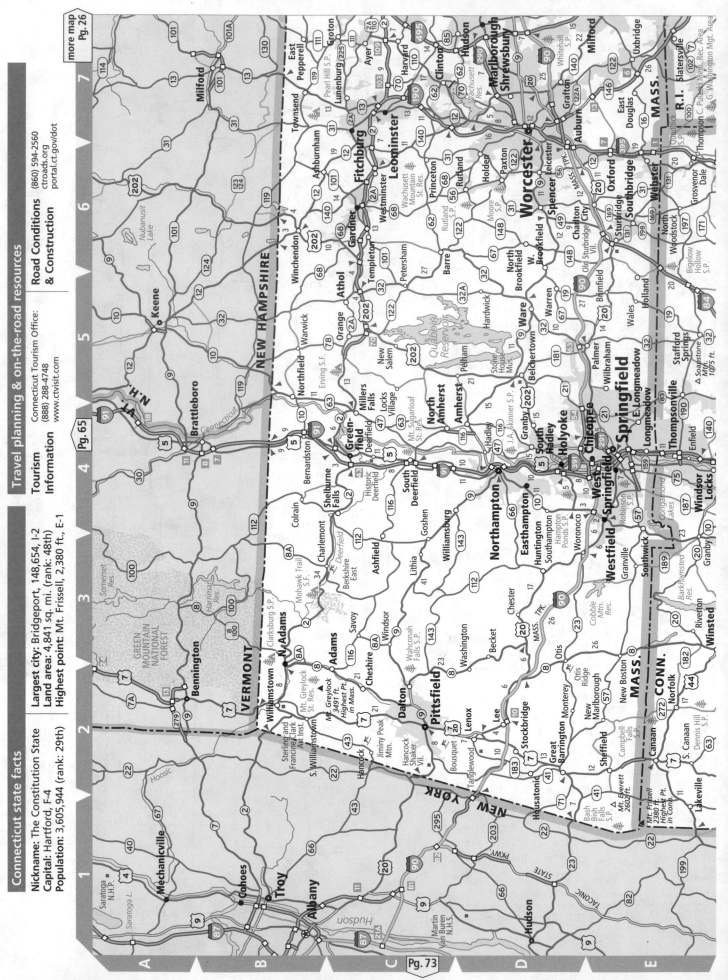

more map Pg. 26

Travel planning & on-the-road resources

Tourism Information
Connecticut Tourism Office:
(888) 288-4748
www.ctvisit.com

Road Conditions & Construction
(860) 594-2560
ctroads.org
portal.ct.gov/dot

Connecticut state facts

Nickname: The Constitution State
Capital: Hartford, F-4
Population: 3,605,944 (rank: 29th)

Largest city: Bridgeport, 148,654, I-2
Land area: 4,841 sq. mi. (rank: 48th)
Highest point: Mt. Frissell, 2,380 ft., E-1

Pg. 65
Pg. 73

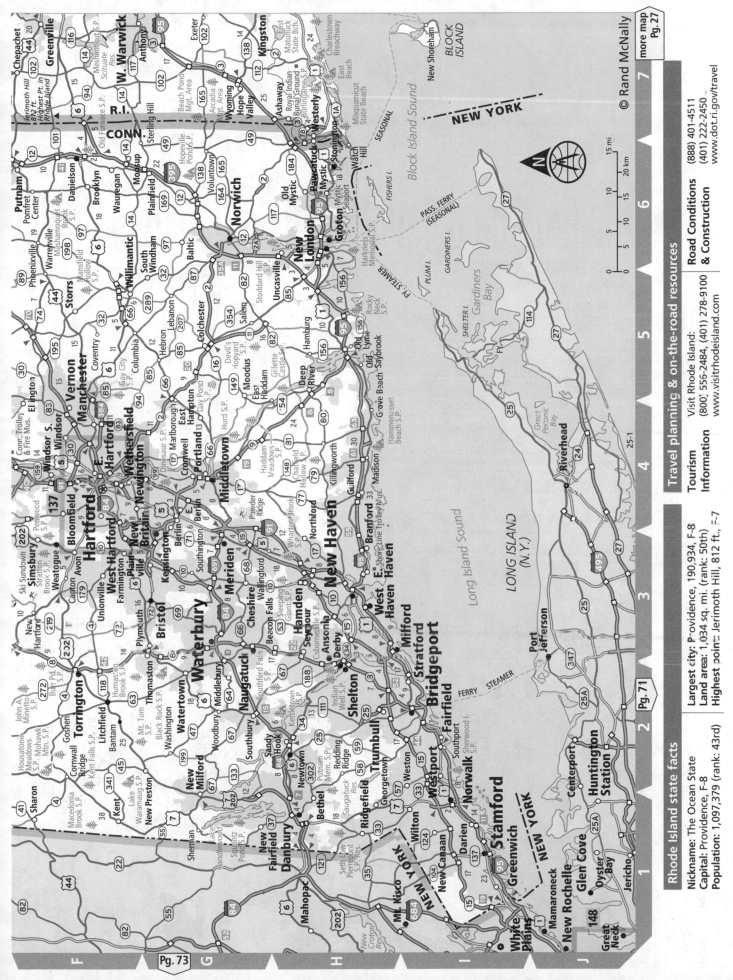

© Rand McNally

NEW YORK

BLOCK ISLAND

Block Island Sound

LONG ISLAND (N.Y.)

Long Island Sound

more map Pg. 27
Pg. 71
Pg. 73

Rhode Island state facts

Nickname: The Ocean State
Capital: Providence, F-8
Population: 1,097,379 (rank: 43rd)

Largest city: Providence, 190,934, F-8
Land area: 1,034 sq. mi. (rank: 50th)
Highest point: Jerimoth Hill, 812 ft., F-7

Travel planning & on-the-road resources

Tourism Information
Visit Rhode Island:
(800) 556-2484, (401) 278-9100
www.visitrhodeisland.com

Road Conditions & Construction
(888) 401-4511
(401) 222-2450
www.dot.ri.gov/travel

Massachusetts state facts

Nickname: The Bay State
Capital: Boston, D-9
Population: 7,029,917 (rank: 15th)
Largest city: Boston, 675,647, D-9
Land area: 7,799 sq. mi. (rank: 45th)
Highest point: Mt. Greylock, 3,491 ft., B-2

more map Pg. 24

Connecticut
Cities and Towns

Smith Mills	G-9
Somerset	F-9
South Deerfield	C-4
South Hadley	D-4
South Yarmouth	G-12
Southampton	D-4
Southbridge	D-6
Spencer	E-4
Springfield	C-9
Stoneham	E-4
Sturbridge	E-6
Sudbury Center	D-8
Swampscott	C-9
Taunton	F-9
Topsfield	B-9
Uxbridge	E-7
Vineyard Haven	G-10
Wakefield	E-8
Walpole	E-8
Waltham	D-8
Ware	D-5
Wareham Center	D-8
Wayland	E-6

Stamford	I-1
Storrs	F-5
Stratford	I-2
Thomaston	G-3
Thompsonville	E-4
Torrington	F-2
Trumbull	H-2
Uncasville	H-6
Unionville	F-3
Vernon	F-4
Waterbury	G-3
Watertown	G-2
Weatogue	F-3
West Hartford	F-4
West Haven	H-3
Westport	I-2
Wethersfield	F-4
Willimantic	F-5
Wilton	I-1
Windsor	F-4
Windsor Locks	E-4
Winsted	E-3

Massachusetts
Cities and Towns

Adams	C-2
Amesbury	B-9
Amherst	B-9
Andover	C-5
Attleboro	E-8
Auburn	D-7
Ayer	C-7
Barnstable	F-11
Bedford	C-8
Belchertown	D-5
Bellingham	D-5
Beverly	C-9
Billerica	C-9
Boston	D-9
Braintree	D-9
Brewster	F-12
Bridgewater	E-9
Brockton	E-9
Brookline	D-9
Buzzards Bay	F-10
Cambridge	D-9
Chicopee	E-4
Clinton	C-7
Cohasset	D-10
Concord	C-8
Dalton	C-2
Danvers	C-9
Dartmouth	D-9
Dedham	D-9
Dennis	F-12
East Douglas	E-9
East Falmouth	E-7
East Longmeadow	G-11
East Pepperell	E-4
Easthampton	B-7
Edgartown	D-4
Everett	H-11
Fairhaven	C-9
Fall River	G-9
Falmouth	F-9
Fitchburg	G-10
Foxborough	C-7
Framingham	E-8
Gardner	C-6
Georgetown	B-9

Rhode Island
Cities and Towns

Anthony	F-7
Bristol	G-8
Central Falls	F-8
Cranston	G-8
East Greenwich	F-8
East Providence	F-7
Exeter	G-8
Greenville	G-8
Jamestown	G-8
Kingston	G-11
Middletown	H-8
Narragansett Pier	H-8
Newport	G-8
North Kingstown	F-8
Pawtucket	G-8
Portsmouth	G-7
Providence	G-8
Tiverton	G-8
Warwick	G-8
West Warwick	G-8
Westerly	H-7
Woonsocket	E-8

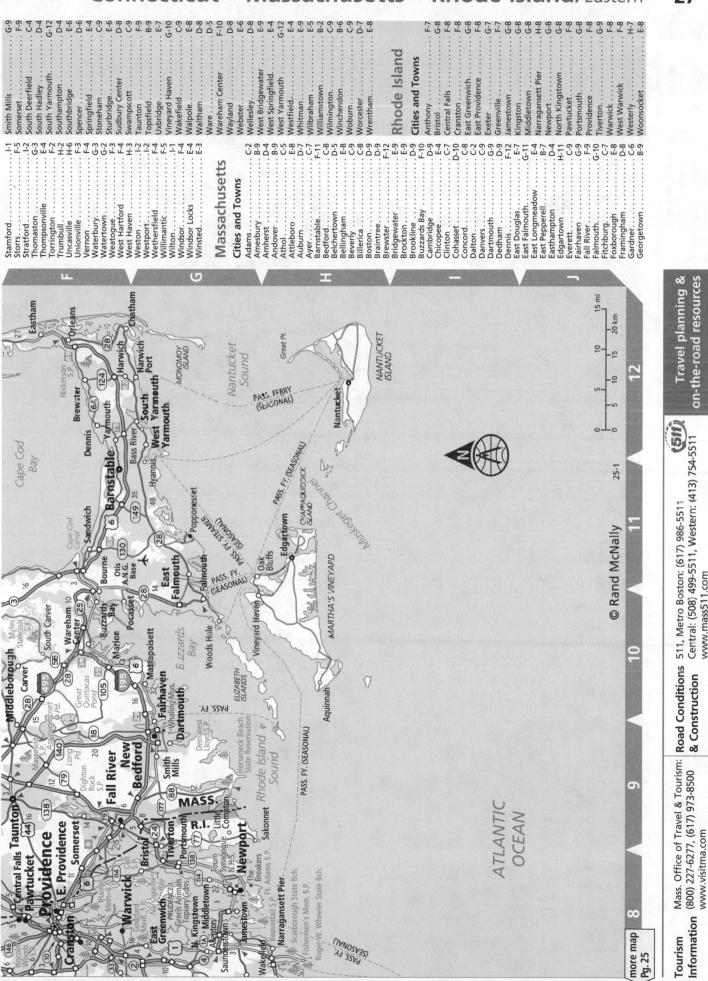

© Rand McNally

more map Pg. 25

Tourism Information Mass. Office of Travel & Tourism: (800) 227-6277, (617) 973-8500 www.visitma.com

Road Conditions & Construction 511, Metro Boston: (617) 986-5511 Central: (508) 499-5511, Western: (413) 754-5511 www.mass511.com

Travel planning & on-the-road resources

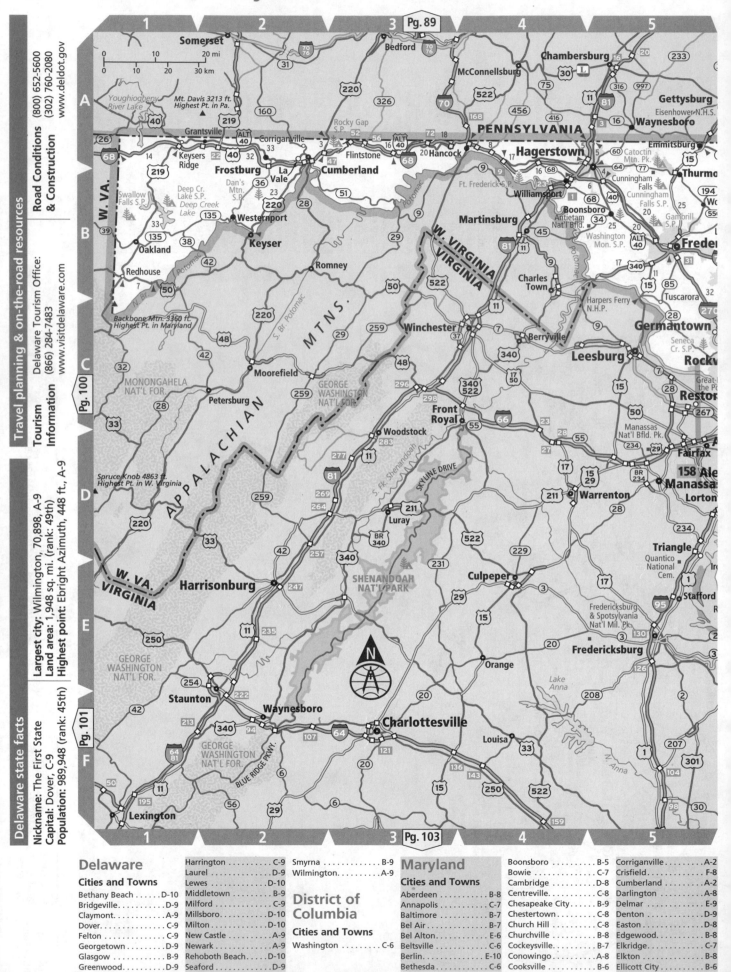

Road Conditions & Construction
(800) 652-5600
(302) 760-2080
www.deldot.gov

Travel planning & on-the-road resources

Tourism Information
Delaware Tourism Office:
(866) 284-7483
www.visitdelaware.com

Delaware state facts

Nickname: The First State
Capital: Dover, C-9
Population: 989,948 (rank: 45th)

Largest city: Wilmington, 70,898, A-9
Land area: 1,948 sq. mi. (rank: 49th)
Highest point: Ebright Azimuth, 448 ft., A-9

NOTE: Maps are not always in alphabetical order.
See Page 1 for map location in this atlas.

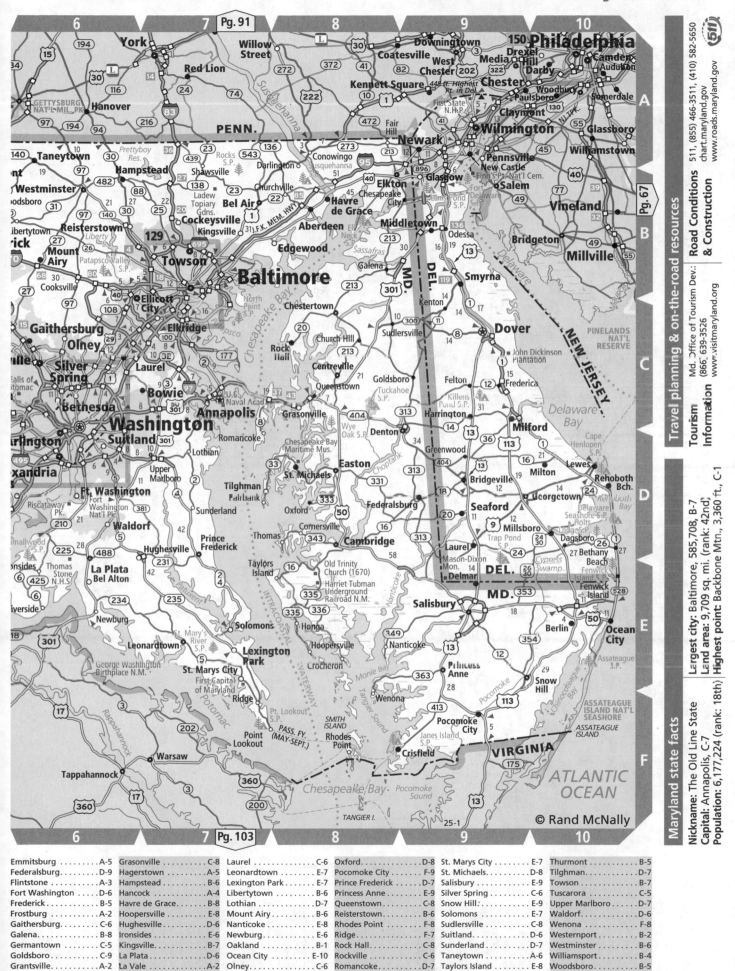

Pg. 91

Pg. 67

Pg. 103

Travel planning & on-the-road resources

Road Conditions & Construction
511, (855) 466-3511, (410) 582-5650
chart.maryland.gov
www.roads.maryland.gov

Tourism Information
Md. Office of Tourism Dev.:
(866) 639-3526
www.visitmaryland.org

Maryland state facts

Largest city: Baltimore, 585,708, B-7
Land area: 9,709 sq. mi. (rank: 42nd)
Highest point: Backbone Mtn., 3,360 ft., C-1

Nickname: The Old Line State
Capital: Annapolis, C-7
Population: 6,177,224 (rank: 18th)

© Rand McNally

Florida state facts	Nickname: The Sunshine State	Population: 18,801,310 (rank: 3rd)	Land area: 53,634 sq. mi. (rank: 26th)
	Capital: Tallahassee, B-1	Largest city: Jacksonville, 949,611, B-4	Highest point: Britton Hill, 345 ft., I-2

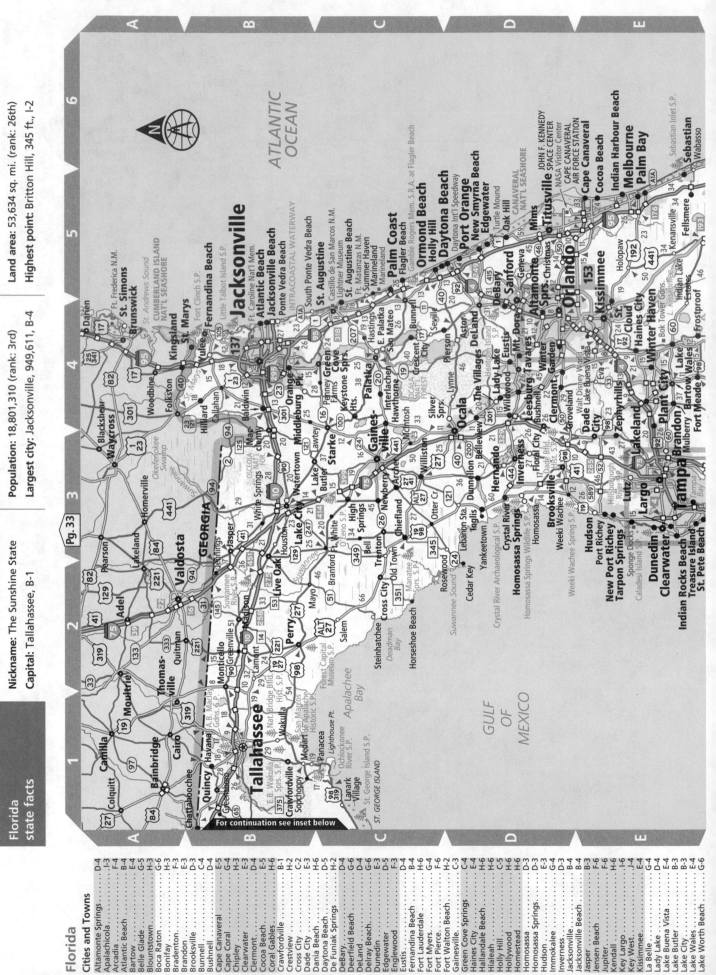

For continuation see inset below

NOTE: Maps are not always in alphabetical order.
See Page 1 for map location in this atlas.

Florida   31

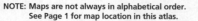

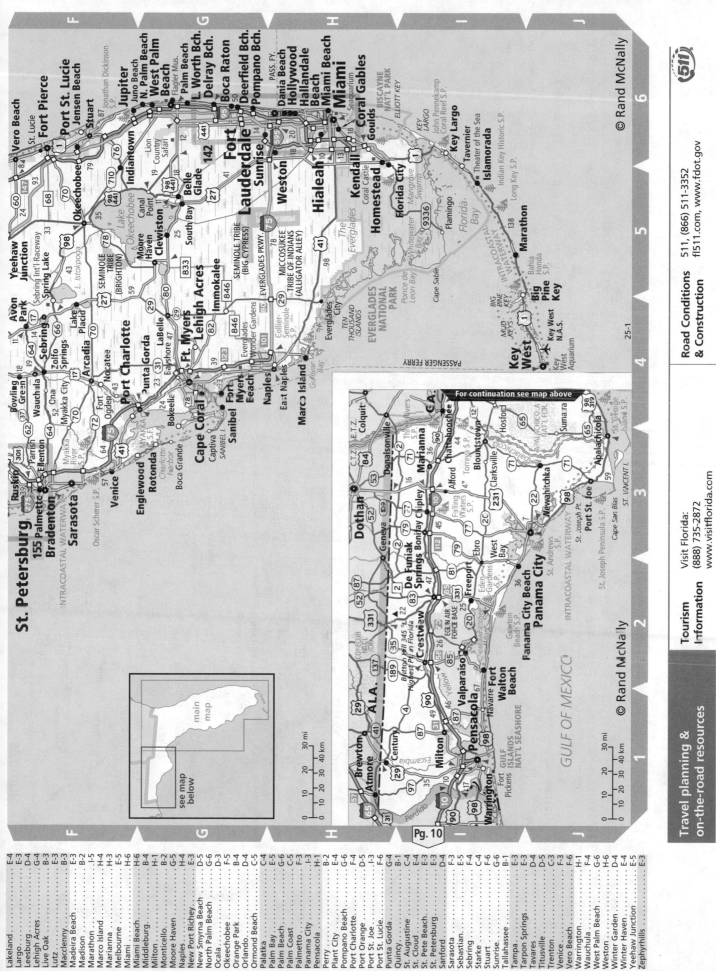

For continuation see map above

Pg. 10

© Rand McNally

© Rand McNally

Tourism Information	Visit Florida: (888) 735-2872 www.visitflorida.com	
Road Conditions & Construction	511, (866) 511-3352 fl511.com, www.fdot.gov	

Travel planning & on-the-road resources

Pg. 75
Pg. 74
Pg. 47
Pg. 10

Georgia state facts

Nickname: The Peach State
Capital: Atlanta, C-2

Population: 10,711,908 (rank: 8th)
Largest city: Atlanta, 498,715, C-2

Land area: 57,701 sq. mi. (rank: 21st)
Highest point: Brasstown Bald, 4,784 ft., A-3

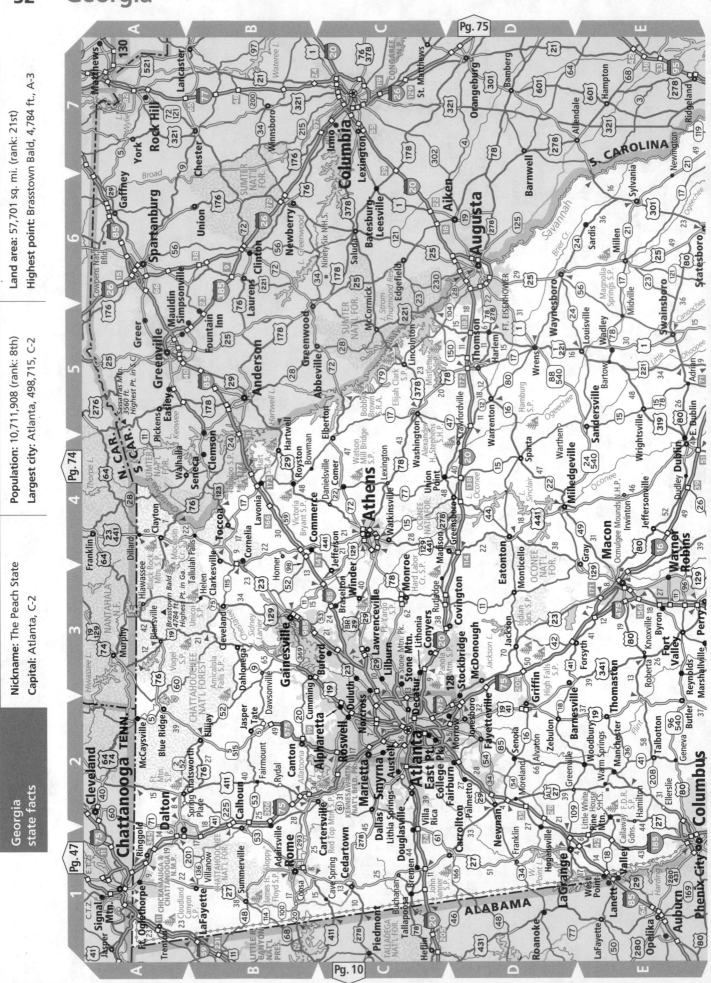

NOTE: Maps are not always in alphabetical order.
See Page 1 for map location in this atlas.

Georgia   33

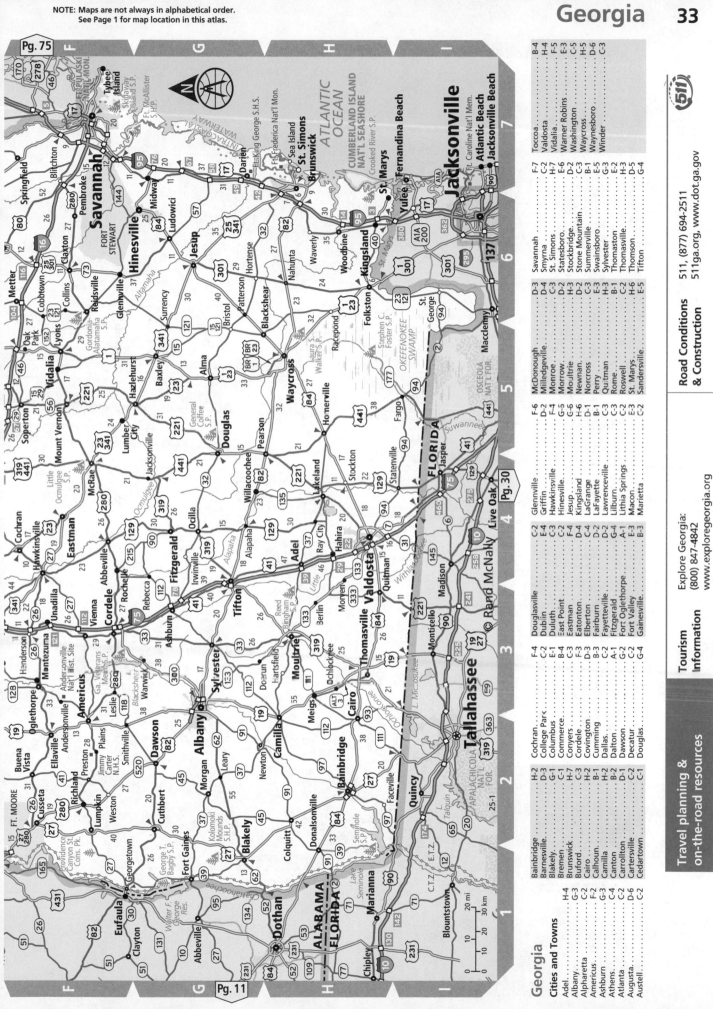

Travel planning & on-the-road resources

Road Conditions & Construction
511, (877) 694-2511
www.dot.ga.gov
511ga.org

Tourism Information
Explore Georgia:
(800) 847-4842
www.exploregeorgia.org

© Rand McNally

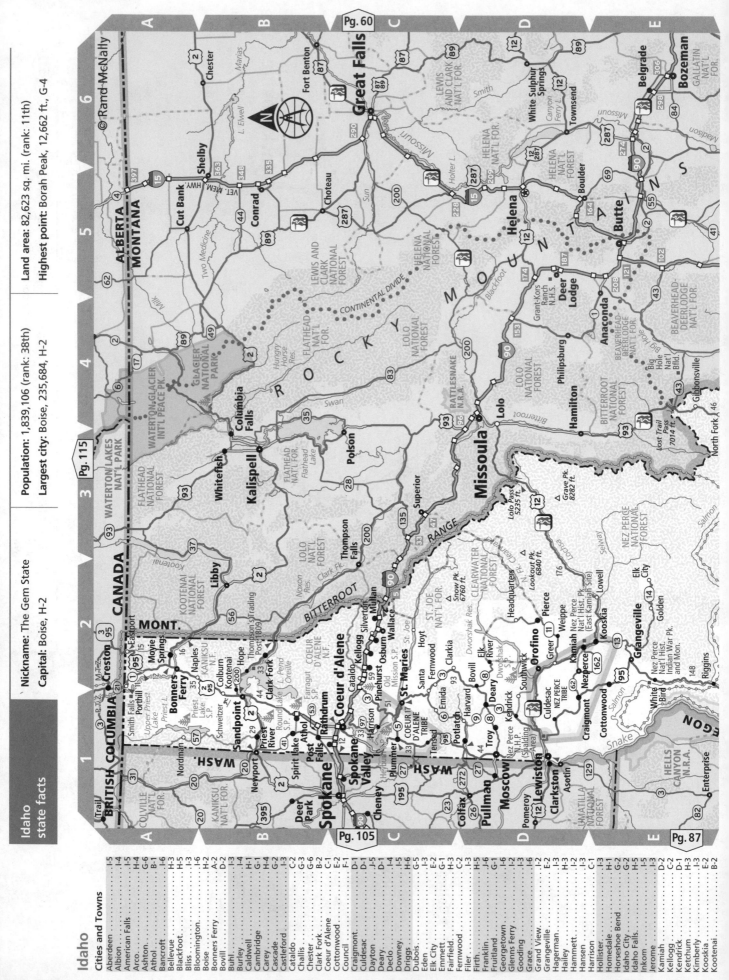

Idaho
state facts

Nickname: The Gem State
Capital: Boise, H-2

Population: 1,839,106 (rank: 38th)
Largest city: Boise, 235,684, H-2

Land area: 82,623 sq. mi. (rank: 11th)
Highest point: Borah Peak, 12,662 ft., G-4

NOTE: Maps are not always in alphabetical order.
See Page 1 for map location in this atlas.

Idaho   35

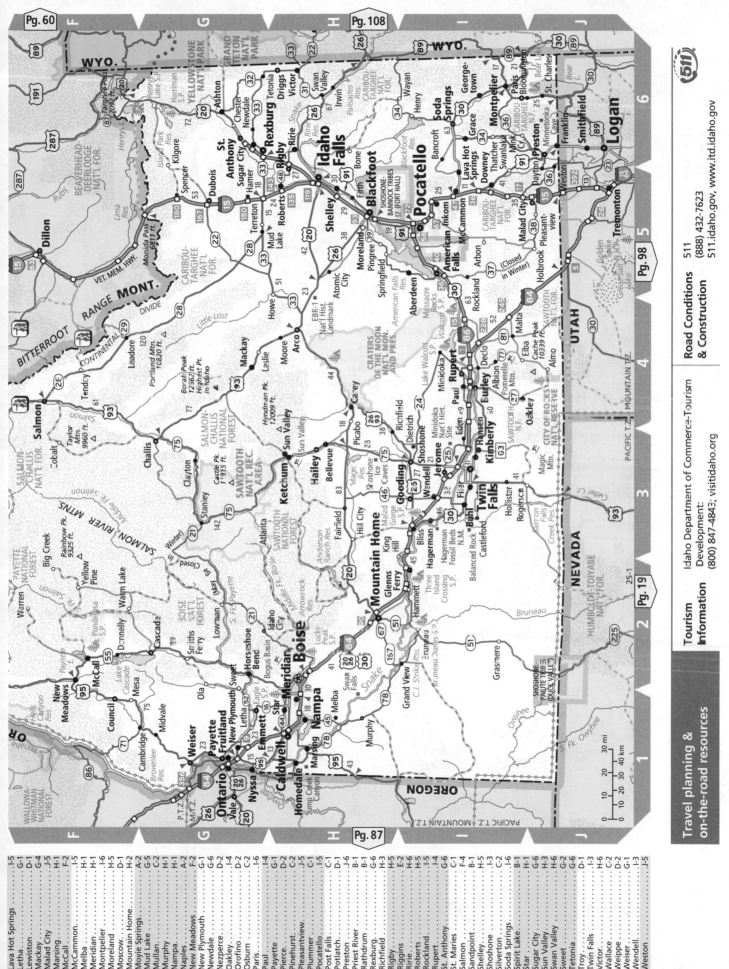

Pg. 60
Pg. 108
Pg. 98
Pg. 19
Pg. 87

Travel planning & on-the-road resources

Tourism Information	Idaho Department of Commerce-Tourism Development: (800) 847-4843; visitidaho.org	Road Conditions & Construction	511 (888) 432-7623 511.idaho.gov, www.itd.idaho.gov

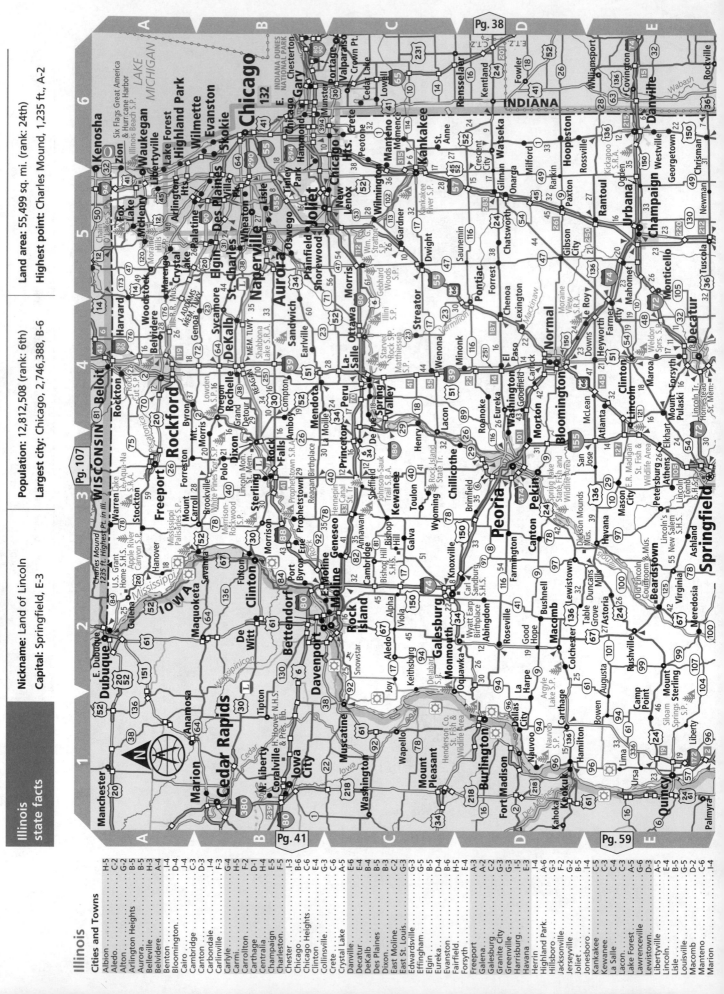

Pg. 38
Pg. 107
Pg. 41
Pg. 59

Illinois state facts

Nickname: Land of Lincoln

Capital: Springfield, E-3

Population: 12,812,508 (rank: 6th)

Largest city: Chicago, 2,746,388, B-6

Land area: 55,499 sq. mi. (rank: 24th)

Highest point: Charles Mound, 1,235 ft., A-2

Illinois

Cities and Towns

NOTE: Maps are not always in alphabetical order.
See Page 1 for map location in this atlas.

Illinois 37

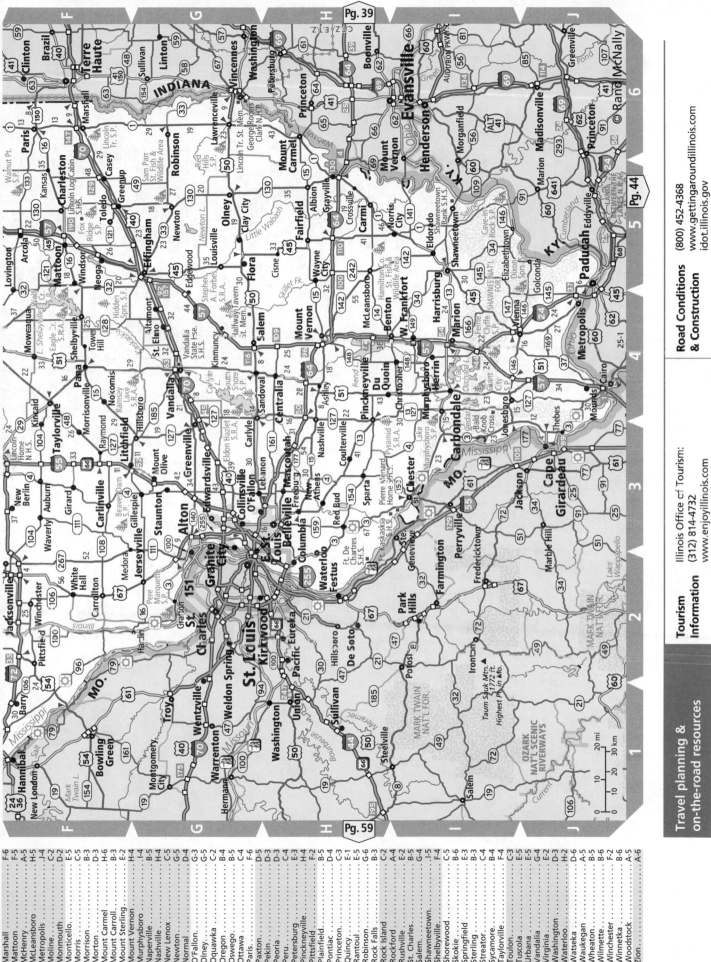

Pg. 39
Pg. 44
Pg. 59

© Rand McNally

Travel planning & on-the-road resources

Tourism Information	Illinois Office of Tourism: (312) 814-4732 www.enjoyillinois.com
Road Conditions & Construction	(800) 452-4368 www.gettingaroundillinois.com idot.illinois.gov

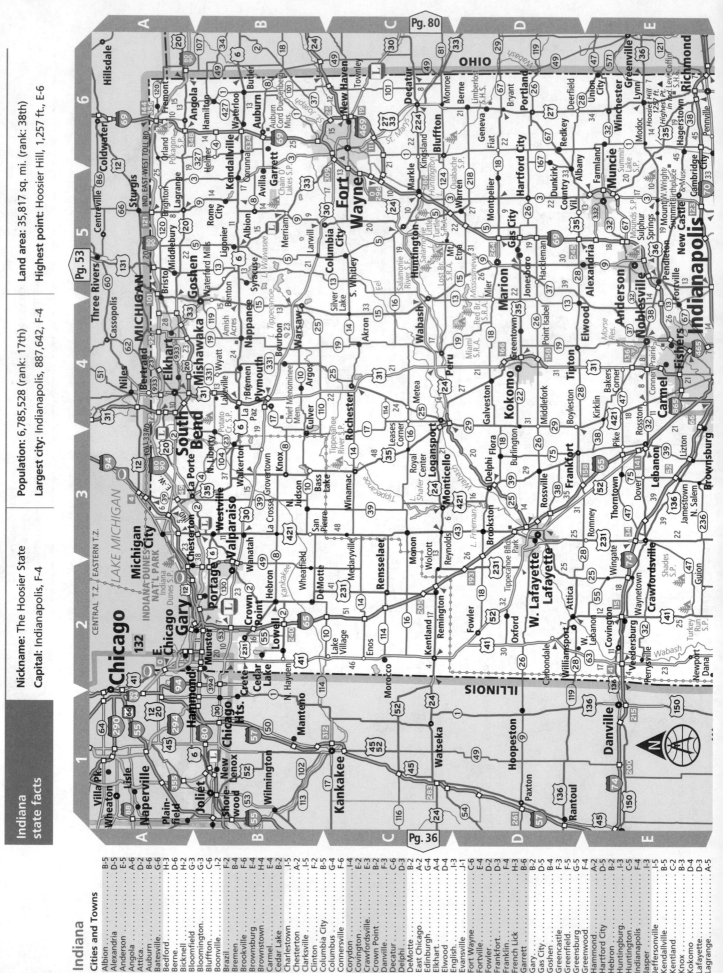

Indiana state facts

Nickname: The Hoosier State

Capital: Indianapolis, F-4

Population: 6,785,528 (rank: 17th)

Largest city: Indianapolis, 887,642, F-4

Land area: 35,817 sq. mi. (rank: 38th)

Highest point: Hoosier Hill, 1,257 ft., E-6

Indiana
Cities and Towns

NOTE: Maps are not always in alphabetical order.
See Page 1 for map location in this atlas.

Indiana 39

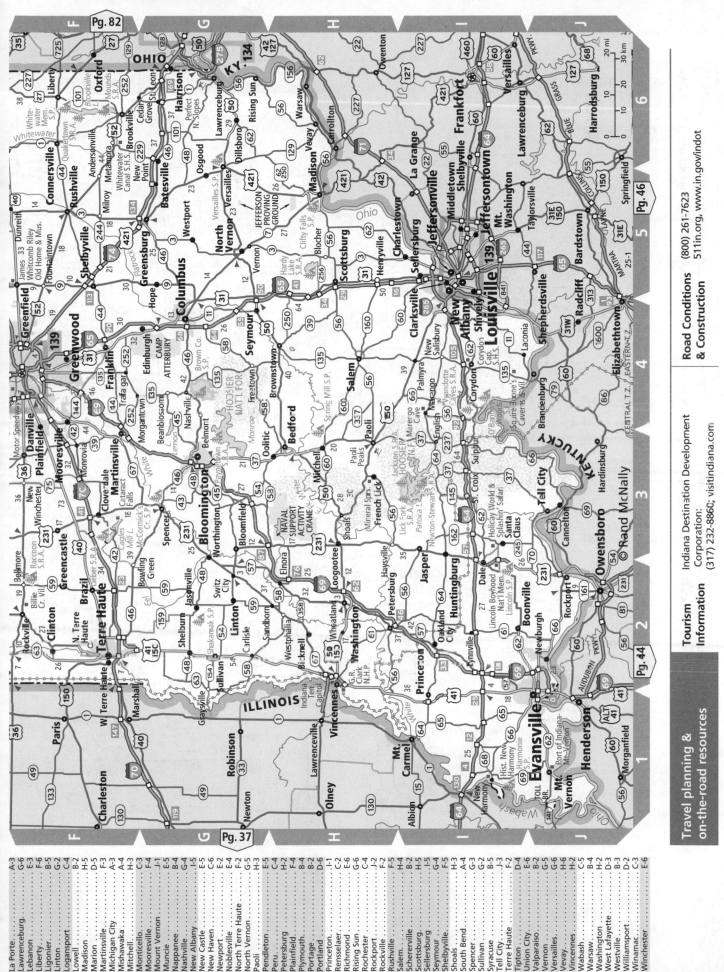

Pg. 82
Pg. 46
Pg. 44
Pg. 37

Travel planning & on-the-road resources

Tourism Information	Indiana Destination Development Corporation: (317) 232-8860; visitindiana.com	Road Conditions & Construction	(800) 261-7623 511in.org, www.in.gov/indot

© Rand McNally

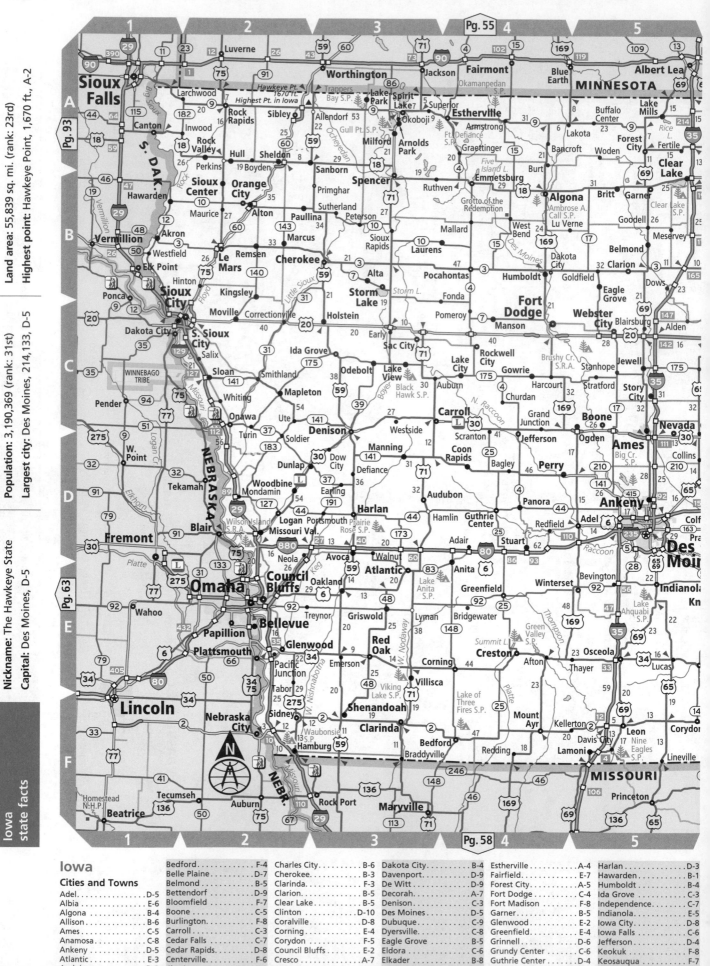

Iowa state facts

Nickname: The Hawkeye State

Capital: Des Moines, D-5

Population: 3,190,369 (rank: 31st)

Largest city: Des Moines, 214,133, D-5

Land area: 55,839 sq. mi. (rank: 23rd)

Highest point: Hawkeye Point, 1,670 ft., A-2

NOTE: Maps are not always in alphabetical order.
See Page 1 for map location in this atlas.

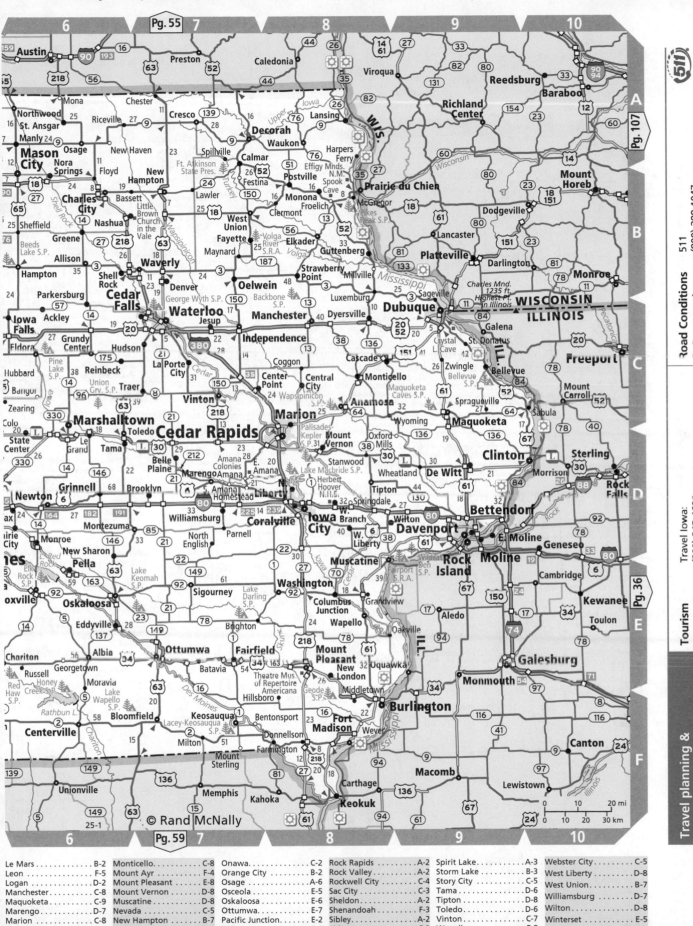

© Rand McNally

Road Conditions & Construction
511
(800) 288-1047
www.511ia.org, iowadot.gov

Tourism Information
Travel Iowa:
(800) 345-4692
www.traveliowa.com

Travel planning & on-the-road resources

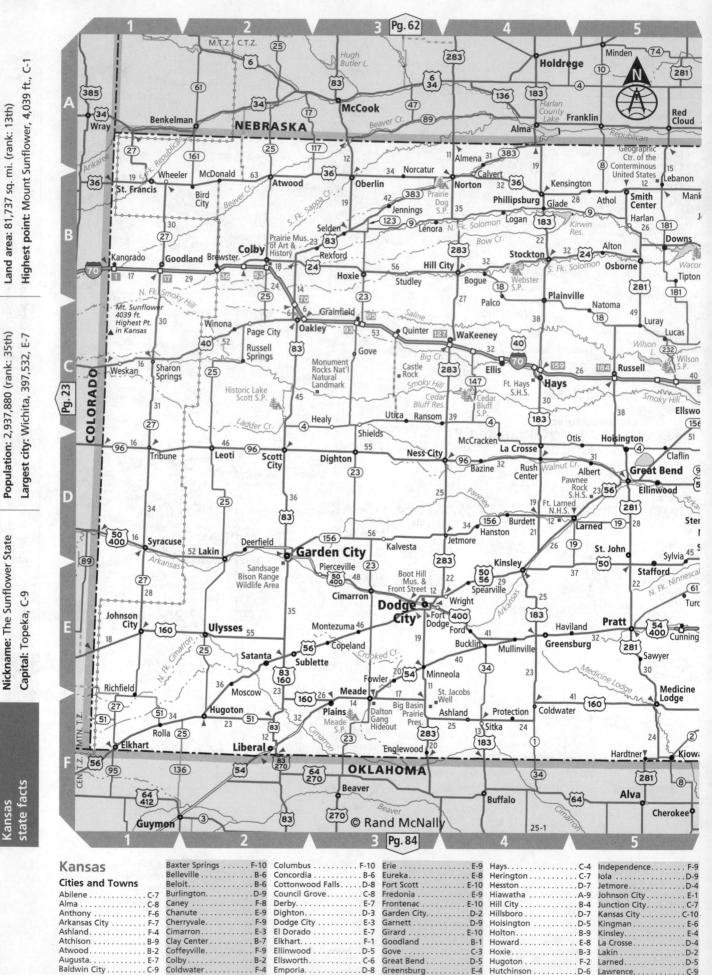

© Rand McNally

Kansas state facts

Land area: 81,737 sq. mi. (rank: 13th)
Highest point: Mount Sunflower, 4,039 ft., C-1

Population: 2,937,880 (rank: 35th)
Largest city: Wichita, 397,532, E-7

Nickname: The Sunflower State
Capital: Topeka, C-9

Kansas

Cities and Towns

NOTE: Maps are not always in alphabetical order.
See Page 1 for map location in this atlas.

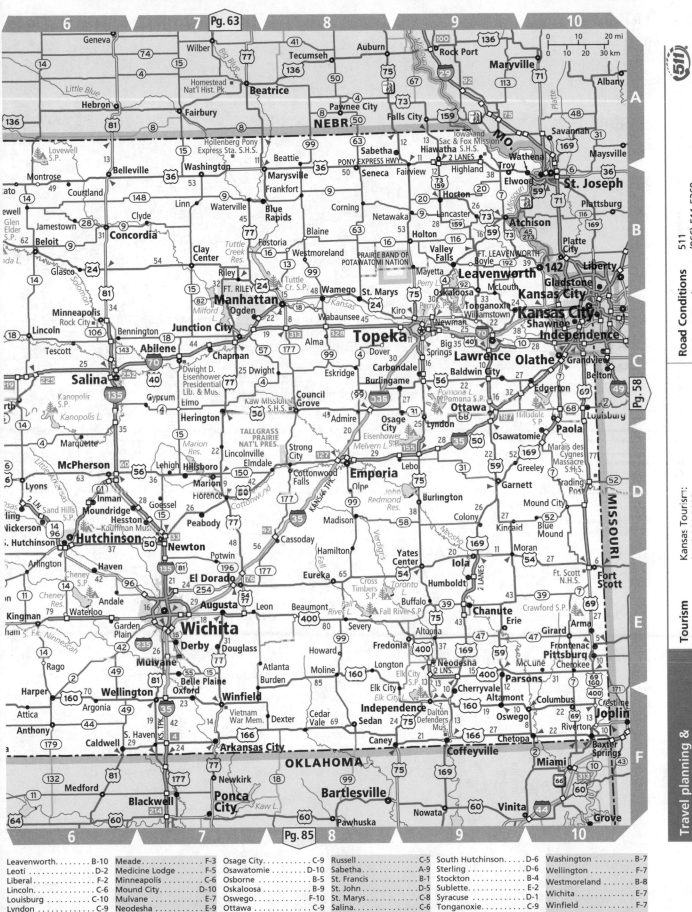

Pg. 63
Pg. 58
Pg. 85

511
(866) 511-5368
www.kandrive.org, www.ksdot.org

Road Conditions & Construction

Kansas Tourism:
(785) 296-2009
www.travelks.com

Tourism Information

Travel planning & on-the-road resources

Kentucky state facts

Nickname: The Bluegrass State
Capital: Frankfort, C-9

Population: 4,505,836 (rank: 26th)
Largest city: Louisville, 633,045, C-8

Land area: 39,481 sq. mi. (rank: 36th)
Highest point: Black Mountain, 4,145 ft., E-12

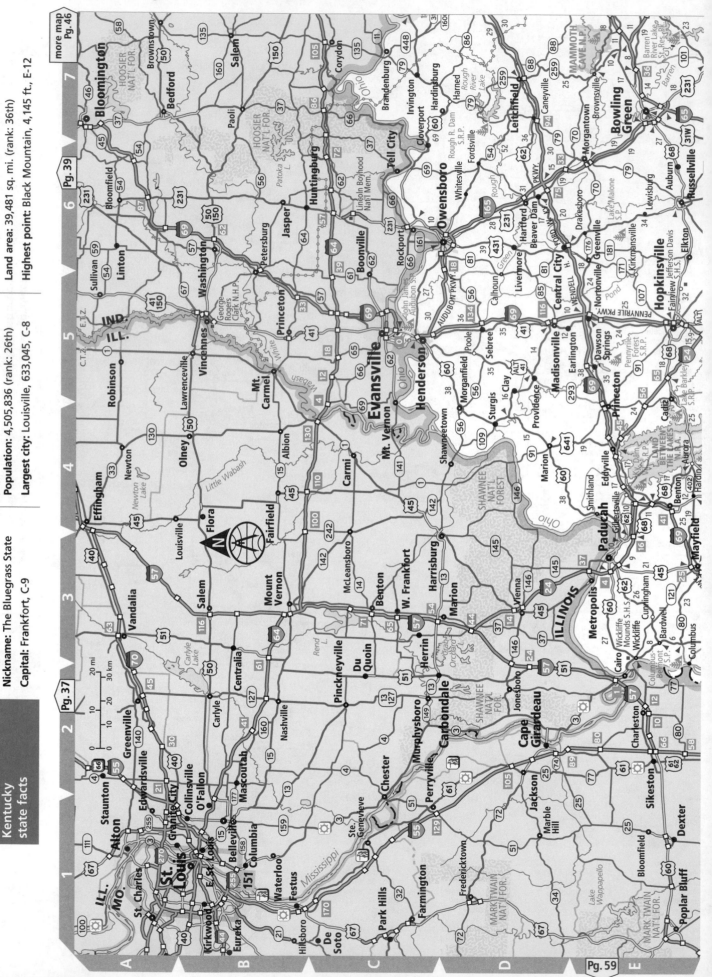

NOTE: Maps are not always in alphabetical order.
See Page 1 for map location in this atlas.

Kentucky • Tennessee/Western   45

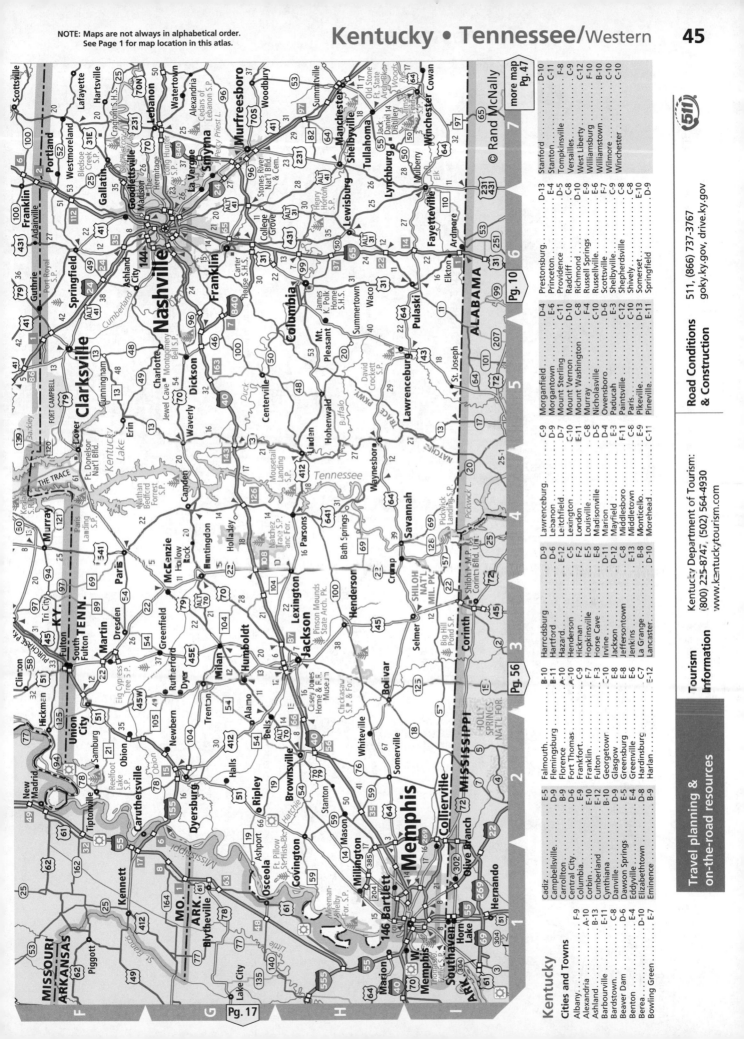

© Rand McNally

more map Pg. 47

Pg. 10

Pg. 56

Pg. 17

Kentucky

Cities and Towns

Tourism Information

Kentucky Department of Tourism:
(800) 225-8747, (502) 564-4930
www.kentuckytourism.com

Road Conditions & Construction

511, (866) 737-3767
goky.ky.gov, drive.ky.gov

Travel planning & on-the-road resources

511

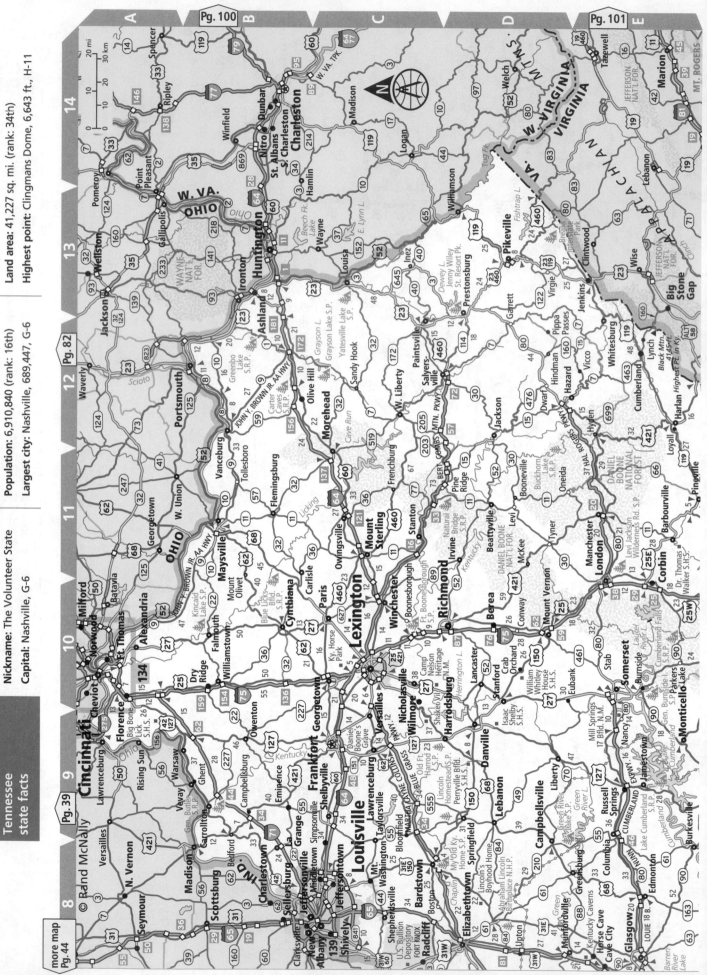

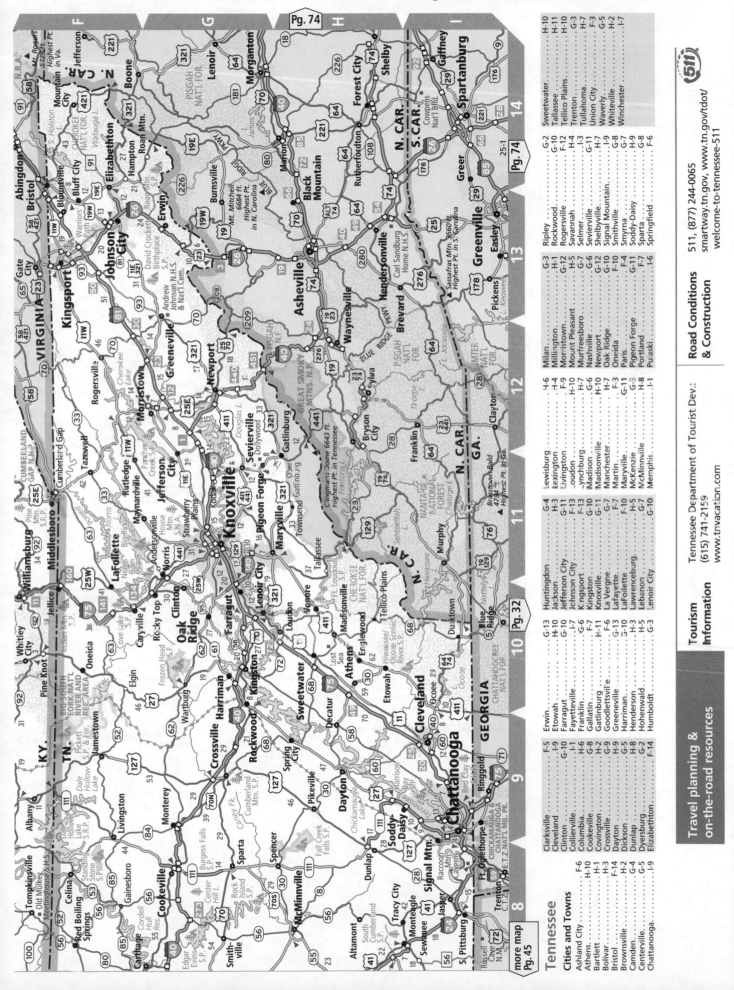

NOTE: Maps are not always in alphabetical order.
See Page 1 for map location in this atlas.

Tennessee

Cities and Towns

Ashland City	F-6
Athens	H-10
Bartlett	H-1
Bolivar	H-3
Brownsville	H-2
Camden	G-4
Centerville	G-5
Chattanooga	I-9
Clarksville	F-5
Cleveland	I-9
Clinton	G-10
Collierville	I-1
Columbia	H-6
Cookeville	G-8
Covington	H-2
Crossville	G-9
Dayton	H-9
Dickson	F-5
Dunlap	H-8
Dyersburg	G-2
Elizabethton	I-9
Erwin	F-5
Etowah	I-9
Farragut	G-10
Fayetteville	H-6
Franklin	G-6
Gallatin	F-7
Gatlinburg	H-11
Goodlettsville	F-6
Greeneville	G-9
Harriman	G-5
Henderson	H-3
Hohenwald	H-5
Humboldt	G-3
Huntingdon	G-3
Jackson	H-3
Jefferson City	G-11
Kingsport	F-13
Kingston	G-10
Knoxville	G-11
La Vergne	F-6
Lafayette	F-7
LaFollette	F-10
Lawrenceburg	H-5
Lebanon	G-7
Lenoir City	G-10
Lewisburg	G-4
Lexington	H-3
Livingston	F-9
Loudon	G-10
Lynchburg	H-6
Madison	G-6
Madisonville	H-10
Manchester	H-7
Martin	F-3
Maryville	G-11
McKenzie	F-4
McMinnville	G-7
Memphis	I-1
Milan	H-6
Millington	H-1
Morristown	F-12
Mount Pleasant	H-5
Murfreesboro	G-7
Nashville	G-6
Newport	H-12
Oak Ridge	G-10
Oneida	F-10
Paris	F-4
Pigeon Forge	H-11
Portland	F-7
Pulaski	I-6
Ripley	G-2
Rockwood	H-1
Rogersville	G-12
Savannah	H-4
Selmer	H-4
Sevierville	G-11
Shelbyville	H-7
Signal Mountain	I-9
Smithville	G-8
Smyrna	G-7
Soddy-Daisy	H-9
Sparta	G-8
Springfield	F-6
Sweetwater	H-10
Tallassee	H-11
Tellico Plains	H-10
Trenton	G-3
Tullahoma	H-7
Union City	F-3
Waverly	G-5
Whiteville	H-2
Winchester	I-7

more map
Pg. 45

Travel planning & on-the-road resources

Tourism Information
Tennessee Department of Tourist Dev.:
(615) 741-2159
www.tnvacation.com

Road Conditions & Construction
511, (877) 244-0065
smartway.tn.gov, www.tn.gov/tdot/
welcome-to-tennessee-511

Louisiana
Cities and Towns

Land area: 43,193 sq. mi. (rank: 33rd)
Highest point: Driskill Mountain, 535 ft., B-3

Population: 4,657,757 (rank: 25th)
Largest city: New Orleans, 383,997, F-7

Nickname: The Pelican State
Capital: Baton Rouge, E-6

Louisiana state facts

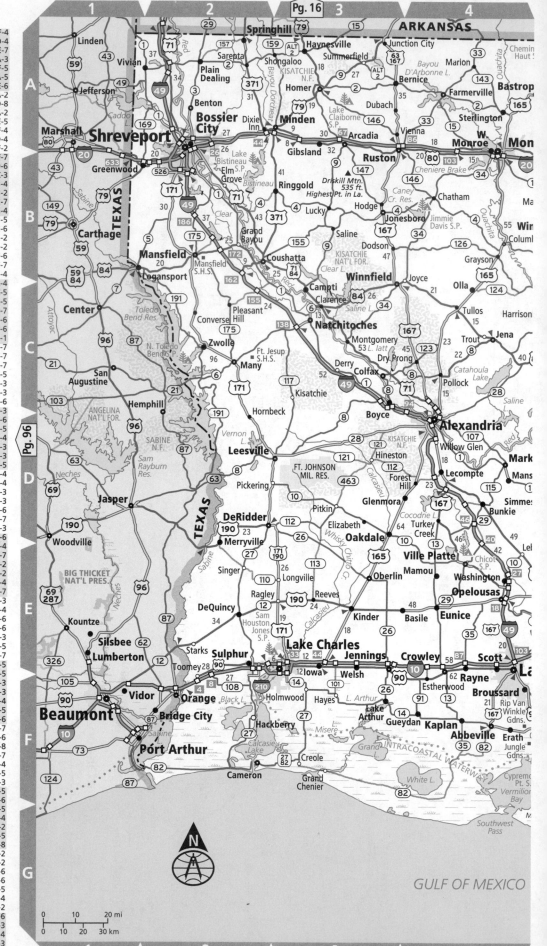

NOTE: Maps are not always in alphabetical order.
See Page 1 for map location in this atlas.

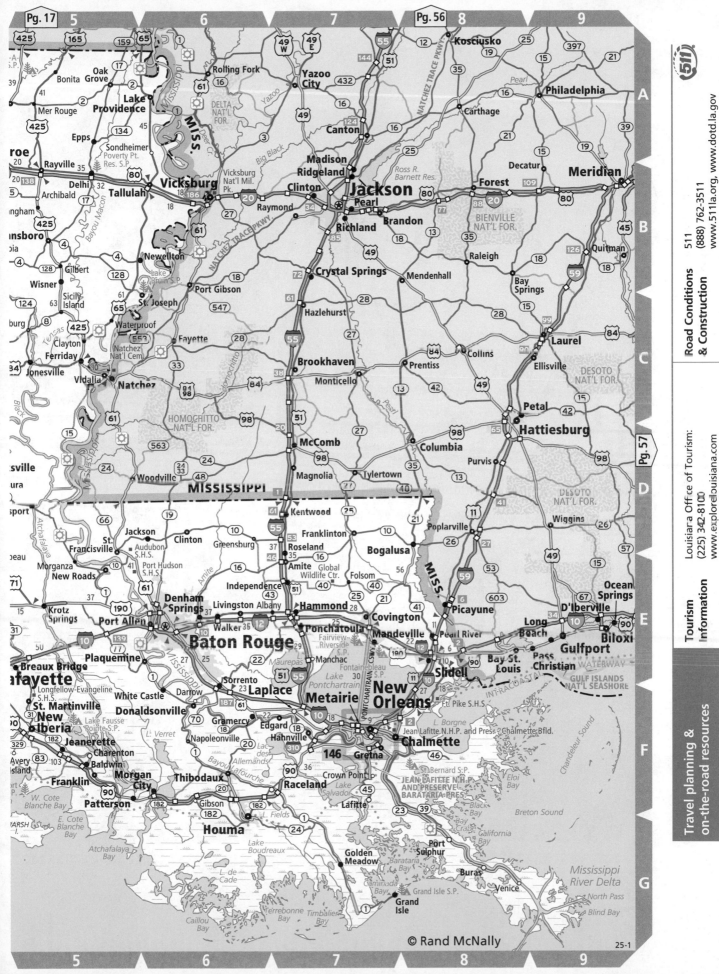

© Rand McNally

Road Conditions & Construction
511
(888) 762-3511
www.511la.org, www.dotd.la.gov

Tourism Information
Louisiana Office of Tourism:
(225) 342-8100
www.explorelouisiana.com

Travel planning & on-the-road resources

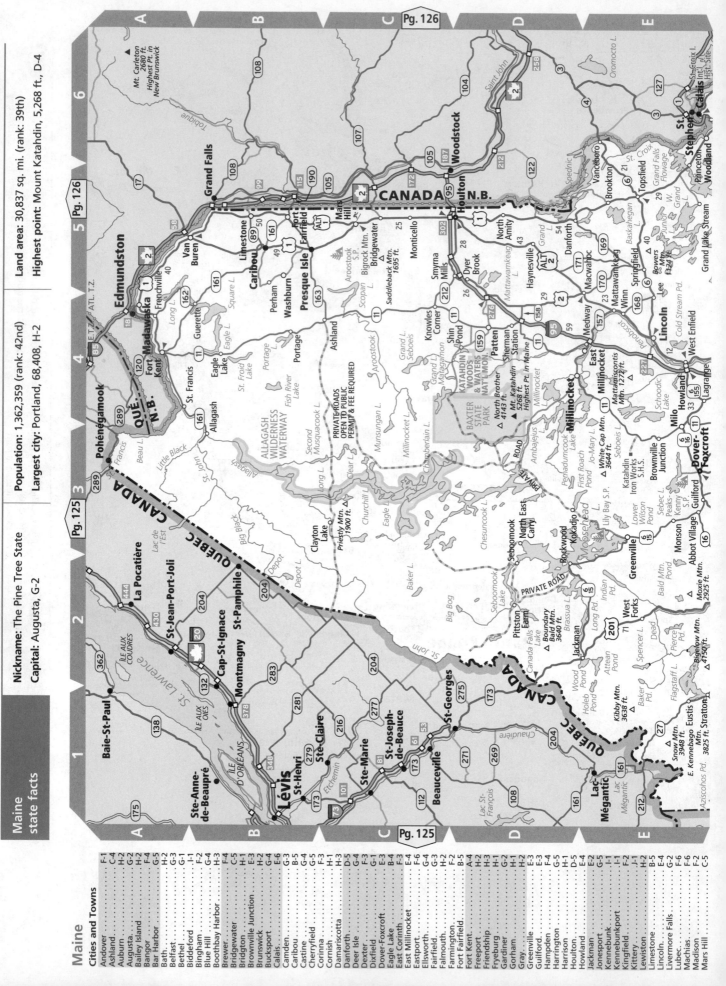

Maine state facts

Nickname: The Pine Tree State	Population: 1,362,359 (rank: 42nd)	Land area: 30,837 sq. mi. (rank: 39th)
Capital: Augusta, G-2	Largest city: Portland, 68,408, H-2	Highest point: Mount Katahdin, 5,268 ft., D-4

Pg. 126
Pg. 126
Pg. 125
Pg. 125

NOTE: Maps are not always in alphabetical order.
See Page 1 for map location in this atlas.

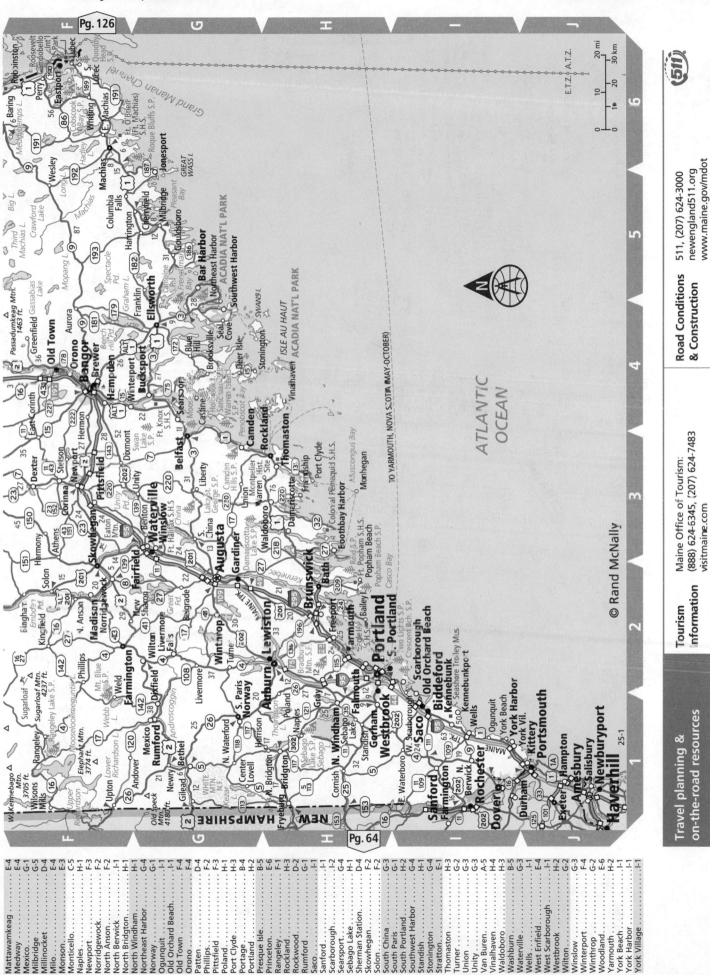

© Rand McNally

Pg. 126

Pg. 64

ATLANTIC OCEAN

TO YARMOUTH, NOVA SCOTIA (MAY–OCTOBER)

NEW HAMPSHIRE

Tourism Information	Maine Office of Tourism: (888) 624-6345, (207) 624-7483 visitmaine.com	**Road Conditions & Construction** 511, (207) 624-3000 newengland511.org www.maine.gov/mdot

Travel planning & on-the-road resources

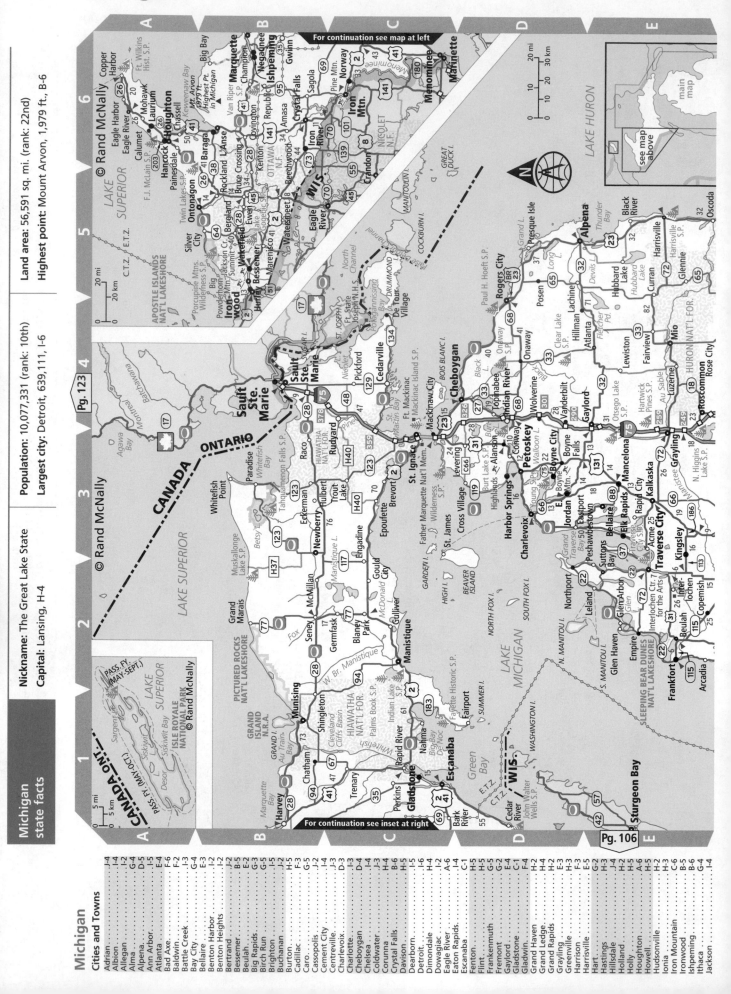

Michigan
Michigan state facts

Nickname: The Great Lake State
Capital: Lansing, H-4

Population: 10,077,331 (rank: 10th)
Largest city: Detroit, 639,111, I-6

Land area: 56,591 sq. mi. (rank: 22nd)
Highest point: Mount Arvon, 1,979 ft., B-6

Michigan
Cities and Towns

NOTE: Maps are not always in alphabetical order.
See Page 1 for map location in this atlas.

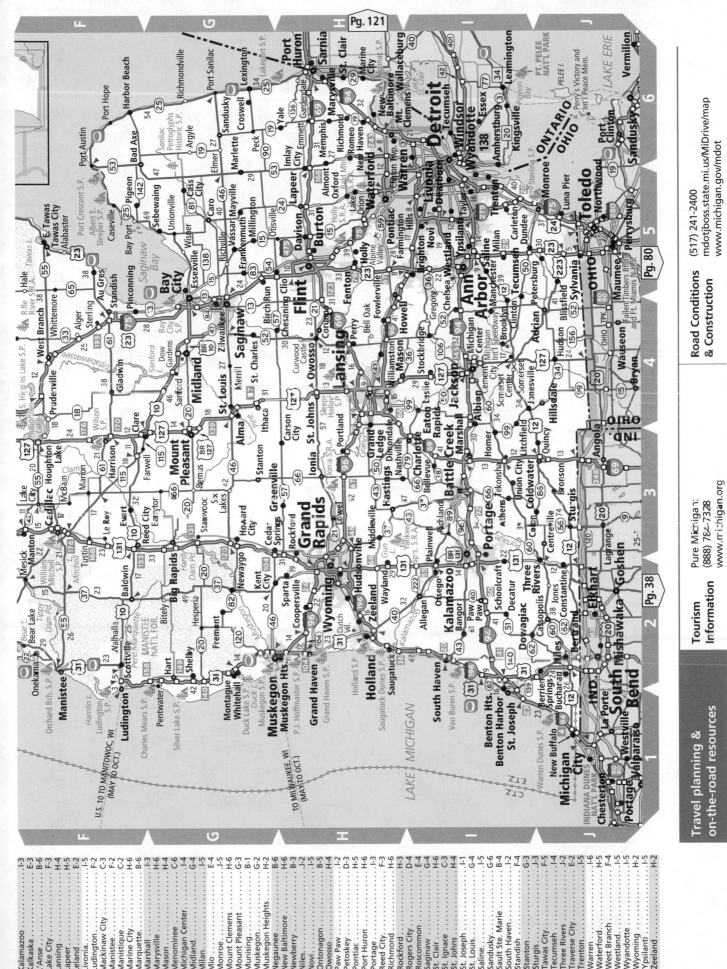

Road Conditions & Construction
(517) 241-2400
mdotjboss.state.mi.us/MiDrive/map
www.michigan.gov/mdot

Tourism Information
Pure Michigan:
(888) 784-7328
www.michigan.org

Travel planning & on-the-road resources

Pg. 106
Pg. 123
Pg. 123
Pg. 119
Pg. 79

Minnesota state facts

Nickname: The North Star State
Capital: St. Paul, H-5

Land area: 79,605 sq. mi. (rank: 22nd)
Population: 5,706,494 (rank: 22nd)
Largest city: Minneapolis, 429,954, H-4

Highest point: Eagle Mountain, 2,301 ft., A-5

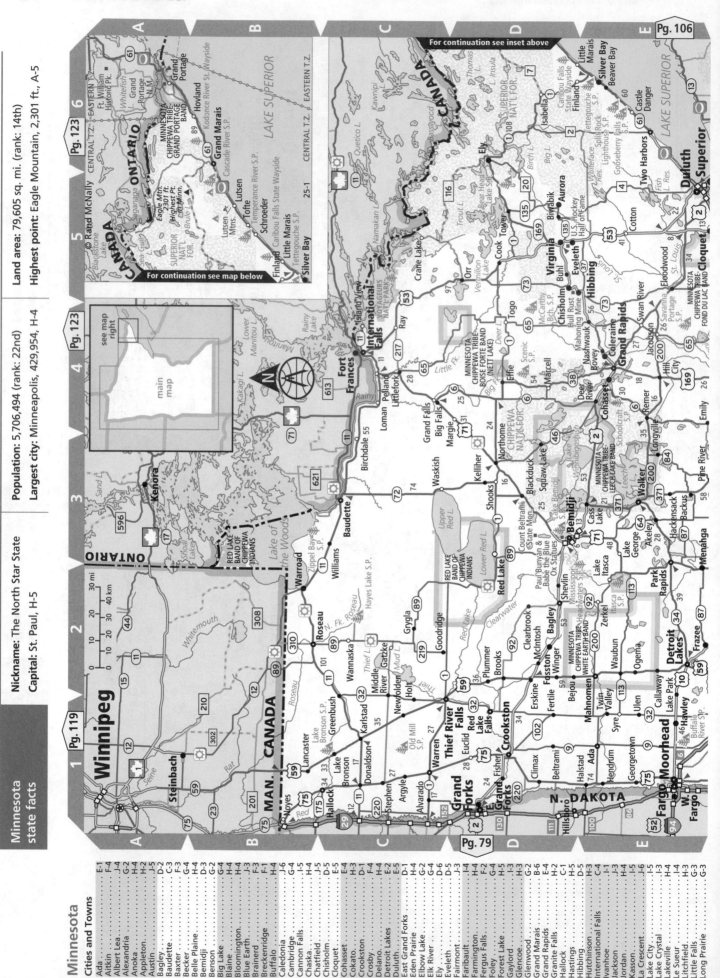

For continuation see inset above

For continuation see map below

© Rand McNally

NOTE: Maps are not always in alphabetical order.
See Page 1 for map location in this atlas.

Minnesota 55

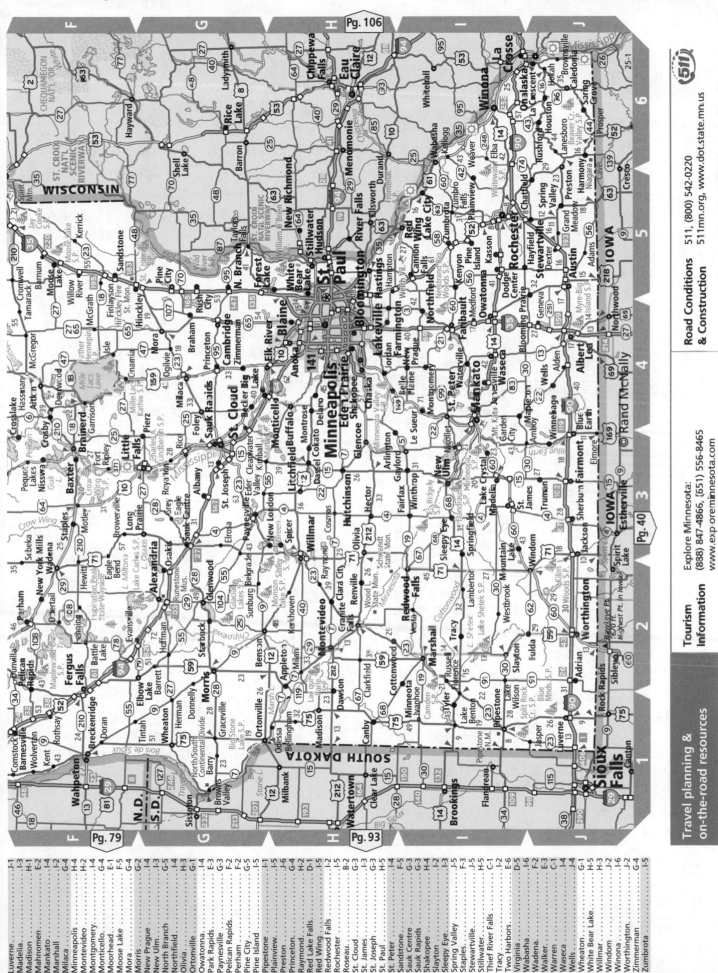

Travel planning & on-the-road resources

Tourism Information
Explore Minnesota:
(888) 847-4866, (651) 556-8465
www.exploreminnesota.com

Road Conditions & Construction
511, (800) 542-0220
511mn.org, www.dot.state.mn.us

© Rand McNally

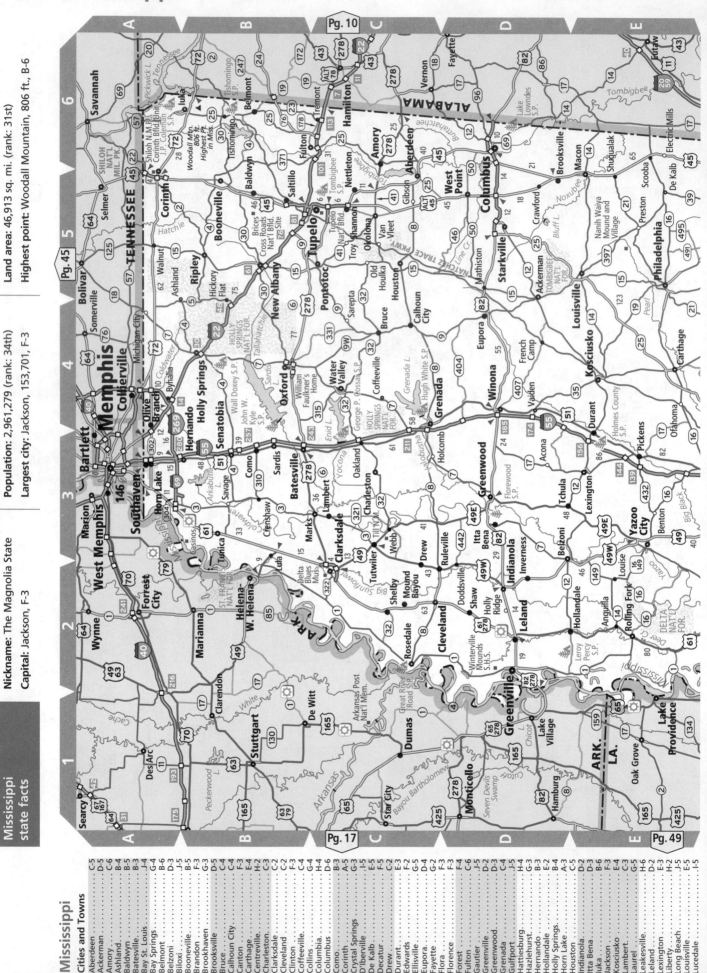

Mississippi state facts

Nickname: The Magnolia State
Capital: Jackson, F-3

Population: 2,961,279 (rank: 34th)
Largest city: Jackson, 153,701, F-3

Land area: 46,913 sq. mi. (rank: 31st)
Highest point: Woodall Mountain, 806 ft., B-6

Pg. 10
Pg. 45
Pg. 17
Pg. 49

NOTE: Maps are not always in alphabetical order.
See Page 1 for map location in this atlas.

Mississippi 57

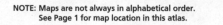

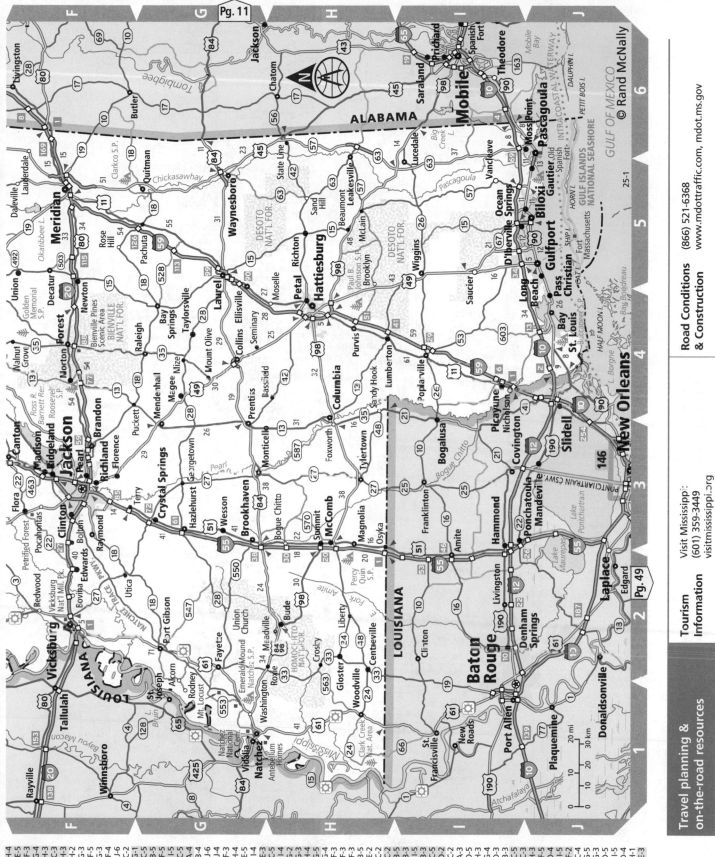

Pg. 11

Pg. 49

© Rand McNally

GULF OF MEXICO

ALABAMA

LOUISIANA

Travel planning & on-the-road resources

Tourism Information	Visit Mississippi: (601) 359-3449 visitmississippi.org
Road Conditions & Construction	(866) 521-6368 www.mdottraffic.com, mdot.ms.gov

Missouri
Cities and Towns

Missouri state facts

Nickname: The Show Me State

Capital: Jefferson City, D-5

Population: 6,154,913 (rank: 19th)

Largest city: Kansas City, 508,090, C-2

Land area: 68,727 sq. mi. (rank: 18th)

Highest point: Taum Sauk Mtn., 1,772 ft., E-7

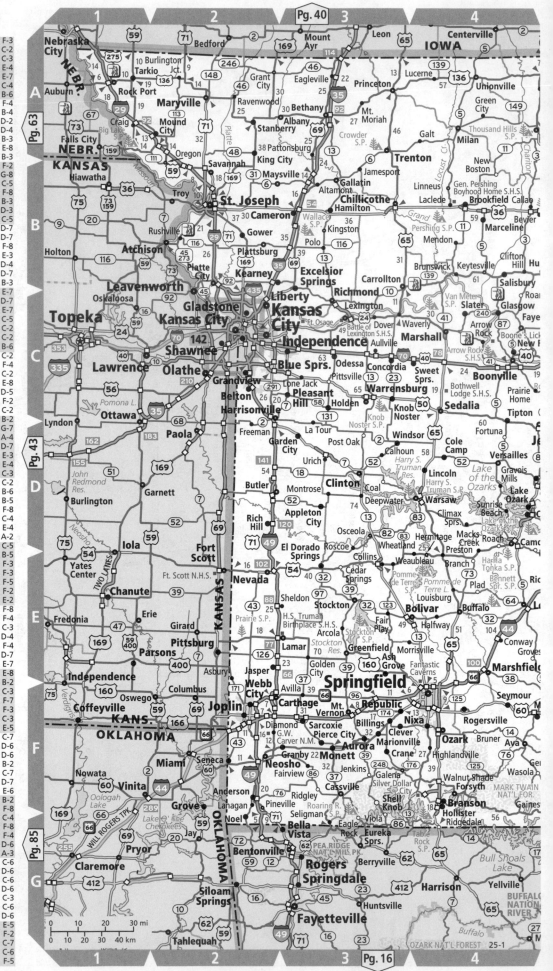

NOTE: Maps are not always in alphabetical order.
See Page 1 for map location in this atlas.

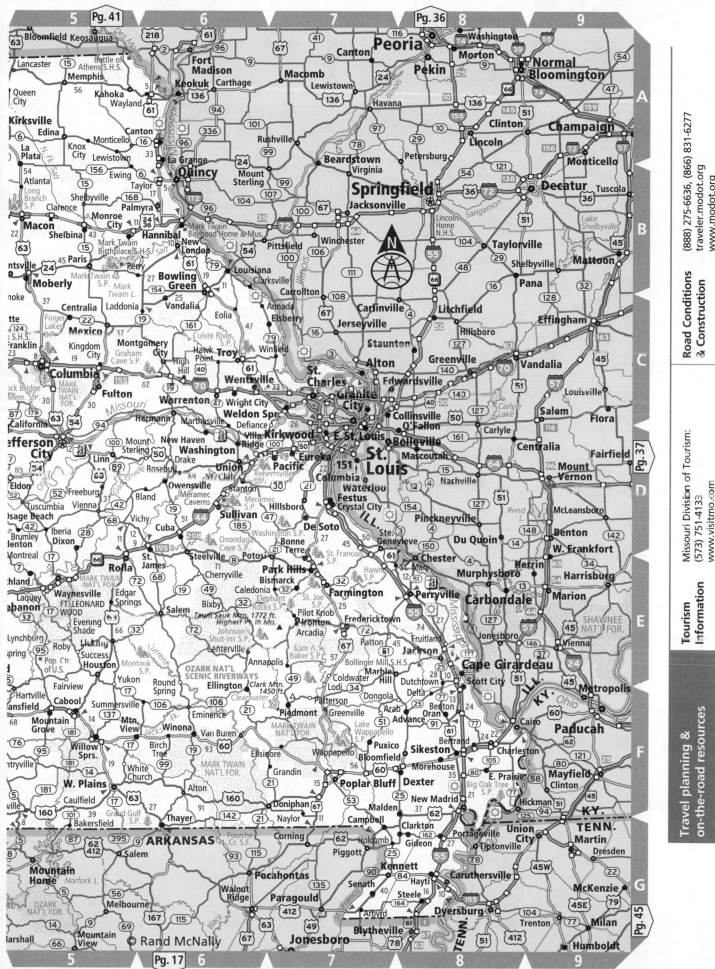

Pg. 41
Pg. 36
Pg. 37
Pg. 45
Pg. 17

Road Conditions & Construction

(888) 275-6636, (866) 831-6277
traveler.modot.org
www.modot.org

Tourism Information

Missouri Division of Tourism:
(573) 751-4133
www.visitmo.com

Travel planning & on-the-road resources

© Rand McNally

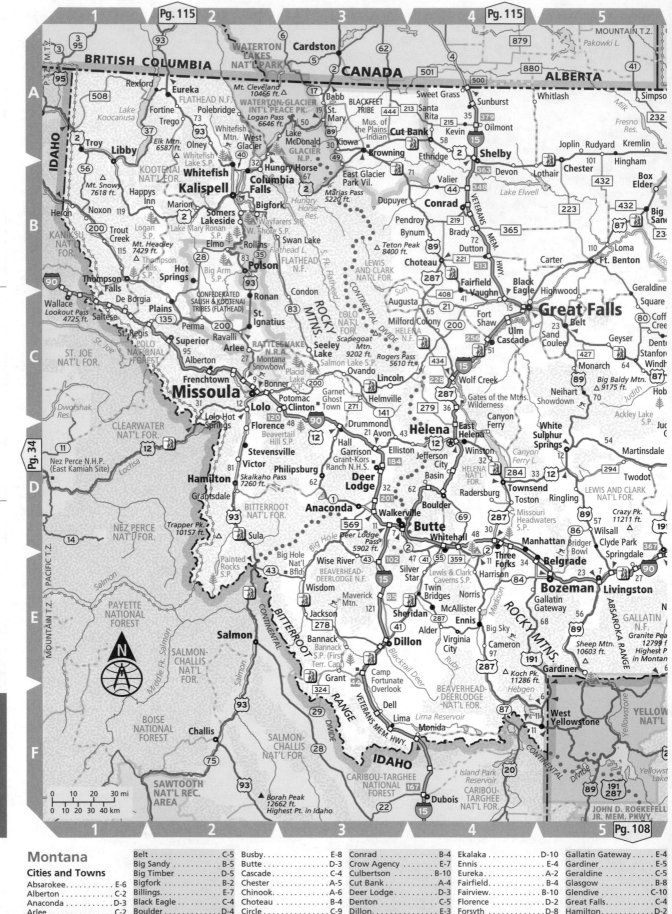

Land area: 145,509 sq. mi. (rank: 4th)
Highest point: Granite Peak, 12,799 ft., E-6

Population: 1,084,225 (rank: 44th)
Largest city: Billings, 117,116, E-7

Nickname: The Treasure State
Capital: Helena, D-4

Montana state facts

Montana

Cities and Towns

NOTE: Maps are not always in alphabetical order.
See Page 1 for map location in this atlas.

Montana **61**

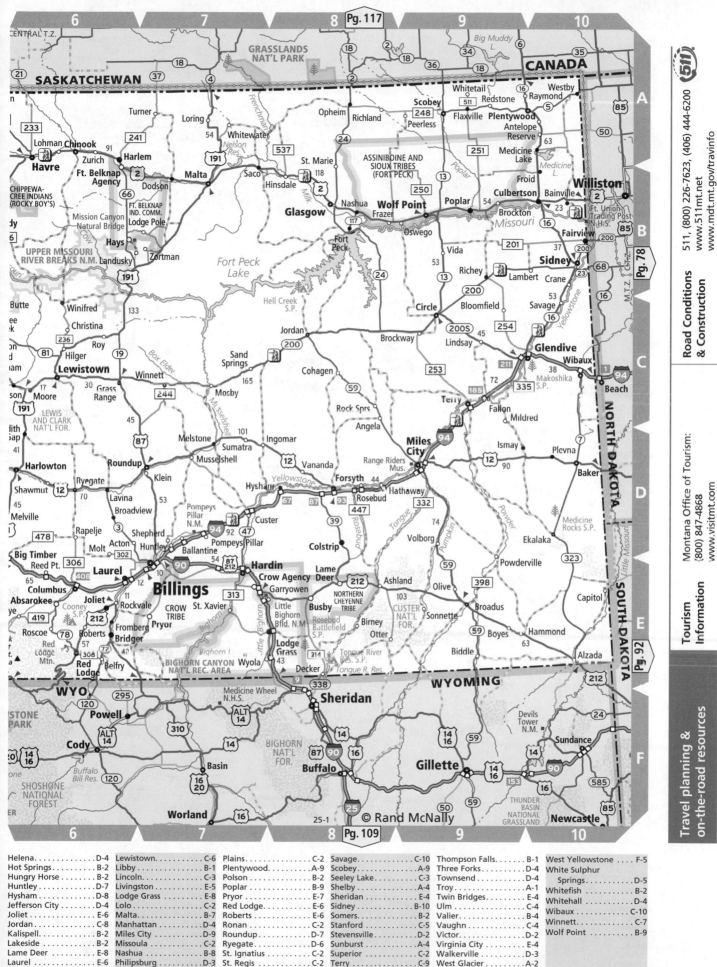

511, (800) 226-7623, (406) 444-6200
www.511mt.net
www.mdt.mt.gov/travinfo

Road Conditions & Construction

Montana Office of Tourism:
(800) 847-4868
www.visitmt.com

Tourism Information

Travel planning & on-the-road resources

© Rand McNally

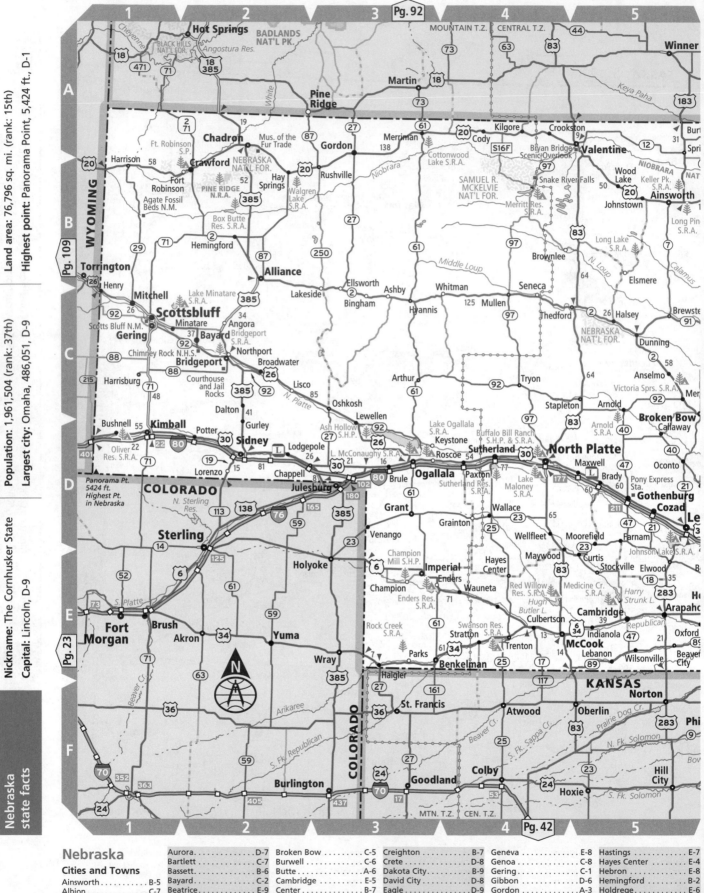

Pg. 92
Pg. 109
Pg. 23
Pg. 42

Nebraska state facts

Nickname: The Cornhusker State
Capital: Lincoln, D-9

Population: 1,961,504 (rank: 37th)
Largest city: Omaha, 486,051, D-9

Land area: 76,796 sq. mi. (rank: 15th)
Highest point: Panorama Point, 5,424 ft., D-1

Nebraska
Cities and Towns

NOTE: Maps are not always in alphabetical order.
See Page 1 for map location in this atlas.

Nebraska 63

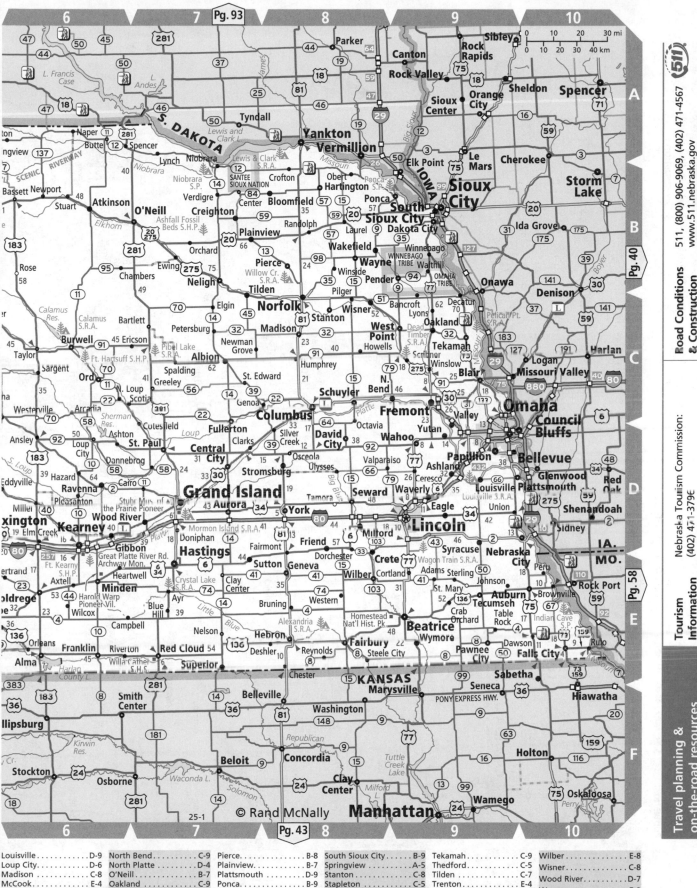

Road Conditions & Construction — 511, (800) 906-9069, (402) 471-4567 — www.511.nebraska.gov — dot.nebraska.gov/travel

Tourism Information — Nebraska Tourism Commission: (402) 471-3796 — visitnebraska.com

Travel planning & on-the-road resources

New Hampshire state facts

Nickname: The Granite State
Capital: Concord, H-5
Population: 1,377,529 (rank: 41st)

Largest city: Manchester, 115,644, H-5
Land area: 8,951 sq. mi. (rank: 44th)
Highest point: Mt. Washington, 6,288 ft., D-6

Travel planning & on-the-road resources

Tourism Information
N.H. Div. of Travel & Tourism Dev.:
(603) 271-2665
www.visitnh.gov

Road Conditions & Construction
(603) 271-3734
newengland511.org
www.dot.nh.gov

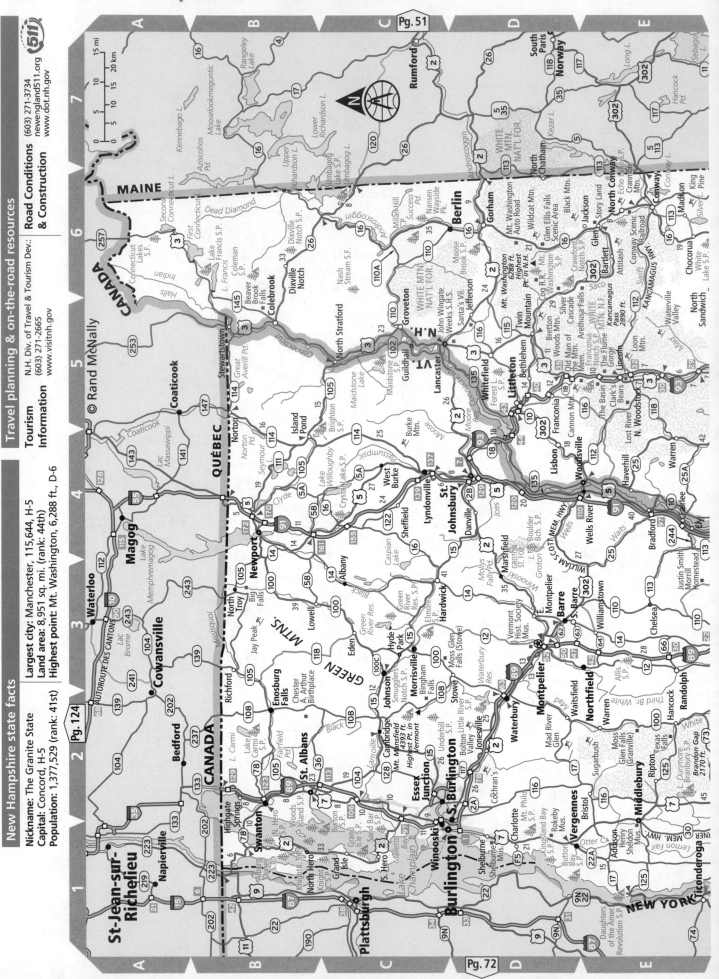

© Rand McNally

NOTE: Maps are not always in alphabetical order.
See Page 1 for map location in this atlas.

New Hampshire • Vermont   65

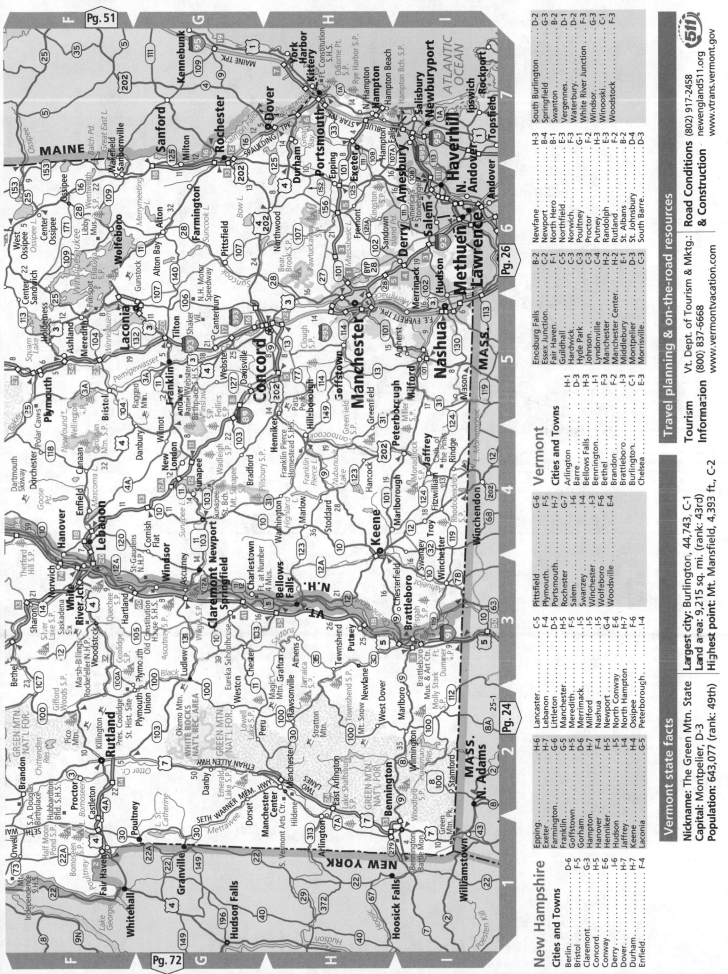

New Hampshire
Cities and Towns

Berlin	D-6
Bristol	F-5
Claremont	G-3
Concord	H-5
Conway	E-6
Derry	I-6
Dover	H-7
Durham	H-7
Enfield	F-4
Epping	H-6
Exeter	H-7
Farmington	G-6
Franklin	G-5
Goffstown	G-5
Gorham	D-7
Hampton	H-7
Hanover	F-4
Henniker	H-5
Hudson	I-5
Jaffrey	I-4
Keene	I-3
Laconia	F-5
Lancaster	H-6
Lebanon	H-7
Littleton	G-6
Manchester	G-5
Meredith	H-5
Merrimack	D-6
Milford	H-7
Nashua	F-4
Newport	H-5
North Conway	I-5
North Hampton	I-4
Ossipee	H-6
Peterborough	G-5
Pittsfield	C-5
Plymouth	F-4
Portsmouth	D-5
Rochester	H-5
Salem	F-5
Swanzey	I-5
Winchester	I-5
Wolfeboro	G-4
Woodsville	E-6

Vermont
Cities and Towns

Arlington	H-1
Barre	D-3
Bellows Falls	H-3
Bennington	I-1
Bethel	F-6
Brandon	E-4
Brattleboro	H-7
Burlington	C-1
Chelsea	E-4
Enosburg Falls	B-2
Essex Junction	C-2
Fair Haven	F-1
Guildhall	C-5
Hardwick	C-3
Hyde Park	C-3
Johnson	D-3
Lyndonville	C-4
Manchester	H-2
Manchester Center	F-2
Middlebury	E-1
Montpelier	C-1
Morrisville	E-3
Newfane	H-3
Newport	B-4
North Hero	B-1
Northfield	C-5
Norwich	F-3
Poultney	G-1
Proctor	F-2
Putney	H-3
Randolph	F-2
Rutland	F-2
St. Albans	B-2
St. Johnsbury	D-4
South Barre	D-3
South Burlington	D-2
Springfield	G-3
Swanton	B-2
Vergennes	D-1
Waterbury	E-3
White River Junction	F-3
Windsor	G-3
Winooski	C-1
Woodstock	F-3

Vermont state facts

Nickname: The Green Mtn. State
Capital: Montpelier, D-3
Population: 643,077 (rank: 49th)
Largest city: Burlington, 44,743, C-1
Land area: 9,215 sq. mi. (rank: 43rd)
Highest point: Mt. Mansfield, 4,393 ft., C-2

Travel planning & on-the-road resources

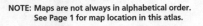

Tourism   Vt. Dept. of Tourism & Mktg.:
Information (800) 837-6668
www.vermontvacation.com

Road Conditions (802) 917-2458
& Construction   newengland511.org
www.vtrans.vermont.gov

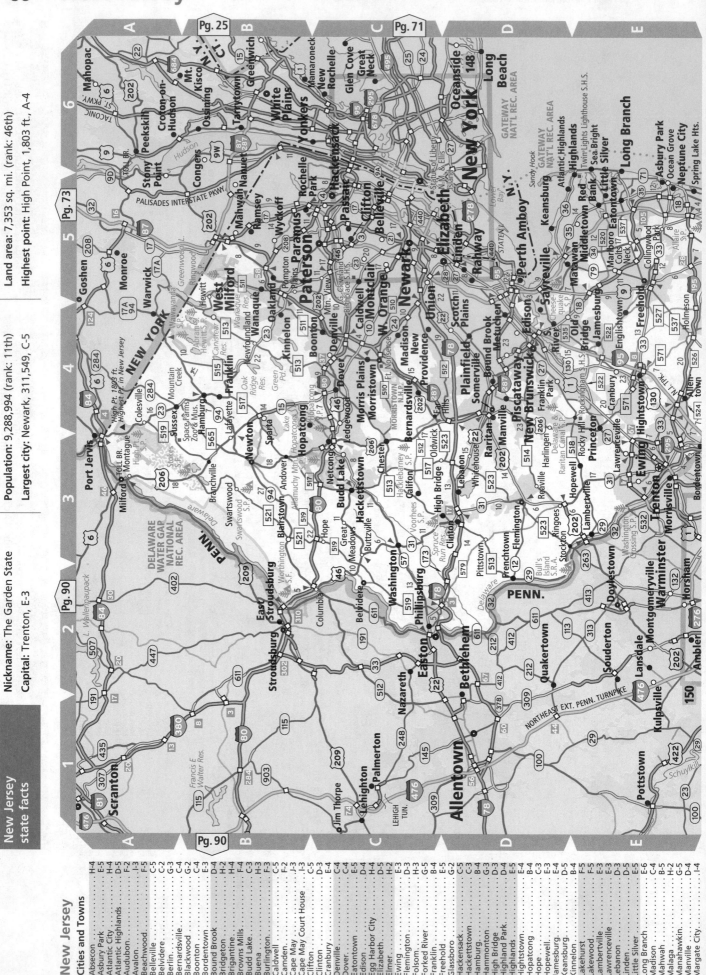

New Jersey state facts

Nickname: The Garden State

Capital: Trenton, E-3

Population: 9,288,994 (rank: 11th)

Largest city: Newark, 311,549, C-5

Land area: 7,353 sq. mi. (rank: 46th)

Highest point: High Point, 1,803 ft., A-4

NOTE: Maps are not always in alphabetical order.
See Page 1 for map location in this atlas.

New Jersey   67

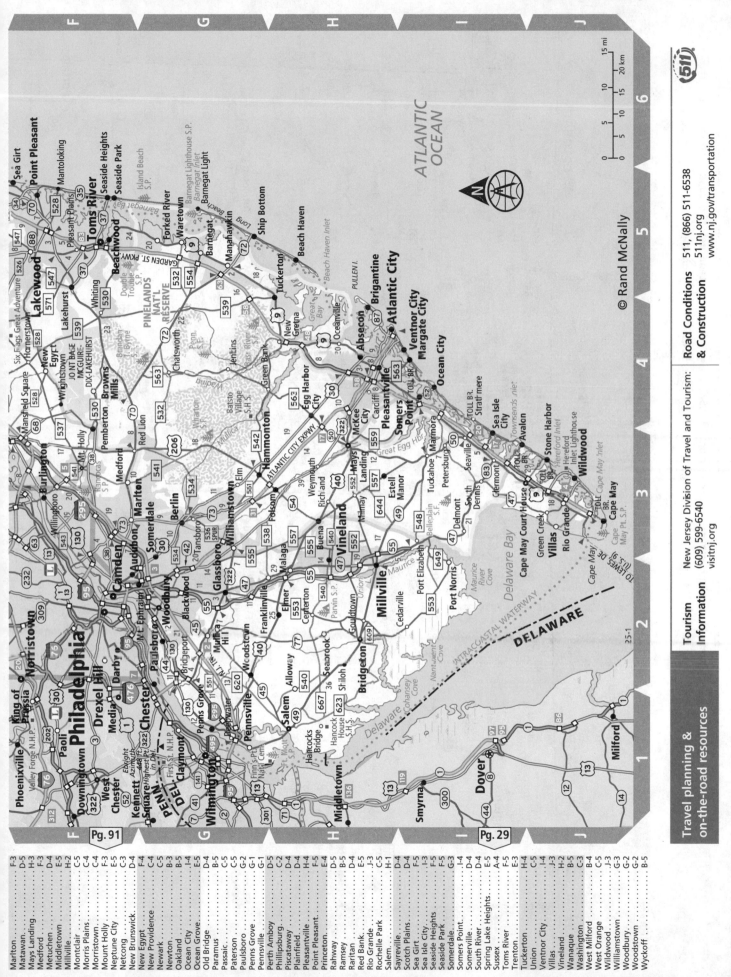

© Rand McNally

Travel planning &
on-the-road resources

Tourism Information	New Jersey Division of Travel and Tourism: (609) 599-6540 visitnj.org	Road Conditions & Construction	511, (866) 511-6538 511nj.org www.nj.gov/transportation

New Mexico state facts

Nickname: Land of Enchantment

Capital: Santa Fe, C-4

Population: 2,117,522 (rank: 36th)

Largest city: Albuquerque, 564,559, D-3

Land area: 121,280 sq. mi. (rank: 5th)

Highest point: Wheeler Peak, 13,161 ft., B-5

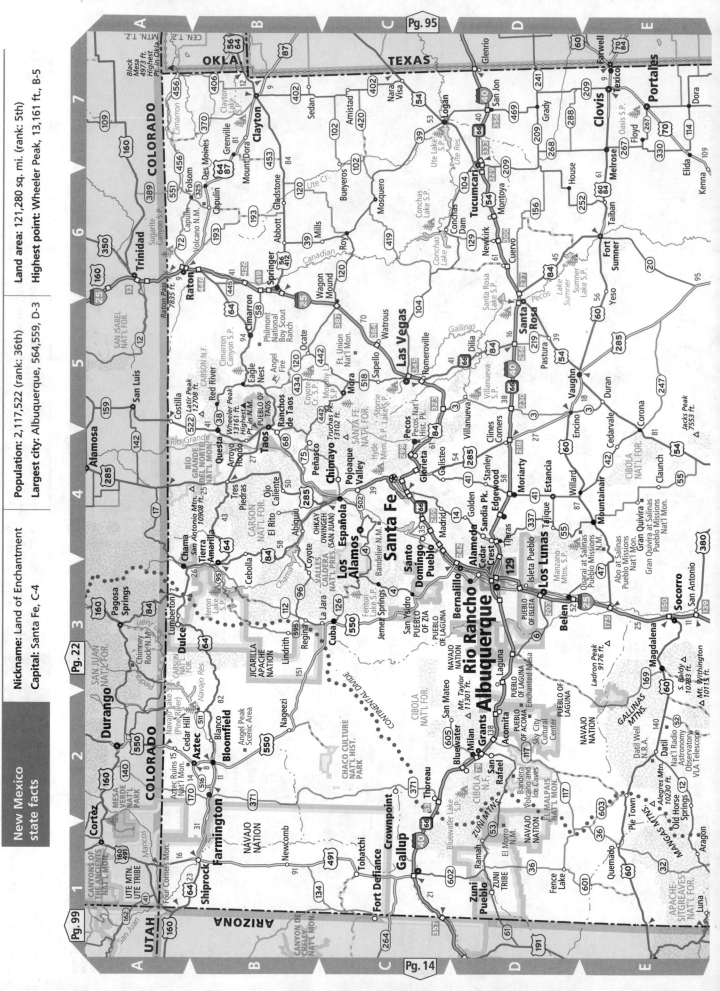

NOTE: Maps are not always in alphabetical order.
See Page 1 for map location in this atlas.

New Mexico   69

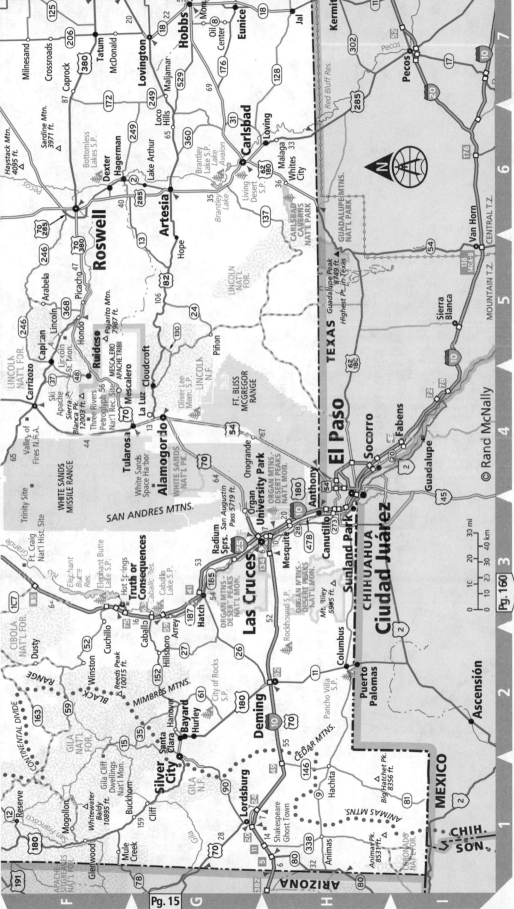

Road Conditions & Construction

511
(800) 432-4269, (505) 795-1401
www.nmroads.com, www.dot.nm.gov

Tourism Information

New Mexico Tourism Department
(505) 795-0343
www.newmexico.org

Travel planning & on-the-road resources

© Rand McNally

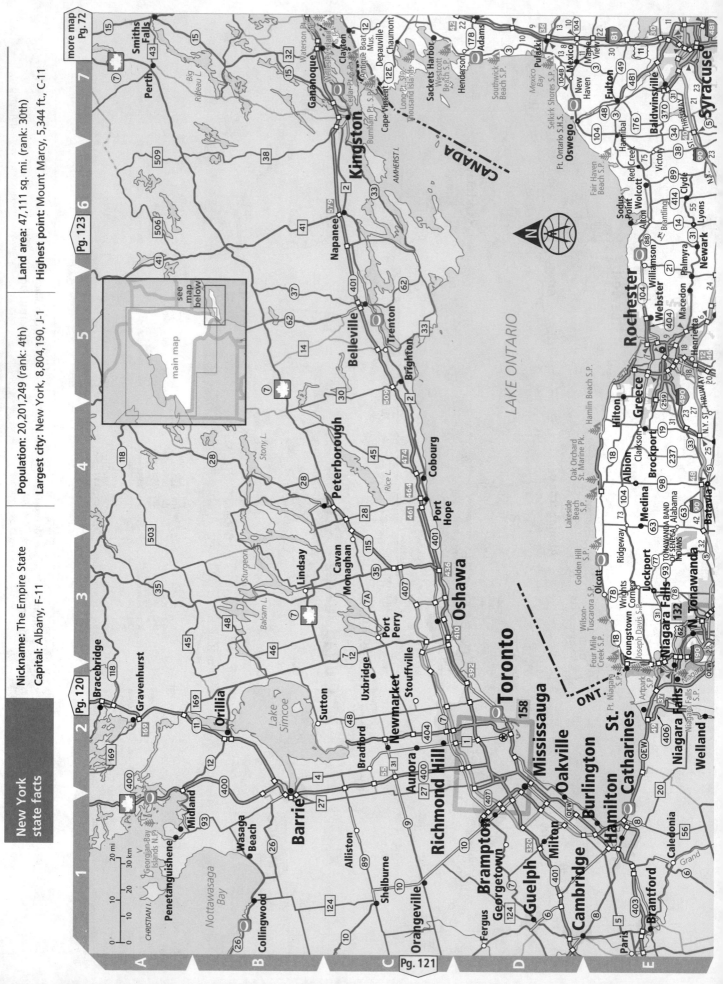

more map Pg. 72
Pg. 123
Pg. 120
Pg. 121

New York state facts

Nickname: The Empire State

Capital: Albany, F-11

Population: 20,201,249 (rank: 4th)

Largest city: New York, 8,804,190, J-1

Land area: 47,111 sq. mi. (rank: 30th)

Highest point: Mount Marcy, 5,344 ft., C-11

CANADA

LAKE ONTARIO

ONT.

Kingston
Napanee
Belleville
Trenton
Brighton
Cobourg
Port Hope
Peterborough
Lindsay
Cavan Monaghan
Port Perry
Oshawa
Uxbridge
Stouffville
Newmarket
Sutton
Aurora
Richmond Hill
Toronto
Mississauga
Oakville
Burlington
Hamilton
St. Catharines
Welland
Niagara Falls
N. Tonawanda
Niagara Falls
Youngstown
Lockport
Olcott
Medina
Albion
Brockport
Batavia
Alabama
Greece
Rochester
Webster
Williamson
Newark
Palmyra
Macedon
Clyde
Lyons
Wolcott
Sodus Point
Oswego
Mexico
Pulaski
Adams
Fulton
Baldwinsville
Syracuse
Fair Haven
Victory
Red Creek
Hannibal
New Haven
Henderson
Sackets Harbor
Cape Vincent
Clayton
Gananoque
Smiths Falls
Perth
Bracebridge
Gravenhurst
Orillia
Barrie
Bradford
Alliston
Shelburne
Orangeville
Georgetown
Guelph
Cambridge
Brampton
Milton
Caledonia
Brantford
Paris
Fergus
Collingwood
Wasaga Beach
Midland
Penetanguishene
Ridgeway
Clarkson

Georgian Bay Islands N.P.
CHRISTIAN I.
Nottawasaga Bay
Lake Simcoe
Stony L.
Rice L.
Balsam L.
Sturgeon
Stoney L.
Thousand Islands
AMHERST I.
Selkirk Shores S.P.
Southwick Beach S.P.
Ft. Ontario S.H.S.
Fair Haven Beach S.P.
Hamlin Beach S.P.
Lakeside Beach S.P.
Golden Hill S.P.
Four Mile Creek S.P.
Wilson-Tuscarora S.P.
Joseph Davis S.P.
Artpark S.P.
Niagara Falls S.P.
Oak Orchard St. Marine Pk.

see map below
main map

NOTE: Maps are not always in alphabetical order.
See Page 1 for map location in this atlas.

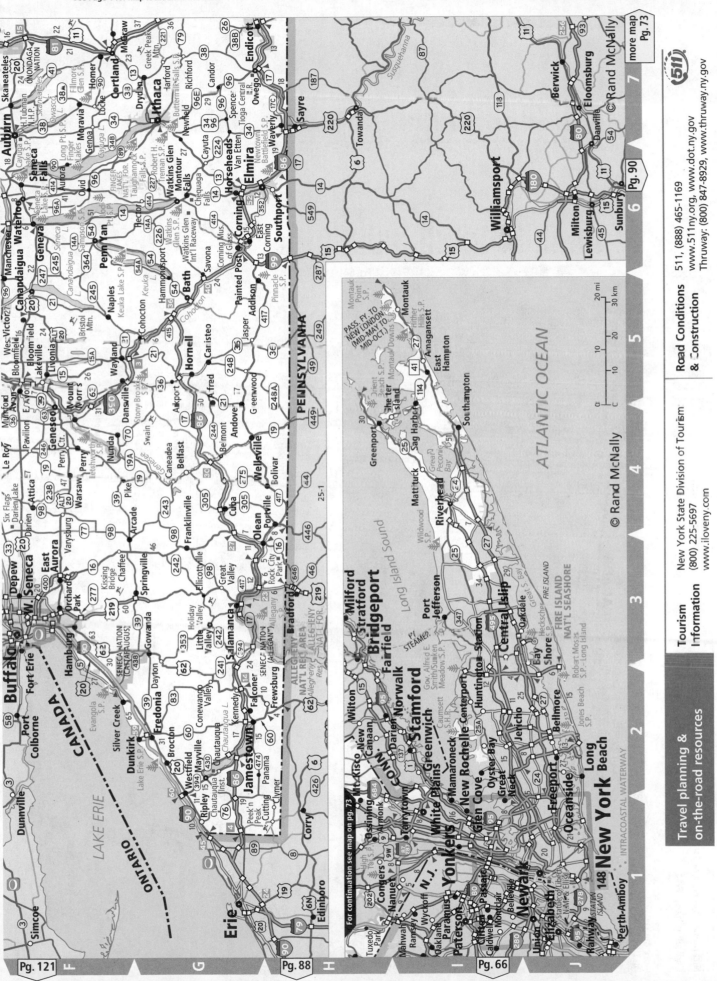

© Rand McNally

© Rand McNally

ATLANTIC OCEAN

LAKE ERIE

PENNSYLVANIA

ONTARIO

CANADA

INTRACOASTAL WATERWAY

Tourism Information	New York State Division of Tourism (800) 225-5697 www.iloveny.com
Road Conditions & Construction	511, (888) 465-1169 www.511ny.org, www.dot.ny.gov Thruway: (800) 847-8929, www.thruway.ny.gov

Travel planning & on-the-road resources

more map Pg. 73

Pg. 90

Pg. 121   Pg. 88   Pg. 66

For continuation see map on pg. 73

New York state facts

Nickname: The Empire State

Capital: Albany, F-11

Population: 20,201,249 (rank: 4th)

Largest city: New York, 8,804,190, J-1

Land area: 47,111 sq. mi. (rank: 30th)

Highest point: Mount Marcy, 5,344 ft., C-11

more map Pg. 70

© Rand McNally

New York

Cities and Towns

Adams	D-7	Le Roy	E-4
Adams Center	D-8	Liberty	H-10
Addison	G-5	Little Falls	E-9
Albany	F-11	Little Valley	G-3
Albion	E-4	Livingston Manor	H-9
Alexandria Bay	B-8	Livonia	F-5
Alfred	G-5	Loch Sheldrake	H-10
Amagansett	I-5	Lockport	E-3
Amenia	H-12	Long Beach	J-2
Amherst	E-3	Lowville	D-8
Amsterdam	F-11	Lyons	E-6
Andover	F-5	Lyons	F-5
Armonk	J-11	Macedon	E-6
Arcade	F-3	Macedon	E-6
Arkport	G-5	Mahopac	I-11
Attica	F-4	Malone	A-10
Auburn	F-5	Mamaroneck	J-11
Avon	F-5	Manchester	F-5
Bainbridge	G-8	Massena	A-9
Baldwinsville	E-7	Mattituck	I-4
Ballston Spa	F-11	Mayville	G-2
Bath	G-5	McGraw	F-7
Batavia	E-4	Mechanicville	F-11
Bay Shore	J-3	Medina	E-4
Beacon	I-11	Mexico	D-7
Belfast	G-4	Middleburgh	G-10
Bellmore	J-2	Middletown	I-10
Belmont	G-4	Middletown	I-10
Binghamton	G-8	Millbrook	H-11
Bolivar	H-4	Millerton	H-12
Bolton Landing	D-11	Monroe	I-11
Boonville	D-9	Montauk	I-5
Brewster	I-12	Monticello	H-10
Brockport	E-4	Montour Falls	G-6
Brocton	G-2	Moravia	F-7
Buffalo	F-3	Mount Kisco	I-11
Cadyville	B-11	Mount Morris	F-4
Cairo	H-11	Naples	F-5
Cambridge	E-12	New Berlin	F-8
Camden	D-8	New Hartford	E-8
Canajoharie	F-10	New Lebanon	F-12
Canandaigua	F-5	New Paltz	I-11
Canastota	E-8	New Rochelle	J-11
Candor	G-7	New Windsor	I-11
Canisteo	G-5	New York	J-1
Canton	B-8	New York Mills	E-8
Carthage	D-8	Newark	E-6
Catskill	G-11	Newburgh	I-11
Cayuta	G-6	Niagara Falls	E-3
Cazenovia	E-8	North Tonawanda	E-3
Centerport	I-2	Northville	D-10
Central Islip	J-3	Norwich	F-8
Champlain	A-12	Norwood	B-9
Claverack	G-11	Nunda	F-4
Clayton	C-7	Oakdale	J-3
Clinton	E-8	Oceanside	J-2
Clyde	E-6	Ogdensburg	B-8
Cobleskill	F-10	Olcott	E-3
Cohocton	G-5	Old Forge	D-9
Cohoes	F-11	Olean	H-3
Congers	H-1	Oneida	E-8
Cooperstown	F-9	Oneonta	G-9
Corinth	E-11	Orchard Park	F-3
Corning	G-6	Ossining	J-11
Cornwall-on-Hudson	I-11	Oswego	D-7
Cortland	F-7	Owego	G-7
Croton Falls	I-12	Oxford	G-8
Croton-on-Hudson	J-11	Oyster Bay	I-2
Crown Point	C-12	Painted Post	G-6
		Palmyra	E-5
		Pawling	I-12
		Peekskill	I-11
		Penn Yan	F-6
		Perry	F-4
		Plattsburgh	B-12
		Port Henry	C-12
		Port Jefferson	I-3

NOTE: Maps are not always in alphabetical order. See Page 1 for map location in this atlas.

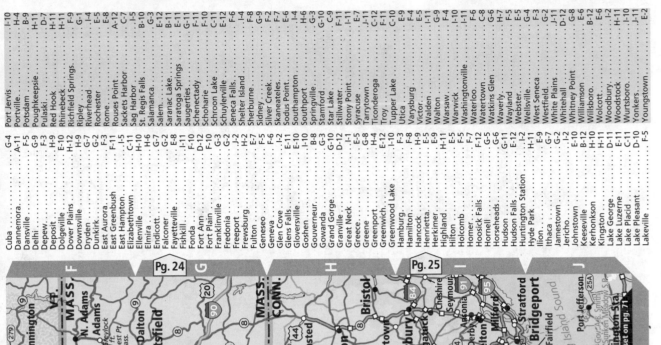

Place	Grid	Place	Grid
Cuba	G-4	Port Jervis	I-10
Dannemora	A-11	Portville	H-4
Dansville	F-5	Potsdam	B-9
Delhi	F-3	Poughkeepsie	D-7
Depew	H-9	Pulaski	H-11
Deposit	E-10	Red Hook	F-9
Dolgeville	H-12	Rhinebeck	H-12
Dover Plains	H-9	Richfield Springs	G-1
Downsville	G-7	Ripley	I-4
Dryden	G-2	Riverhead	E-5
Dunkirk	F-3	Rochester	E-8
East Aurora	F-11	Rome	A-12
East Greenbush	I-5	Rouses Point	C-7
East Hampton	C-11	Sackets Harbor	B-10
Elizabethtown	H-10	Sag Harbor	G-3
Ellenville	G-7	St. Regis Falls	E-12
Elmira	G-2	Salamanca	B-11
Endicott	E-8	Salem	E-8
Falconer	B-11	Saranac Lake	G-11
Fayetteville	G-11	Saratoga Springs	G-11
Fishkill	F-10	Saugerties	F-10
Fonda	F-10	Schenectady	E-12
Fort Ann	C-11	Schoharie	F-6
Fort Plain	F-6	Schroon Lake	E-12
Franklinville	G-3	Schuylerville	I-4
Fredonia	G-2	Seneca Falls	F-8
Freeport	J-2	Shelter Island	H-2
Frewsburg	H-2	Sherburne	E-7
Fulton	F-5	Sidney	F-5
Geneseo	F-6	Silver Creek	F-6
Geneva	I-2	Skaneateles	I-2
Glen Cove	I-2	Sodus Point	E-11
Glens Falls	E-11	Southampton	I-10
Gloversville	E-10	Southport	H-6
Goshen	I-10	Springville	G-3
Gouverneur	B-8	Star Lake	C-9
Gowanda	G-10	Stillwater	E-7
Grand Gorge	G-3	Stony Point	J-11
Granville	D-12	Syracuse	F-11
Great Neck	I-1	Tarrytown	C-12
Greene	E-7	Ticonderoga	F-11
Greenport	J-11	Troy	C-10
Greenwich	I-10	Tupper Lake	F-4
Greenwood Lake	H-8	Utica	E-9
Hamburg	F-4	Varysburg	H-9
Hamilton	E-9	Victor	E-5
Hancock	H-9	Walden	I-11
Henrietta	E-5	Walton	F-4
Herkimer	E-9	Warsaw	I-10
Highland	H-11	Warwick	H-11
Hilton	E-5	Washingtonville	E-5
Holcomb	F-7	Waterloo	E-5
Homer	F-12	Watertown	G-6
Hoosick Falls	G-5	Watkins Glen	G-11
Hornell	G-11	Waverly	E-12
Horseheads	J-2	Wayland	I-2
Hudson	H-11	Webster	H-11
Hudson Falls	E-12	West Seneca	E-9
Huntington Station	I-2	Westfield	G-7
Ilion	E-9	White Plains	I-2
Ithaca	G-7	Whitehall	D-12
Jamestown	I-2	Whitney Point	E-6
Jericho	J-2	Williamson	B-12
Johnstown	E-10	Willsboro	H-10
Keeseville	B-12	Wolcott	H-11
Kerhonkson	H-10	Woodbury	I-2
Kingston	G-11	Woodstock	E-11
Lake George	D-11	Wurtsboro	H-10
Lake Luzerne	E-11	Yonkers	I-2
Lake Placid	G-2	Youngstown	F-5
Lake Pleasant	D-10		
Lakeville	F-5		

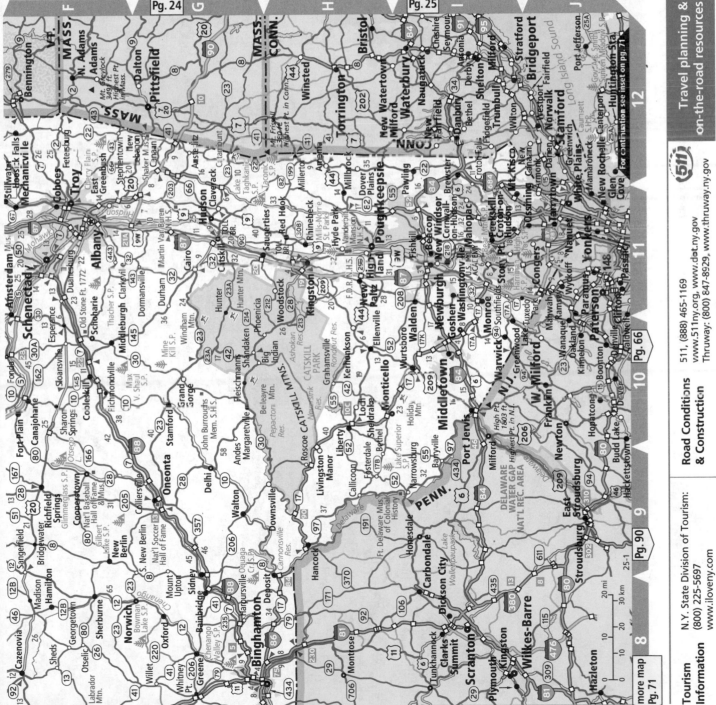

Pg. 24 · Pg. 25 · Pg. 66 · Pg. 90 · more map Pg. 71 · For continuation see inset on pg. 71

Travel planning & on-the-road resources

511

Road Conditions & Construction	**Tourism Information**
511, (888) 465-1169	N.Y. State Division of Tourism:
www.511ny.org, www.dot.ny.gov	(800) 225-5697
Thruway: (800) 847-8929, www.thruway.ny.gov	www.iloveny.com

North Carolina state facts

Nickname: The Tar Heel State

Capital: Raleigh, C-8

Population: 10,439,388 (rank: 9th)

Largest city: Charlotte, 874,579, D-5

Land area: 48,607 sq. mi. (rank: 29th)

Highest point: Mount Mitchell, 6,684 ft., C-3

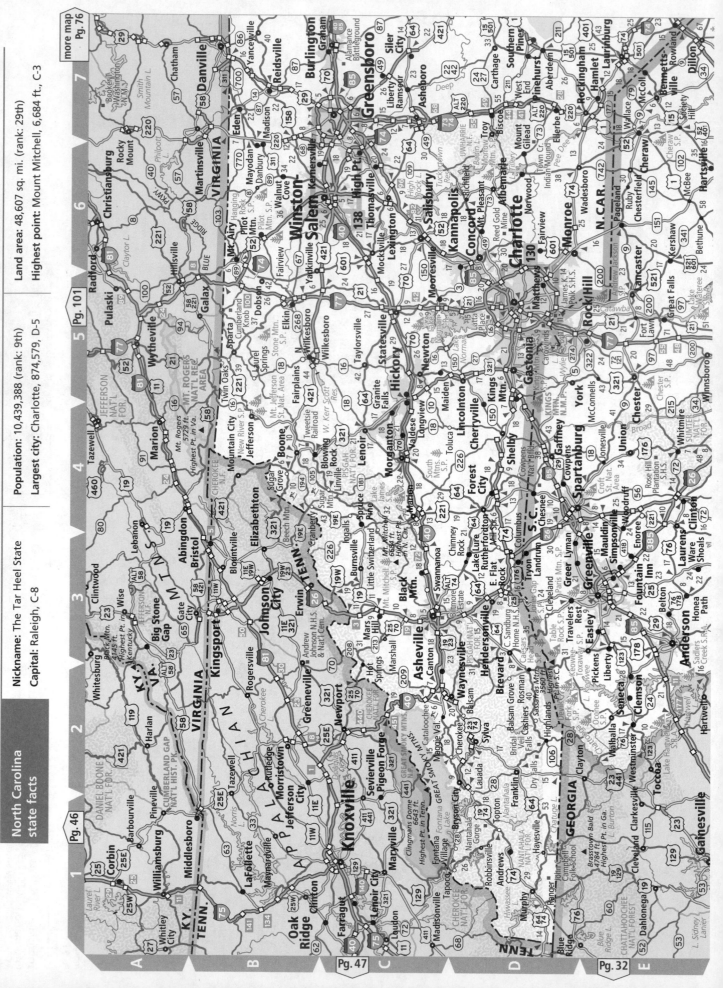

NOTE: Maps are not always in alphabetical order.
See Page 1 for map location in this atlas.

North Carolina • South Carolina/Western   75

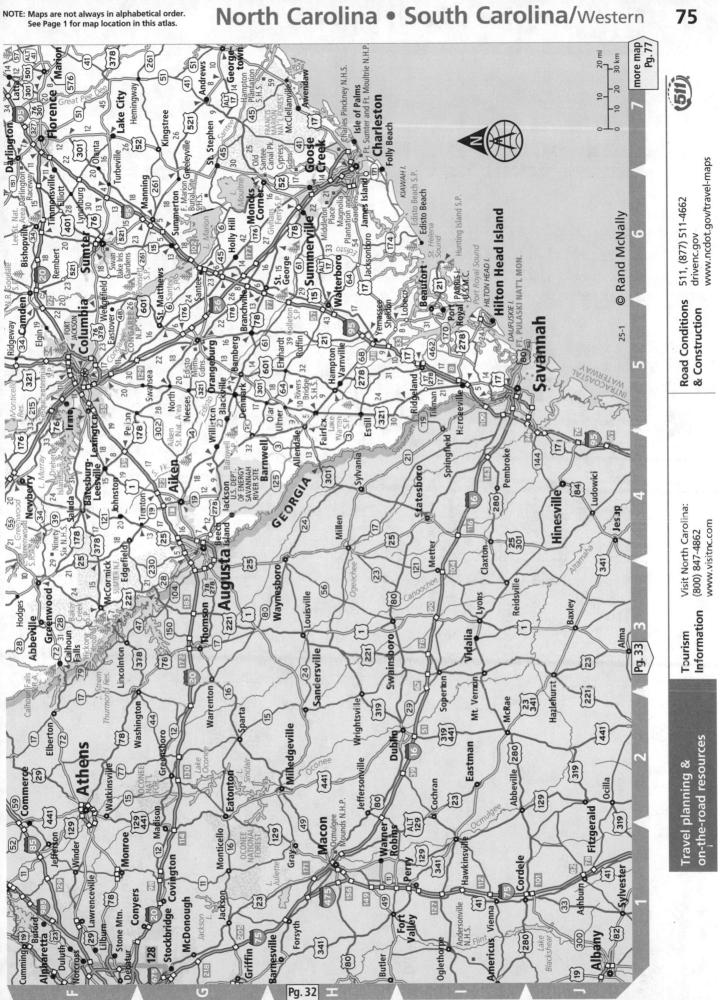

more map
Pg. 77

© Rand McNally

511

Road Conditions
& Construction

511, (877) 511-4662
drivenc.gov
www.ncdot.gov/travel-maps

Tourism
Information

Visit North Carolina:
(800) 847-4862
www.visitnc.com

Travel planning &
on-the-road resources

North Carolina

Cities and Towns

South Carolina

Cities and Towns

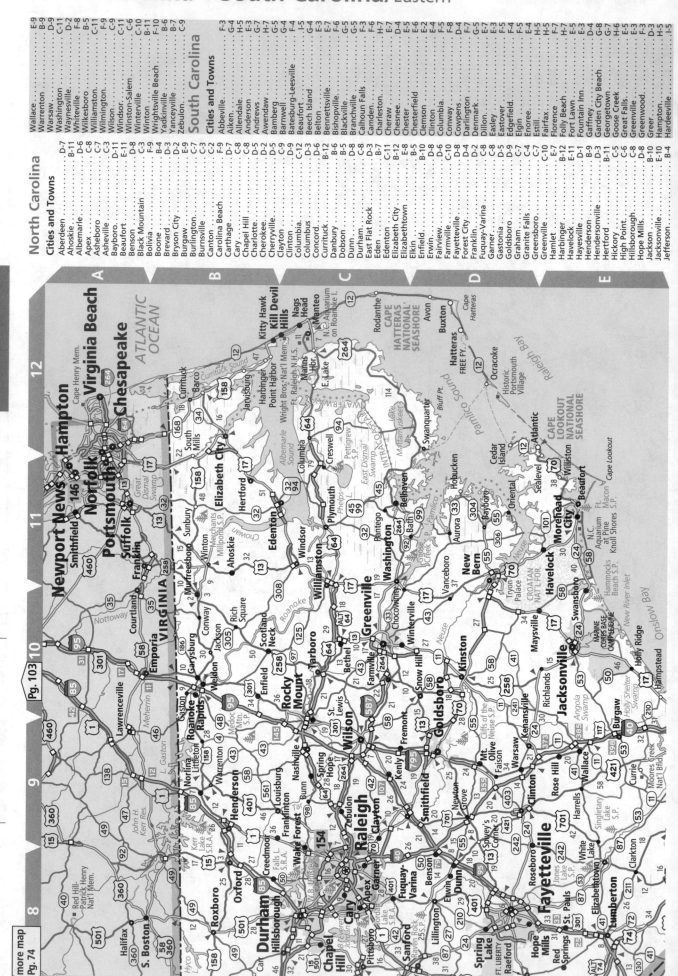

South Carolina state facts

Nickname: The Palmetto State
Capital: Columbia, F-5
Population: 5,118,425 (rank: 23rd)
Largest city: Charleston, 150,227, H-7
Land area: 30,056 sq. mi. (rank: 40th)
Highest point: Sassafras Mtn., 3,560 ft., D-3

more map Pg. 74
Pg. 103

NOTE: Maps are not always in alphabetical order.
See Page 1 for map location in this atlas.

Place	Grid
Hartsville	E-6
Hilton Head Island	I-5
Holly Hill	G-6
Honea Path	E-3
Irmo	F-5
Isle of Palms	H-7
Jackson	G-4
James Island	H-6
Johnston	F-4
Jonesville	E-4
Kershaw	E-6
Kingstree	G-7
Lake City	F-7
Lancaster	E-5
Landrum	D-3
Latta	E-7
Laurens	E-3
Lexington	F-5
Liberty	E-3
Little River	F-8
Loris	F-8
Lyman	D-3
Manning	F-7
Marion	E-7
Mauldin	E-3
McBee	E-6
McColl	E-7
McCormick	F-3
Moncks Corner	G-6
Murrells Inlet	G-8
Myrtle Beach	G-8
Newberry	F-4
North	G-5
North Myrtle Beach	F-8
Orangeburg	G-5
Pageland	E-6
Pickens	E-3
Port Royal	I-5
Ridgeland	I-5
Rock Hill	D-5
St. George	G-5
St. Matthews	G-5
St. Stephen	G-7
Saluda	F-4
Santee	G-6
Seneca	E-2
Simpsonville	E-3
Socastee	G-8
Society Hill	E-7
Spartanburg	D-3
Summerton	F-6
Summerville	G-6
Sumter	F-6
Timmonsville	F-7
Travelers Rest	D-3
Turbeville	F-6
Union	E-4
Varnville	H-4
Walhalla	E-2
Walterboro	H-5
Ware Shoals	E-3
Westminster	E-2
Whitmire	E-4
Williston	G-4
Winnsboro	E-5
Woodruff	E-4
Yemassee	H-5
York	D-5

Place	Grid
Kannapolis	D-6
Kenansville	D-9
Kernersville	B-6
Kill Devil Hills	C-12
Kings Mountain	D-5
Kinston	D-10
Kitty Hawk	B-12
Laurinburg	E-7
Lenoir	C-4
Lexington	C-6
Liberty	C-7
Lillington	D-8
Lincolnton	D-5
Longview	C-5
Louisburg	C-9
Lumberton	E-8
Maiden	C-5
Manteo	C-12
Marion	C-4
Marshall	C-3
Matthews	D-5
Mayodan	B-6
Mocksville	C-6
Monroe	D-6
Mooresville	C-5
Morehead City	E-11
Morganton	C-4
Mount Airy	B-6
Mount Olive	D-9
Murfreesboro	B-10
Murphy	D-1
Nags Head	C-12
Nashville	C-9
New Bern	D-11
Newton	C-5
North Wilkesboro	B-5
Oak Island	F-9
Oxford	B-8
Pinehurst	D-7
Pittsboro	C-8
Plymouth	C-11
Raeford	D-8
Raleigh	C-8
Red Springs	E-8
Reidsville	B-7
Roanoke Rapids	B-10
Robbinsville	D-1
Rockingham	E-7
Rocky Mount	C-9
Roxboro	B-8
Rutherfordton	D-4
Salisbury	C-6
Sanford	D-8
Scotland Neck	B-10
Shallotte	F-9
Shelby	D-4
Siler City	C-7
Smithfield	D-9
Snow Hill	D-10
Southern Pines	D-7
Sparta	B-5
Spring Lake	D-8
Statesville	C-5
Swannanoa	C-3
Swanquarter	D-12
Sylva	D-2
Tabor City	F-8
Tarboro	C-10
Taylorsville	C-5
Thomasville	C-6
Troy	D-7
Valdese	C-4
Wadesboro	D-6
Wake Forest	C-9

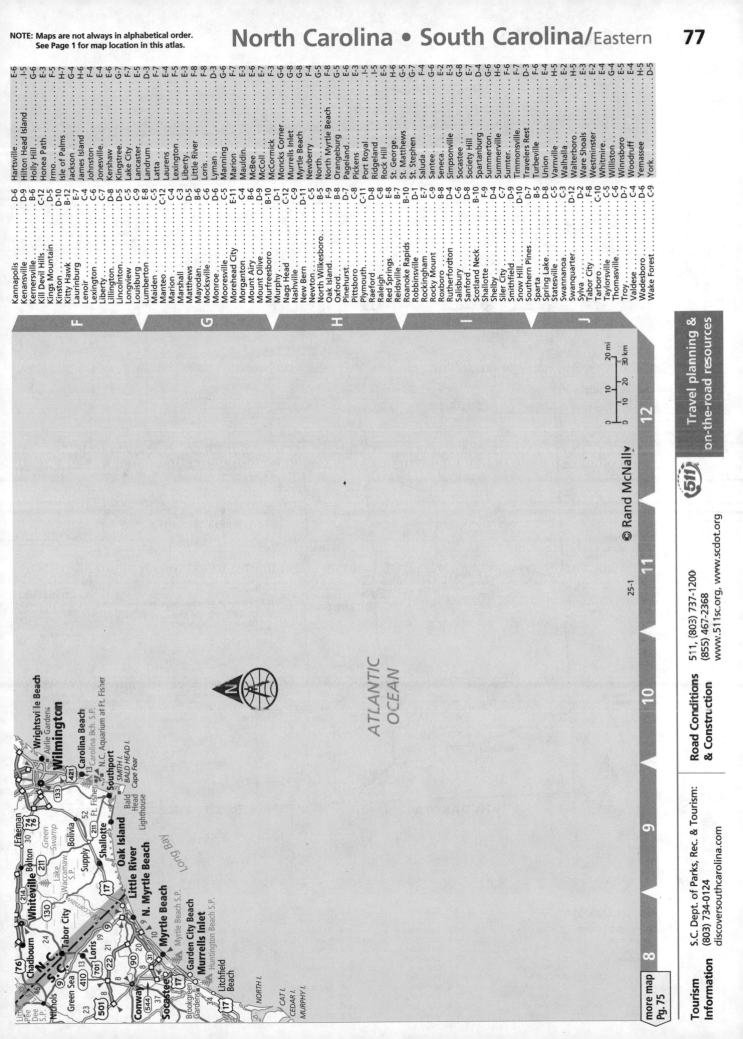

ATLANTIC OCEAN

Wilmington · Wrightsville Beach · Airlie Gardens · Carolina Beach · Carolina Bch. S.P. · N.C. Aquarium at Ft. Fisher · Southport · SMITH I. · BALD HEAD I. · Cape Fear · Ft. Fisher · Bald Head Lighthouse · Oak Island · Shallotte · Little River · N. Myrtle Beach · Myrtle Beach · Myrtle Beach S.P. · Garden City Beach · Murrells Inlet · Huntington Beach S.P. · Litchfield Beach · Brookgreen Gardens · Socastee · Conway · Loris · Tabor City · Whiteville · Chadbourn · Bolivia · Supply · Bolton · Freeman · Green Sea · Nichols · Long Bay · Waccamaw S.F. · Green Swamp · Lake Waccamaw S.P. · NORTH I. · CAT I. · CEDAR I. · MURPHY I.

N.C. / S.C.

more map Pg. 75

20 mi · 30 km · 0 10 20

25-1

© Rand McNally

Tourism Information
S.C. Dept. of Parks, Rec. & Tourism:
(803) 734-0124
discoversouthcarolina.com

Road Conditions & Construction
511, (803) 737-1200
(855) 467-2368
www.511sc.org, www.scdot.org

511 — Travel planning & on-the-road resources

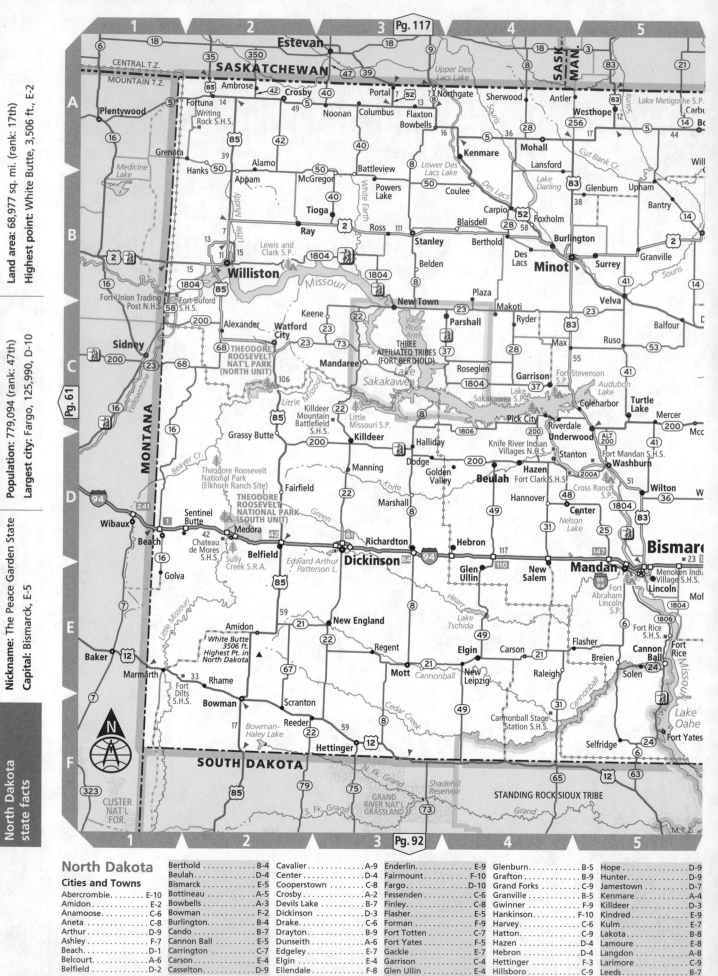

Pg. 117
Pg. 92
Pg. 61

North Dakota state facts

Land area: 68,977 sq. mi. (rank: 17th)
Highest point: White Butte, 3,506 ft, E-2
Population: 779,094 (rank: 47th)
Largest city: Fargo, 125,990, D-10
Nickname: The Peace Garden State
Capital: Bismarck, E-5

NOTE: Maps are not always in alphabetical order.
See Page 1 for map location in this atlas.

North Dakota 79

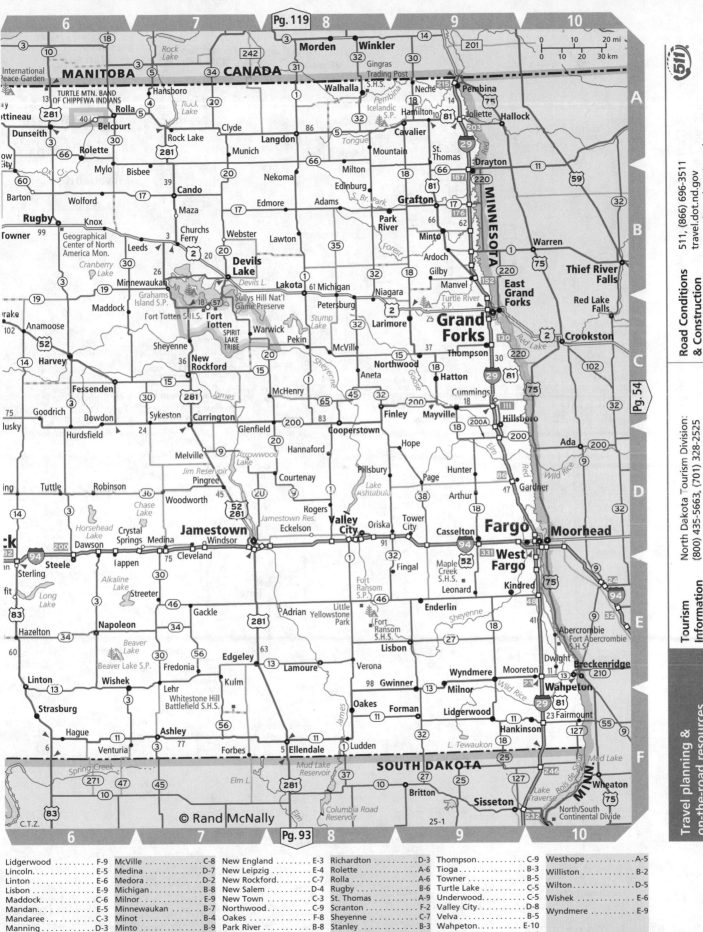

Road Conditions & Construction

511, (866) 696-3511
travel.dot.nd.gov
www.dot.nd.gov/travel

Tourism Information

North Dakota Tourism Division:
(800) 435-5663, (701) 328-2525
www.ndtourism.com

Travel planning & on-the-road resources

© Rand McNally

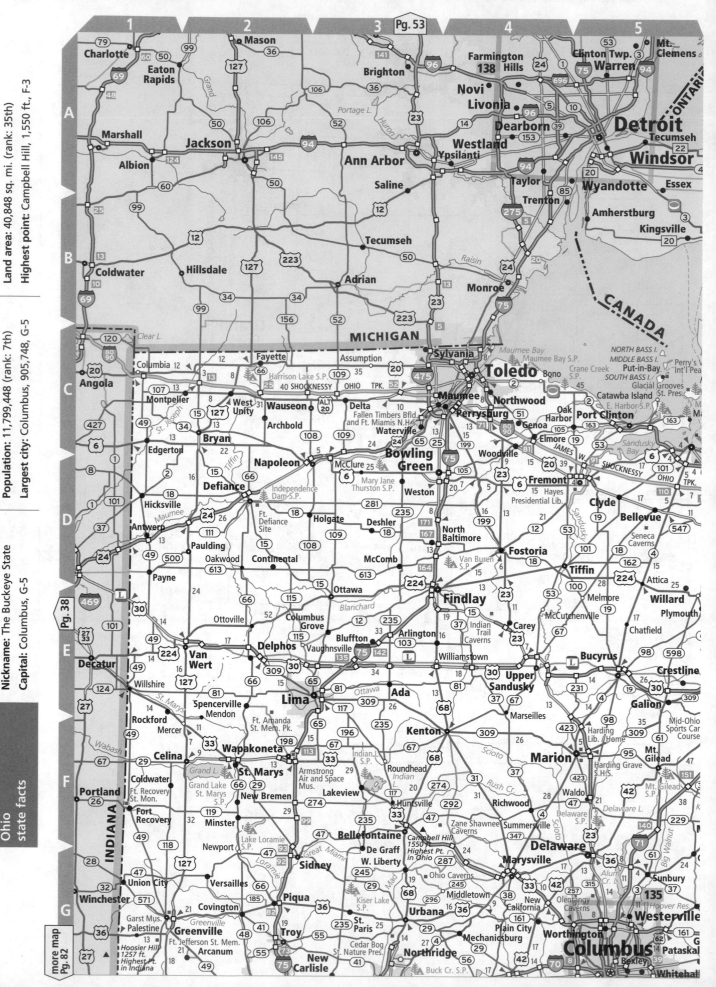

Pg. 53

Land area: 40,848 sq. mi. (rank: 35th)
Highest point: Campbell Hill, 1,550 ft., F-3

Population: 11,799,448 (rank: 7th)
Largest city: Columbus, 905,748, G-5

Nickname: The Buckeye State
Capital: Columbus, G-5

Ohio state facts

more map Pg. 82

NOTE: Maps are not always in alphabetical order.
See Page 1 for map location in this atlas.

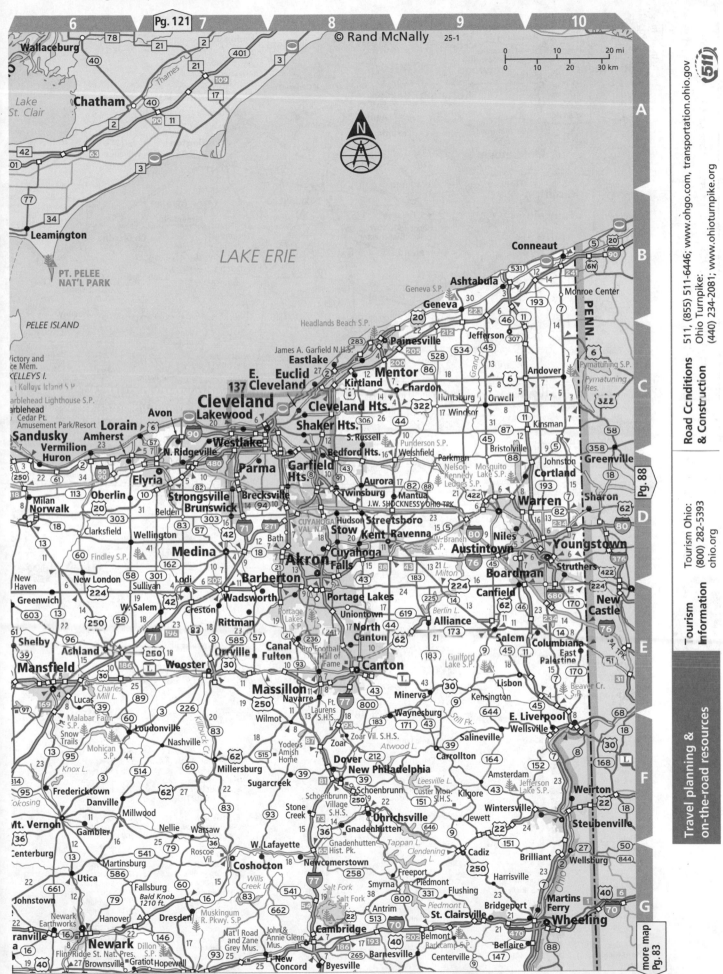

© Rand McNally 25-1

Road Conditions & Construction — 511, (855) 511-6446; www.ohgo.com, transportation.ohio.gov
Ohio Turnpike: (440) 234-2081; www.ohioturnpike.org

Tourism Information — Tourism Ohio: (800) 282-5393 ohio.org

Travel planning & on-the-road resources

Ohio state facts

Nickname: The Buckeye State
Capital: Columbus, G-5

Population: 11,799,448 (rank: 7th)
Largest city: Columbus, 905,748, G-5

Land area: 40,848 sq. mi. (rank: 35th)
Highest point: Campbell Hill, 1,550 ft., F-3

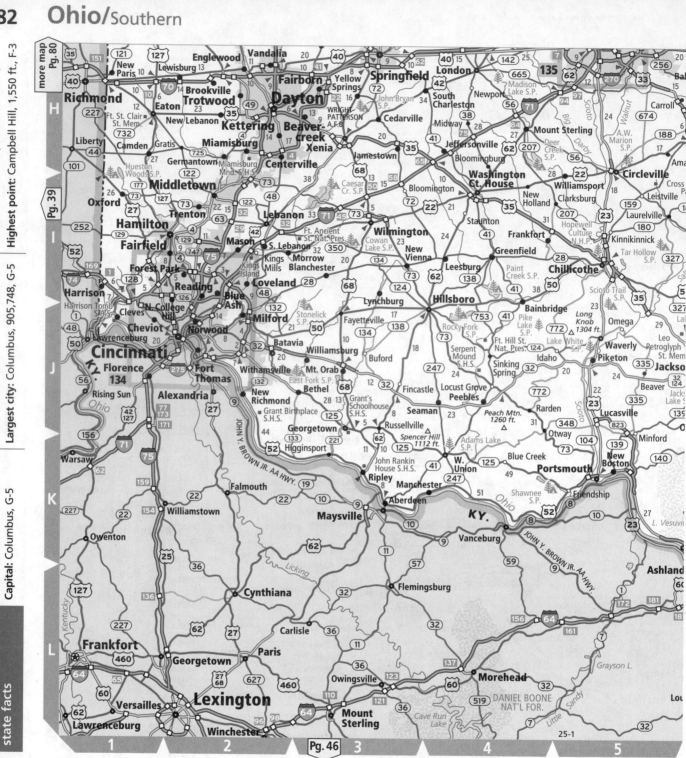

Ohio

Cities and Towns

Pg. 80 more map

Pg. 39

Pg. 46

Pg. 46

NOTE: Maps are not always in alphabetical order.
See Page 1 for map location in this atlas.

511, (855) 511-6446; www.ohgo.com, transportation.ohio.gov
Ohio Turnpike:
(440) 234-2081; www.ohioturnpike.org

Road Conditions & Construction

Tourism Ohio: (800) 282-5393
ohio.org

Tourism Information

Travel planning & on-the-road resources

© Rand McNally

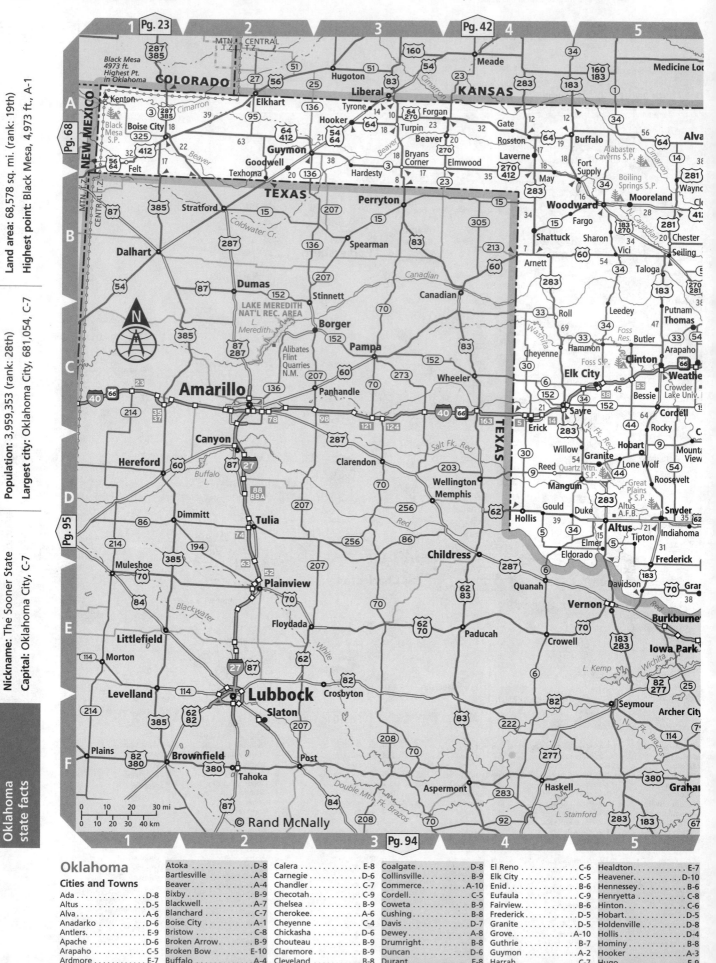

Pg. 23
Pg. 42
Pg. 68
Pg. 95
Pg. 94

Oklahoma state facts

Nickname: The Sooner State
Capital: Oklahoma City, C-7

Population: 3,959,353 (rank: 28th)
Largest city: Oklahoma City, 681,054, C-7

Land area: 68,578 sq. mi. (rank: 19th)
Highest point: Black Mesa, 4,973 ft., A-1

© Rand McNally

Oklahoma

Cities and Towns

NOTE: Maps are not always in alphabetical order.
See Page 1 for map location in this atlas.

Oklahoma **85**

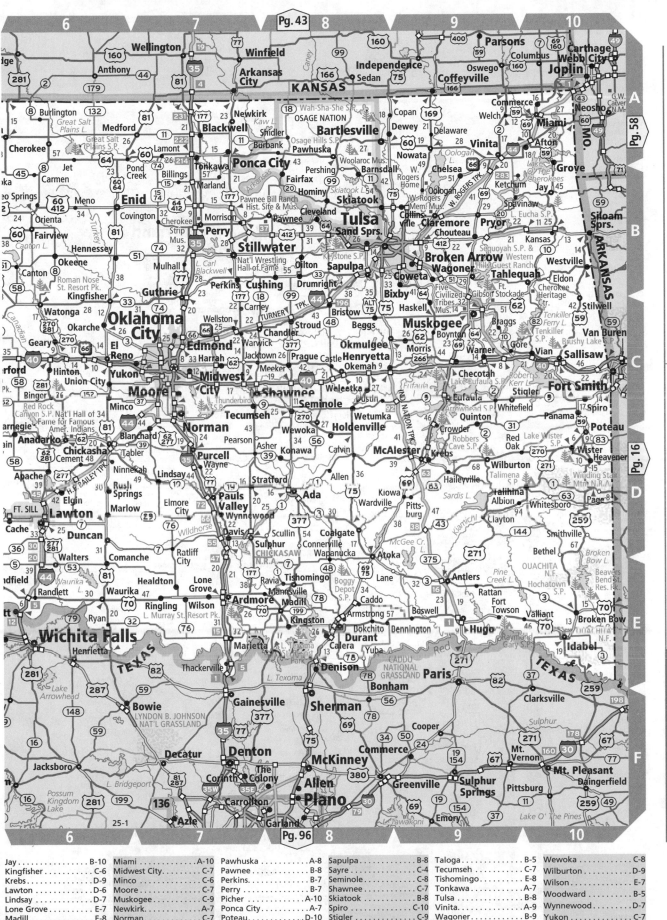

Road Conditions & Construction — (844) 465-4997, okroads.org, oklahoma.gov/odot/travel.html

Tourism Information — Oklahoma Tourism Department: (800) 652-6552, (405) 522-9500, www.travelok.com

Travel planning & on-the-road resources

Oregon

Oregon state facts

Nickname: The Beaver State

Capital: Salem, C-2

Population: 4,237,256 (rank: 27th)

Largest city: Portland, 652,503, B-3

Land area: 95,963 sq. mi. (rank: 10th)

Highest point: Mount Hood, 11,239 ft., B-4

Cities and Towns

Pg. 104
Pg. 18

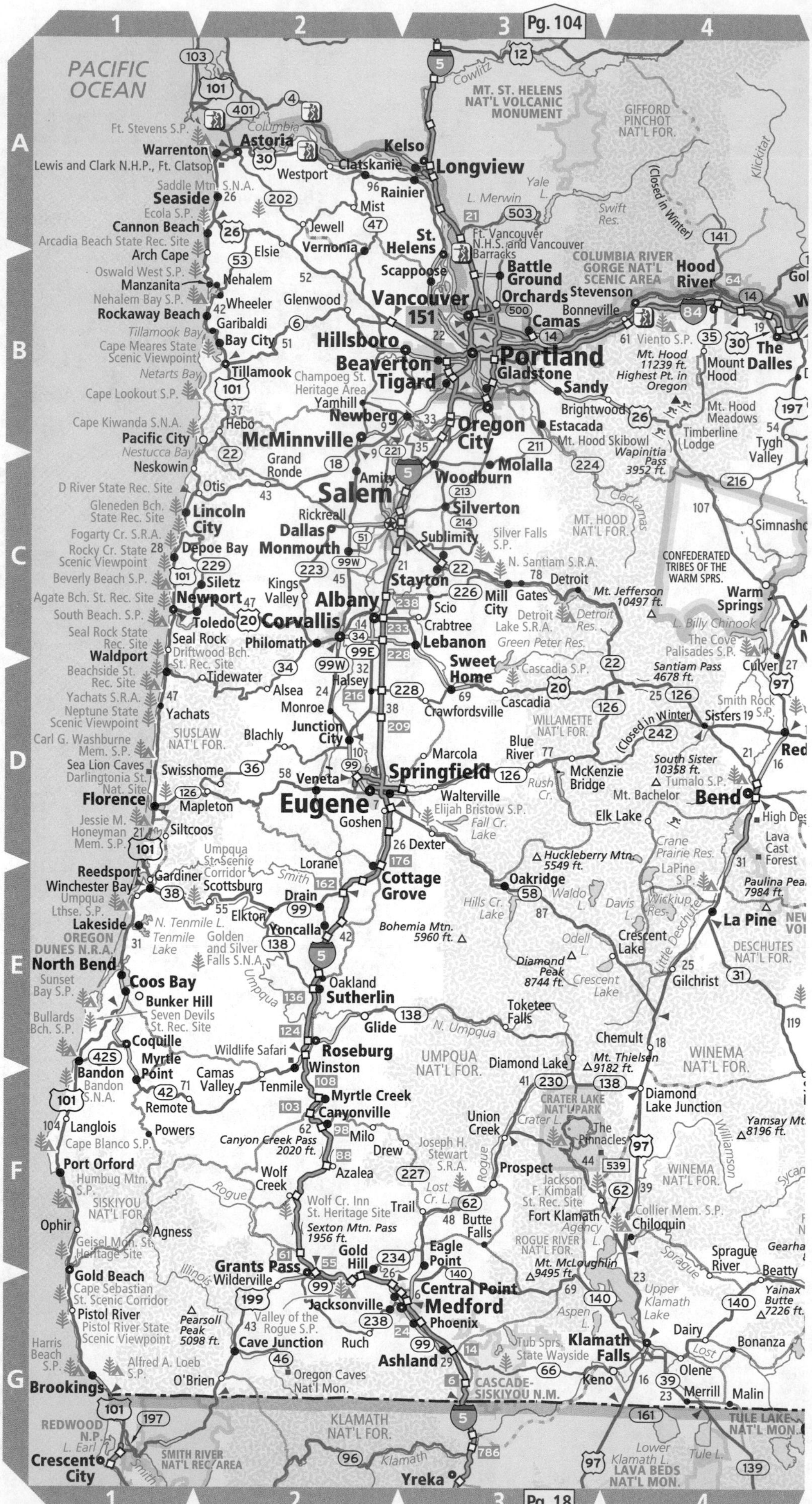

NOTE: Maps are not always in alphabetical order.
See Page 1 for map location in this atlas.

Oregon 87

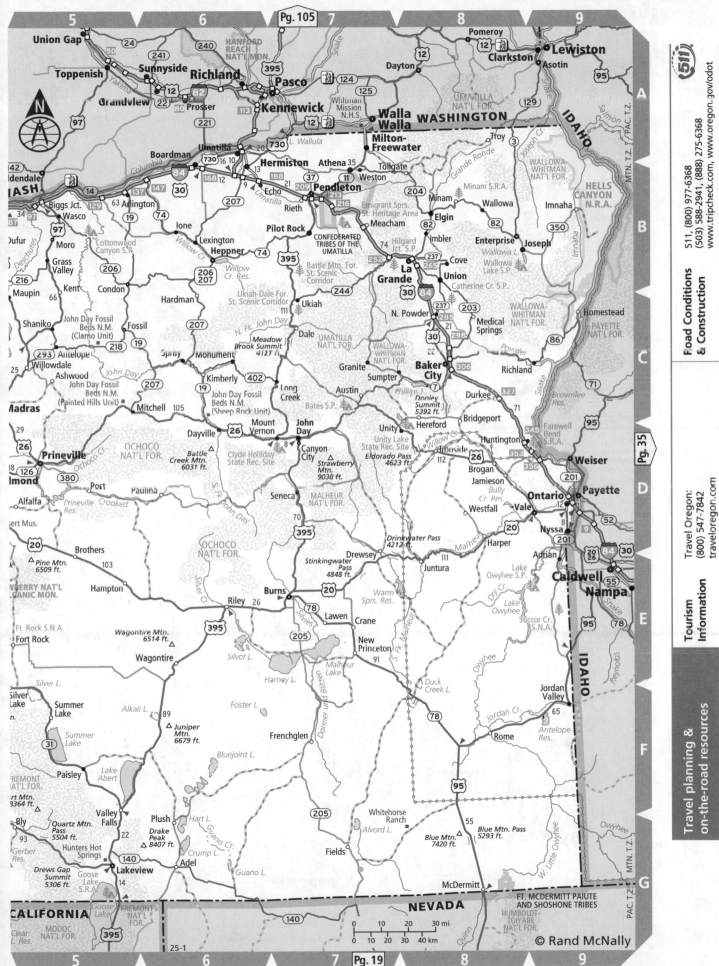

Pg. 105
Pg. 35
Pg. 19

Road Conditions & Construction
511, (800) 977-6368
(503) 588-2941, (888) 275-6368
www.tripcheck.com, www.oregon.gov/odot

Tourism Information
Travel Oregon:
(800) 547-7842
traveloregon.com

Travel planning & on-the-road resources

© Rand McNally

Pennsylvania state facts

Nickname: The Keystone State
Capital: Harrisburg, G-9

Population: 13,002,700 (rank: 5th)
Largest city: Philadelphia, 1,603,797, H-13

Land area: 44,730 sq. mi. (rank: 32nd)
Highest point: Mount Davis, 3,213 ft., I-4

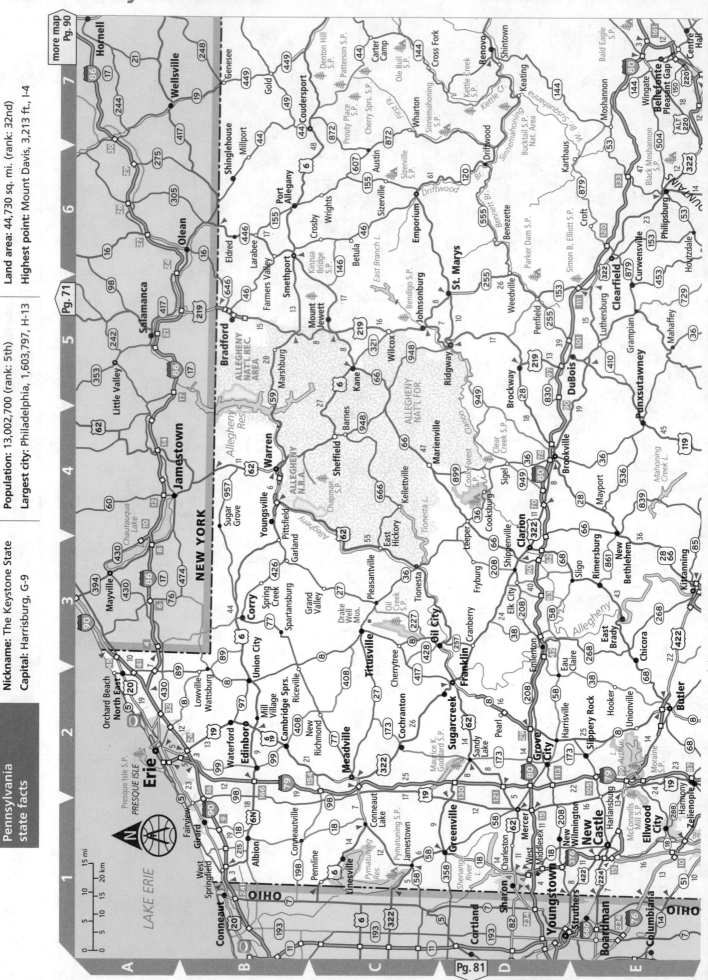

more map Pg. 90

Pg. 71

Pg. 81

NOTE: Maps are not always in alphabetical order.
See Page 1 for map location in this atlas.

Pennsylvania/Western 89

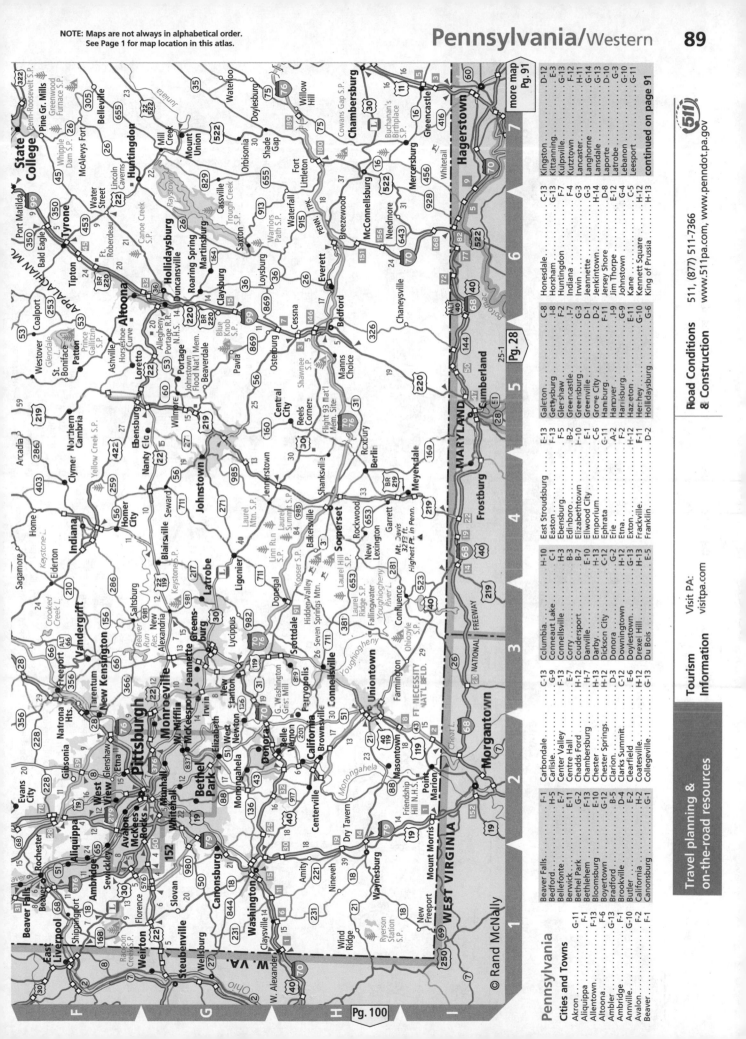

more map Pg. 91

Pg. 28

Pg. 100

continued on page 91

Pennsylvania
Cities and Towns

City	Grid
Akron	G-11
Aliquippa	F-1
Allentown	F-13
Altoona	F-6
Ambler	G-13
Ambridge	F-1
Annville	G-10
Avalon	F-2
Beaver	F-1
Beaver Falls	F-1
Bedford	H-5
Bellefonte	E-7
Berwick	E-11
Bethel Park	G-2
Bethlehem	E-10
Bloomsburg	E-10
Boyertown	F-6
Bradford	B-5
Brookville	D-4
Butler	E-2
California	H-2
Canonsburg	G-1
Carbondale	C-13
Carlisle	G-9
Center Valley	F-13
Centre Hall	E-7
Chadds Ford	H-12
Chambersburg	H-7
Chester	H-13
Chester Springs	H-12
Clarion	D-3
Clarks Summit	C-12
Clearfield	E-6
Coatesville	H-2
Collegeville	G-13
Columbia	C-13
Conneaut Lake	G-9
Connellsville	F-13
Corry	E-7
Coudersport	H-12
Danville	H-7
Darby	H-13
Dickson City	H-12
Downingtown	C-12
Doylestown	E-6
Drexel Hill	H-12
Du Bois	G-13
East Stroudsburg	H-10
Easton	C-1
Ebensburg	H-3
Edinboro	B-7
Elizabethtown	I-10
Ellwood City	H-13
Emporium	C-12
Ephrata	G-11
Erie	A-2
Etna	H-12
Exton	E-11
Frackville	F-1
Franklin	E-5
Galeton	E-13
Gettysburg	F-13
Gibsonia	F-5
Greencastle	B-2
Greensburg	I-10
Greenville	C-6
Grove City	C-6
Hamburg	G-11
Hanover	A-2
Harrisburg	H-12
Hazleton	E-11
Hershey	F-11
Hollidaysburg	D-2
Honesdale	C-8
Horsham	I-8
Huntingdon	F-2
Indiana	I-7
Irwin	G-3
Jeannette	G-3
Jenkintown	D-1
Jersey Shore	F-11
Jim Thorpe	D-8
Johnstown	G-9
Kane	E-11
Kennett Square	C-5
King of Prussia	G-6
Kingston	C-13
Kittanning	G-13
Kulpsville	F-7
Kutztown	F-4
Lancaster	G-3
Langhorne	H-11
Lansdale	G-14
Lansdowne	H-14
Laporte	D-8
Latrobe	D-10
Lebanon	G-3
Leesport	G-11

Travel planning & on-the-road resources

Tourism Information
Visit PA:
visitpa.com

Road Conditions & Construction
511, (877) 511-7366
www.511pa.com, www.penndot.pa.gov

© Rand McNally

Pennsylvania state facts

Nickname: The Keystone State
Capital: Harrisburg, G-9

Population: 13,002,700 (rank: 5th)
Largest city: Philadelphia, 1,603,797, H-13

Land area: 44,730 sq. mi. (rank: 32nd)
Highest point: Mount Davis, 3,213 ft., I-4

© Rand McNally

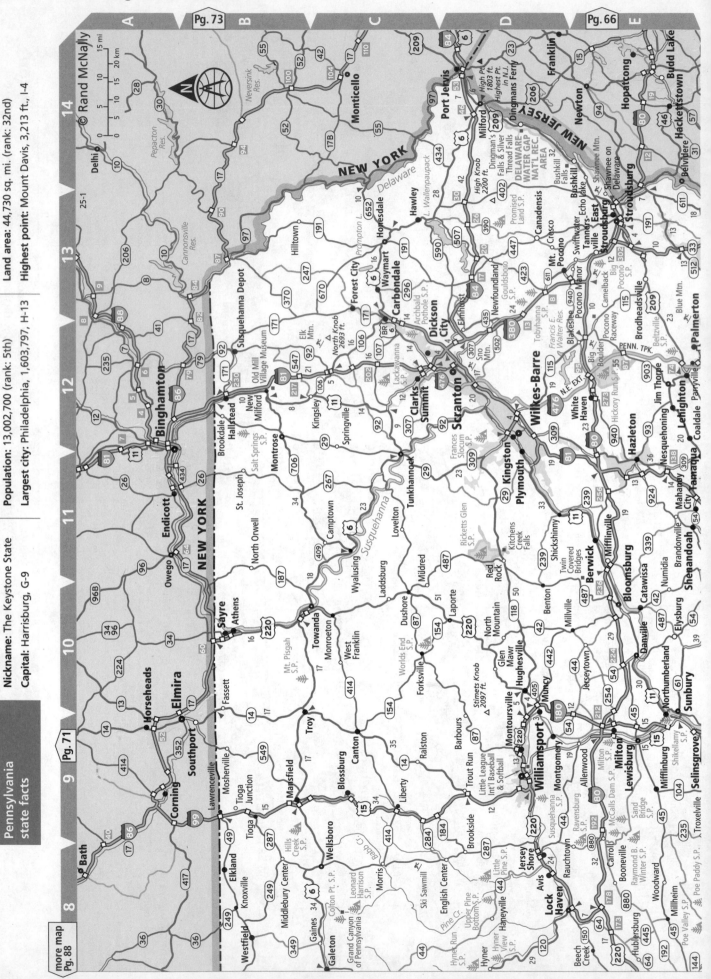

more map Pg. 88

NOTE: Maps are not always in alphabetical order.
See Page 1 for map location in this atlas.

Pennsylvania/Eastern 91

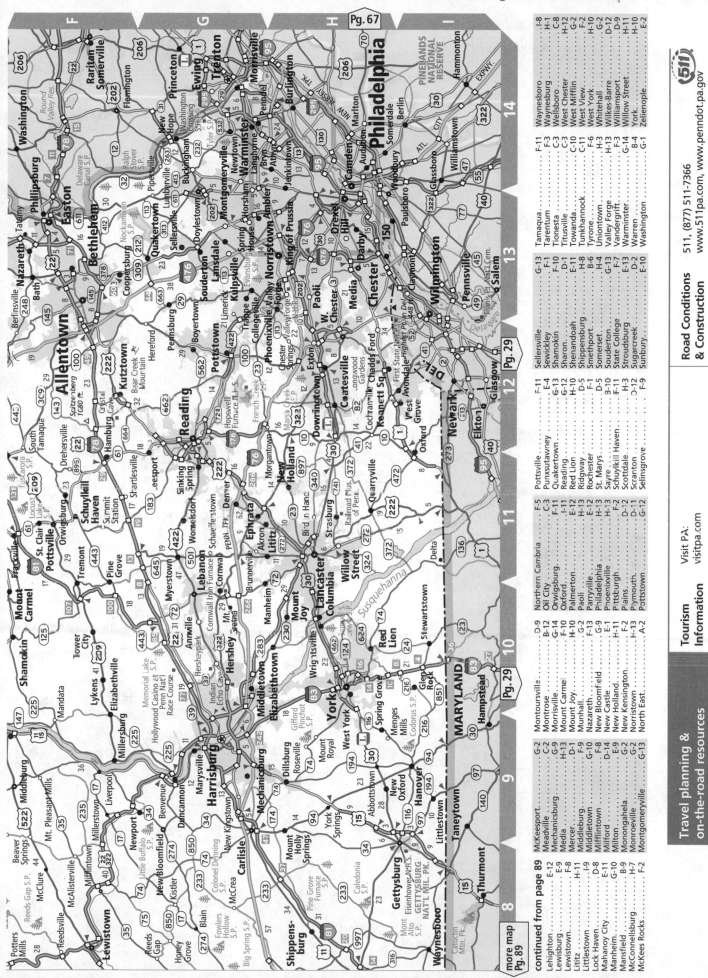

Pg. 67
Pg. 29
Pg. 29
more map
Pg. 89

Travel planning & on-the-road resources

Road Conditions & Construction	511, (877) 511-7366 www.511pa.com, www.penndot.pa.gov
Tourism Information	Visit PA: visitpa.com

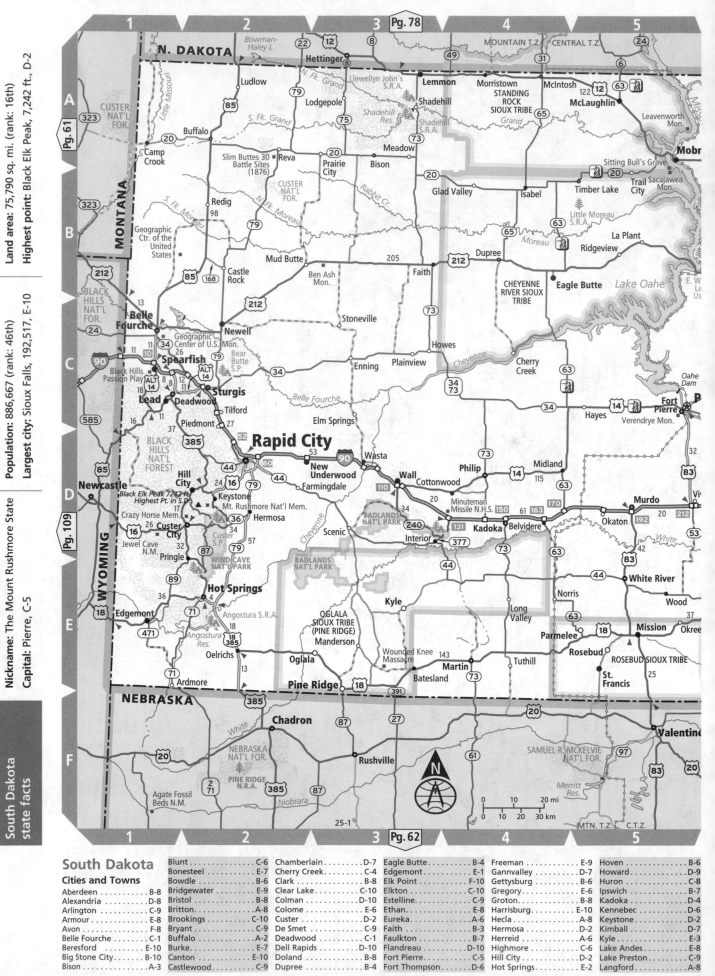

Land area: 75,790 sq. mi. (rank: 16th)
Highest point: Black Elk Peak, 7,242 ft., D-2

Population: 886,667 (rank: 46th)
Largest city: Sioux Falls, 192,517, E-10

Nickname: The Mount Rushmore State
Capital: Pierre, C-5

South Dakota state facts

South Dakota
Cities and Towns

NOTE: Maps are not always in alphabetical order.
See Page 1 for map location in this atlas.

South Dakota 93

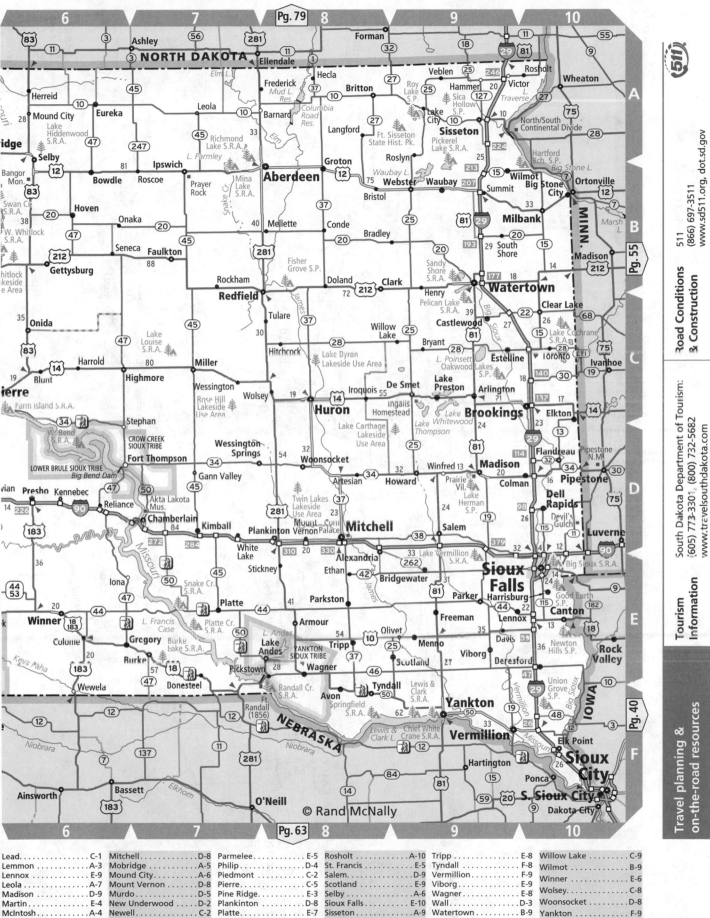

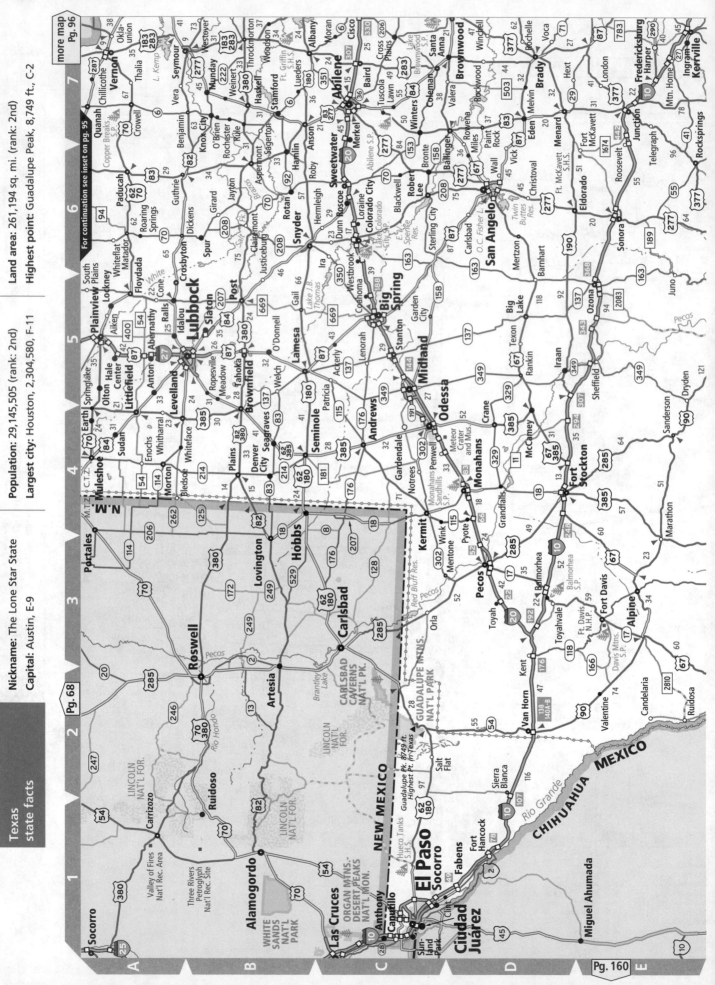

more map Pg. 96

For continuation see inset on pg. 95

Pg. 68

Pg. 160

Texas state facts

Nickname: The Lone Star State
Capital: Austin, E-9

Population: 29,145,505 (rank: 2nd)
Largest city: Houston, 2,304,580, F-11

Land area: 261,194 sq. mi. (rank: 2nd)
Highest point: Guadalupe Peak, 8,749 ft., C-2

NOTE: Maps are not always in alphabetical order.
See Page 1 for map location in this atlas.

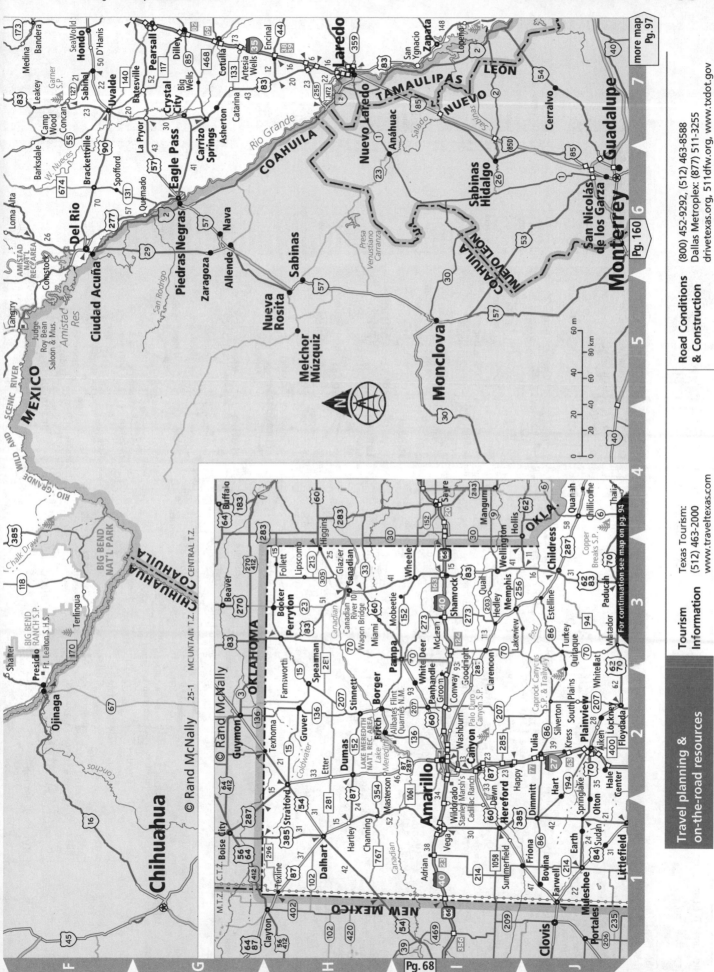

more map
Pg. 97

Pg. 160

Road Conditions
& Construction

(800) 452-9292, (512) 463-8588
Dallas Metroplex: (877) 511-3255
drivetexas.org, 511dfw.org, www.txdot.gov

Tourism
Information

Texas Tourism:
(512) 463-2000
www.traveltexas.com

Travel planning &
on-the-road resources

© Rand McNally

For continuation see map on pg. 94

Pg. 68

Texas state facts

Nickname: The Lone Star State
Capital: Austin, E-9
Population: 29,145,505 (rank: 2nd)
Largest city: Houston, 2,304,580, F-11
Land area: 261,194 sq. mi. (rank: 2nd)
Highest point: Guadalupe Peak, 8,749 ft., C-2

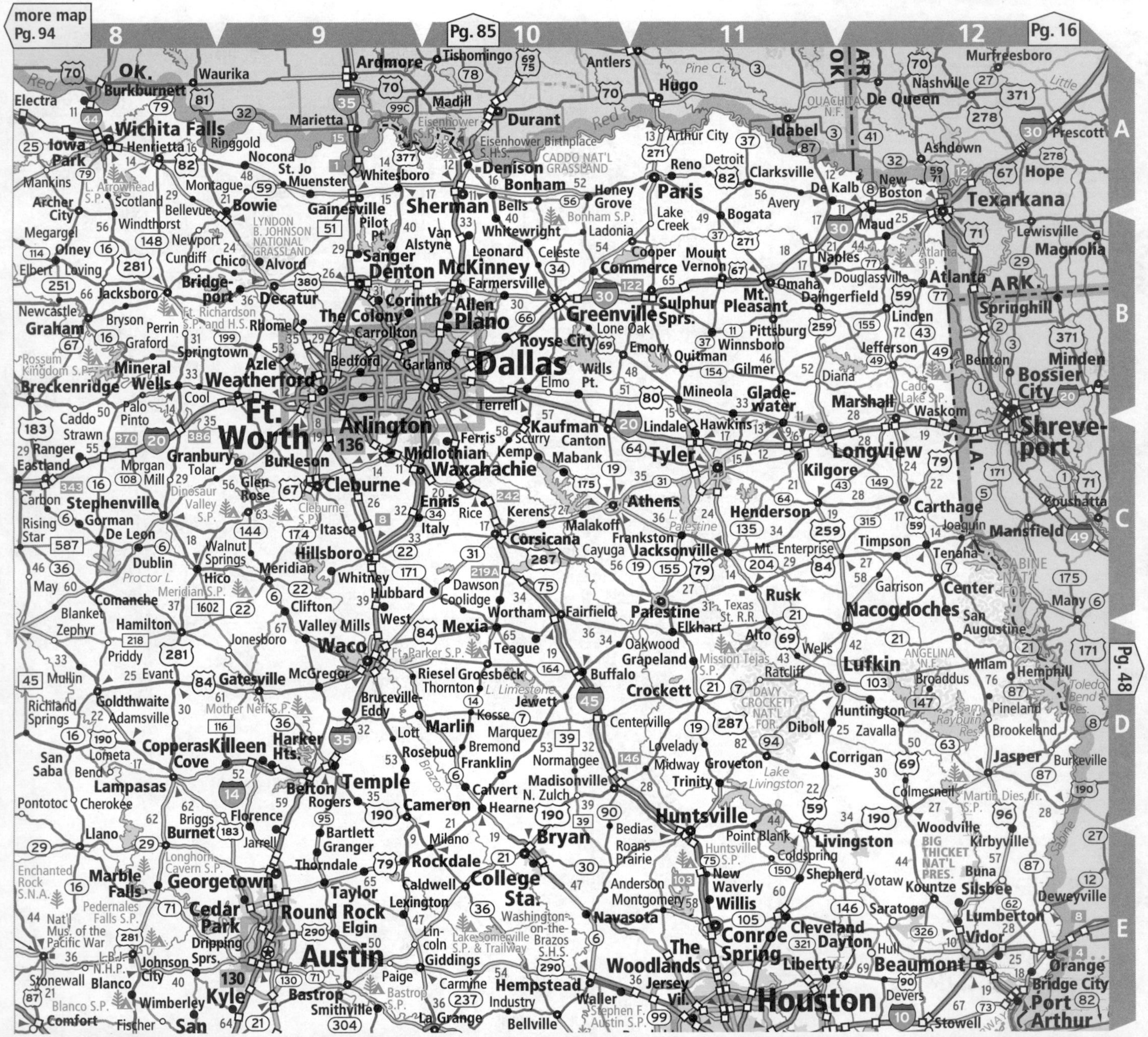

Texas

Cities and Towns

more map Pg. 94
Pg. 16
Pg. 85
Pg. 48

NOTE: Maps are not always in alphabetical order.
See Page 1 for map location in this atlas.

Texas/Eastern 97

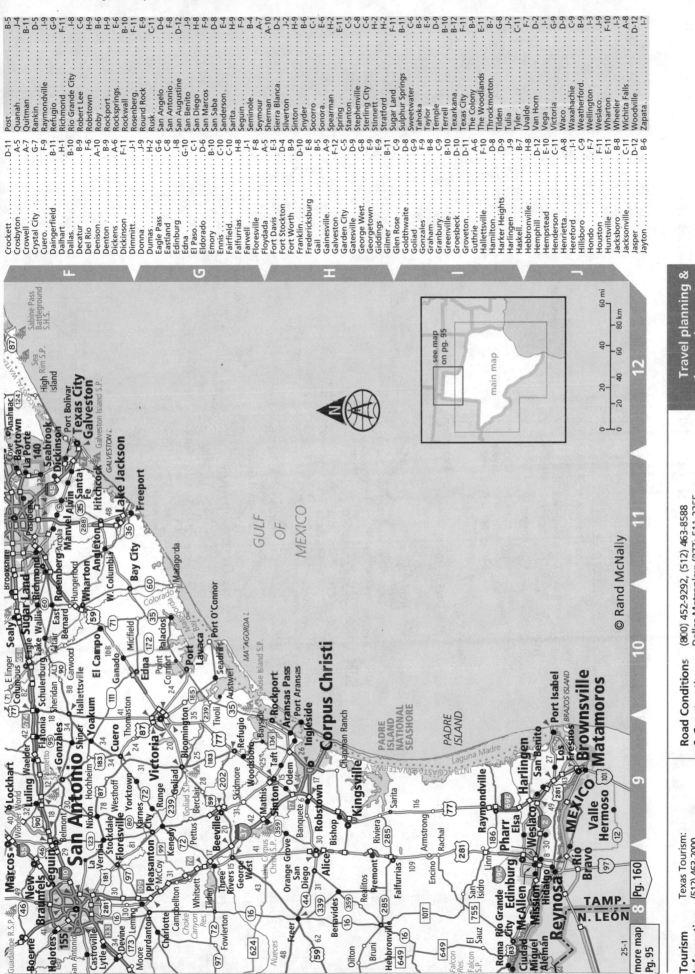

© Rand McNally

Travel planning & on-the-road resources

Tourism Information
Texas Tourism:
(512) 463-2000
www.traveltexas.com

Road Conditions & Construction
(800) 452-9292, (512) 463-8588
Dallas Metroplex: (877) 511-3255
drivetexas.org, 511dfw.org, www.txdot.gov

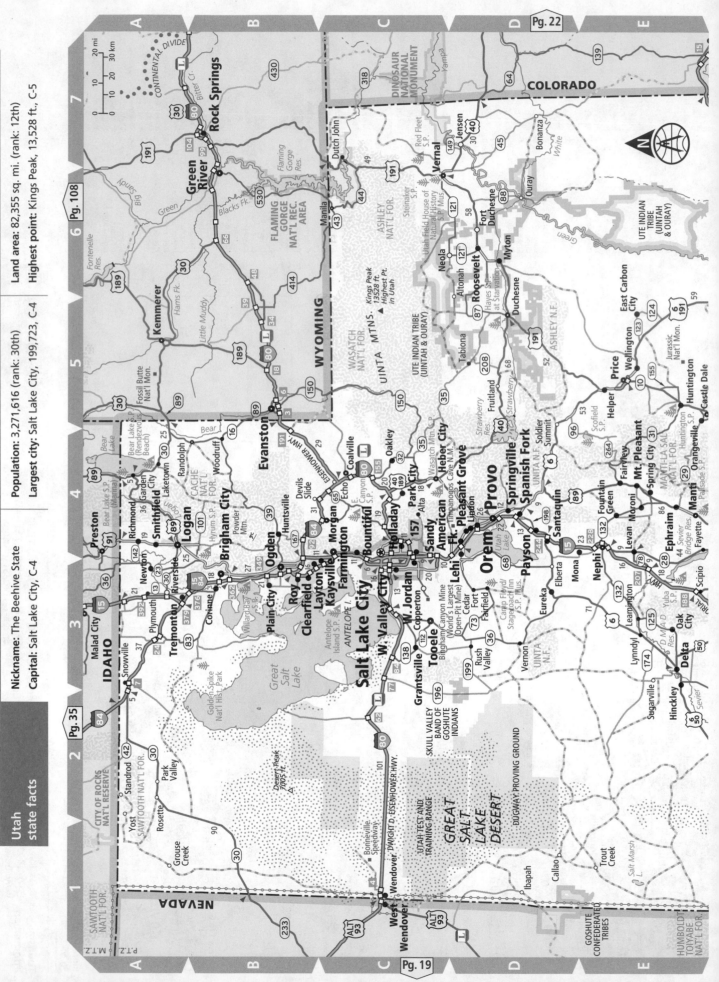

Utah state facts

Nickname: The Beehive State

Capital: Salt Lake City, C-4

Population: 3,271,616 (rank: 30th)

Largest city: Salt Lake City, 199,723, C-4

Land area: 82,355 sq. mi. (rank: 12th)

Highest point: Kings Peak, 13,528 ft, C-5

NOTE: Maps are not always in alphabetical order.
See Page 1 for map location in this atlas.

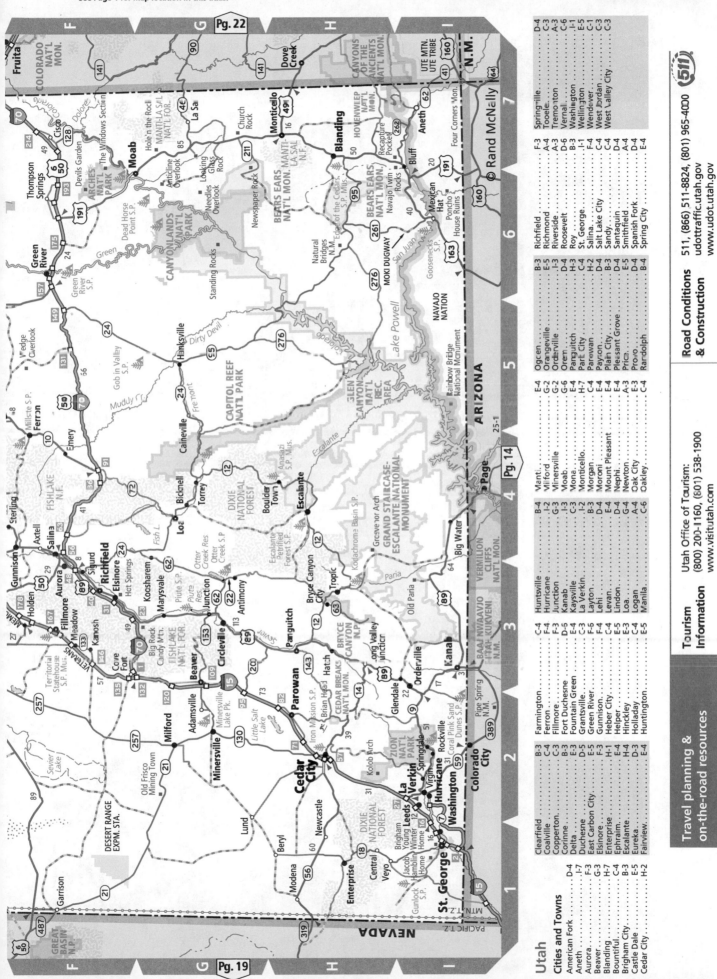

© Rand McNally

Travel planning & on-the-road resources

Tourism Information
Utah Office of Tourism:
(800) 200-1160, (801) 538-1900
www.visitutah.com

Road Conditions & Construction
511, (866) 511-8824, (801) 965-4000
udottraffic.utah.gov
www.udot.utah.gov

more map Pg. 102

Virginia state facts

Nickname: Old Dominion

Capital: Richmond, G-11

Population: 8,631,393 (rank: 12th)

Largest city: Virginia Beach, 459,470, H-13

Land area: 39,472 sq. mi. (rank: 37th)

Highest point: Mount Rogers, 5,729 ft., I-4

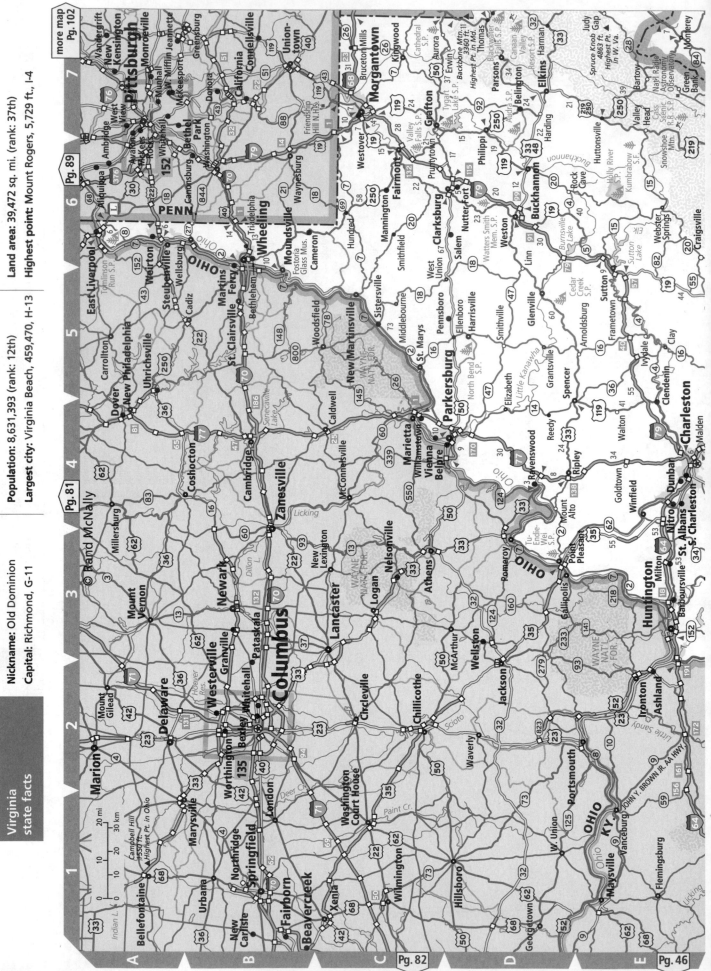

Pg. 89
Pg. 81
Pg. 82
Pg. 46

NOTE: Maps are not always in alphabetical order.
See Page 1 for map location in this atlas.

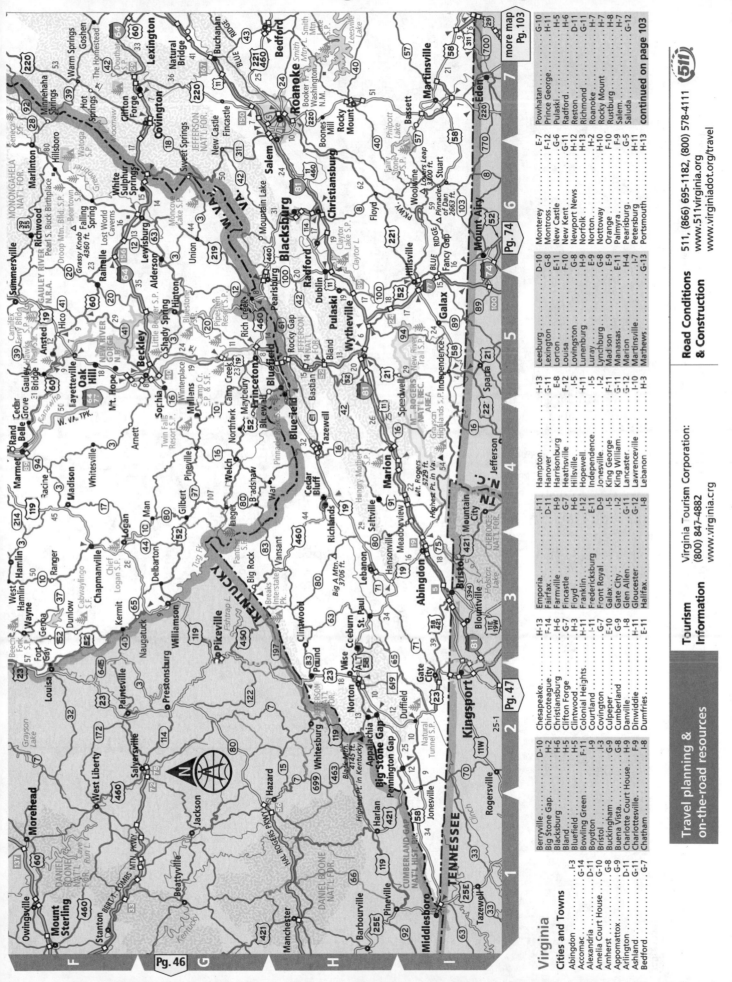

more map Pg. 103

Pg. 74

Pg. 47

Pg. 46

Virginia
Cities and Towns

continued on page 103

Tourism Information
Virginia Tourism Corporation:
(800) 847-4882
www.virginia.org

Road Conditions & Construction
511, (866) 695-1182, (800) 578-4111
www.511virginia.org
www.virginiadot.org/travel

Travel planning & on-the-road resources

511

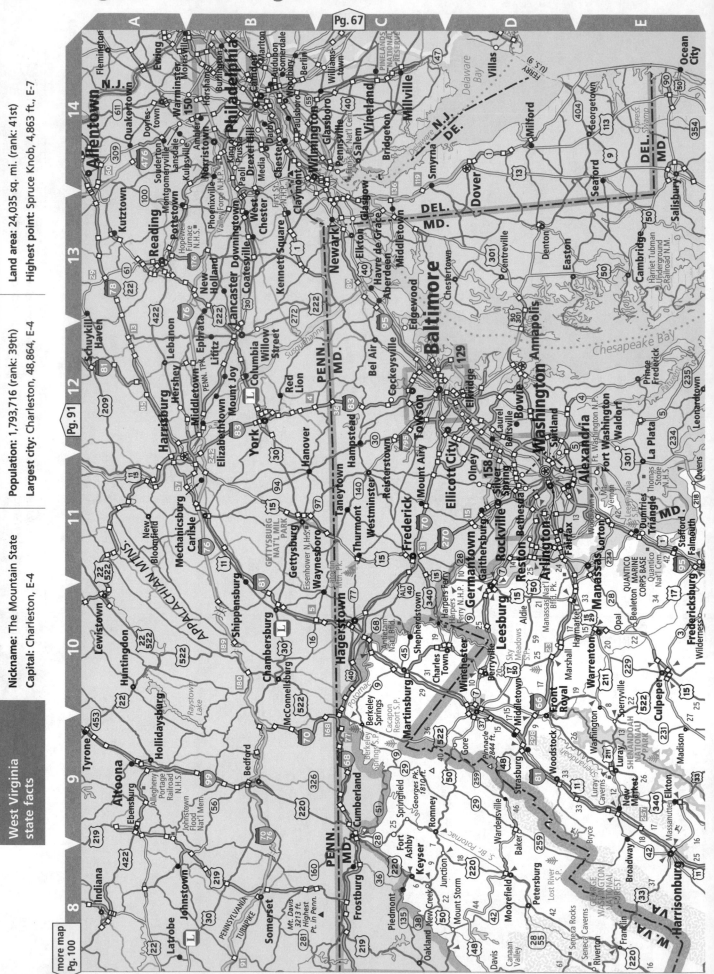

Pg. 67

Pg. 91

West Virginia state facts

Nickname: The Mountain State

Capital: Charleston, E-4

Population: 1,793,716 (rank: 39th)

Largest city: Charleston, 48,864, E-4

Land area: 24,035 sq. mi. (rank: 41st)

Highest point: Spruce Knob, 4,863 ft., E-7

more map Pg. 100

NOTE: Maps are not always in alphabetical order.
See Page 1 for map location in this atlas.

Virginia • West Virginia/Eastern   103

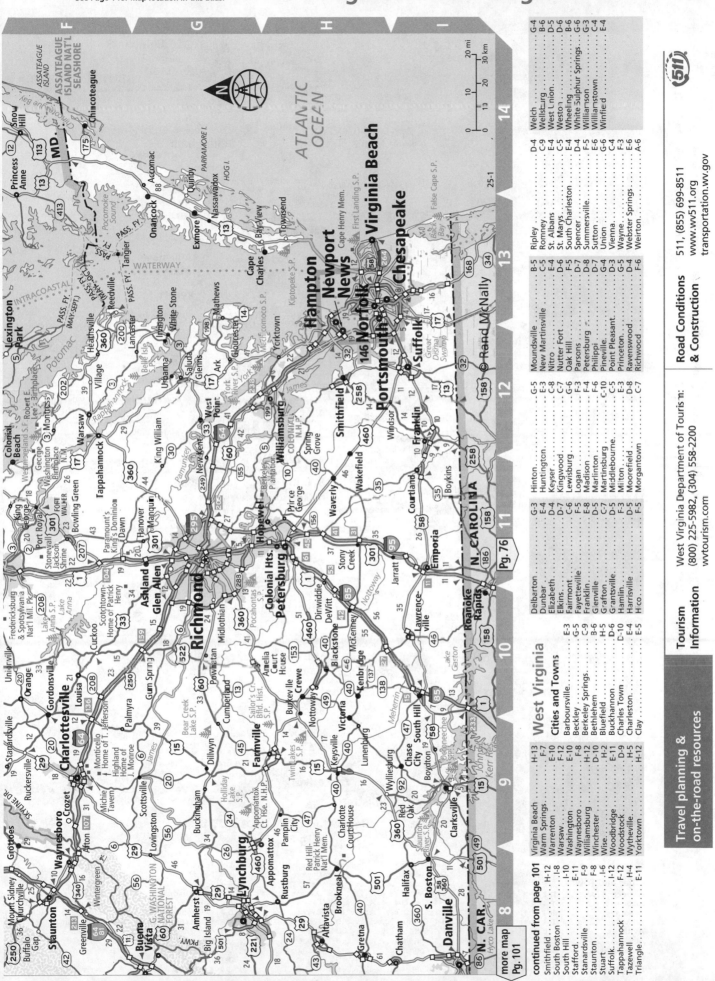

Pg. 76

more map
Pg. 101

Travel planning &
on-the-road resources

Tourism
Information

West Virginia Department of Tourism:
(800) 225-5982, (304) 558-2200
wvtourism.com

Road Conditions
& Construction

511, (855) 699-8511
www.wv511.org
transportation.wv.gov

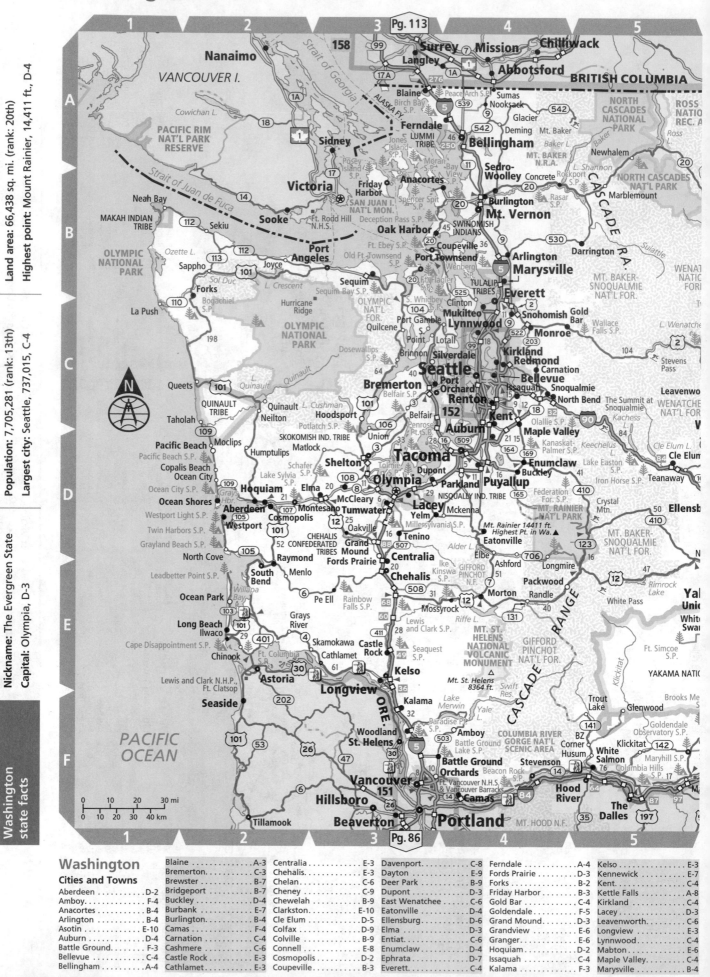

Land area: 66,438 sq. mi. (rank: 20th)
Highest point: Mount Rainier, 14,411 ft., D-4

Population: 7,705,281 (rank: 13th)
Largest city: Seattle, 737,015, C-4

Nickname: The Evergreen State
Capital: Olympia, D-3

Washington state facts

Washington
Cities and Towns

NOTE: Maps are not always in alphabetical order.
See Page 1 for map location in this atlas.

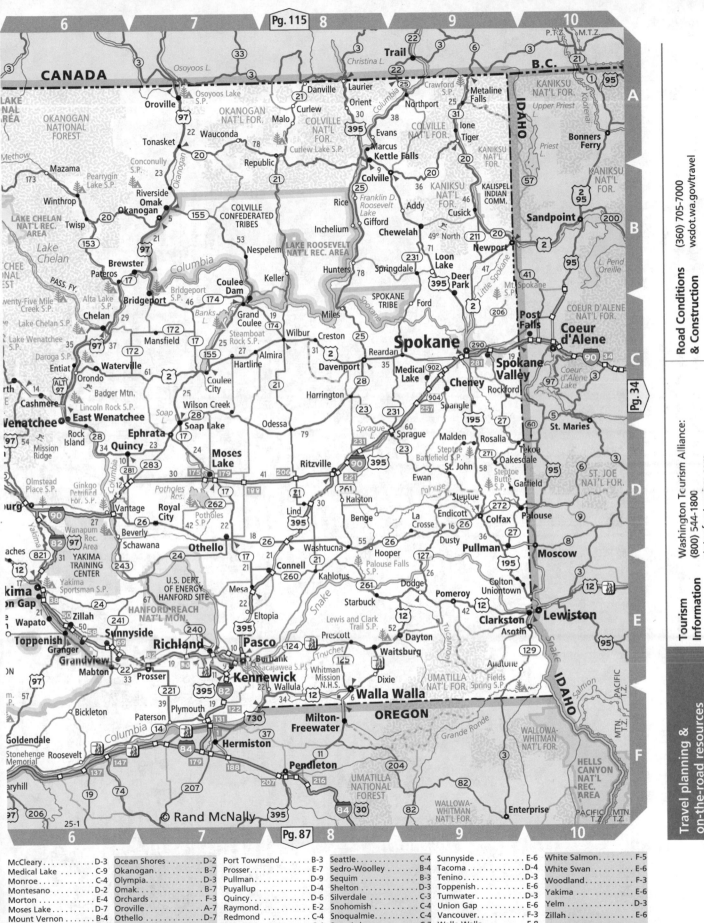

Pg. 115
Pg. 87
Pg. 34

Road Conditions & Construction

(360) 705-7000
wsdot.wa.gov/travel

Tourism Information

Washington Tourism Alliance:
(800) 544-1800
stateofwatourism.com

Travel planning & on-the-road resources

© Rand McNally

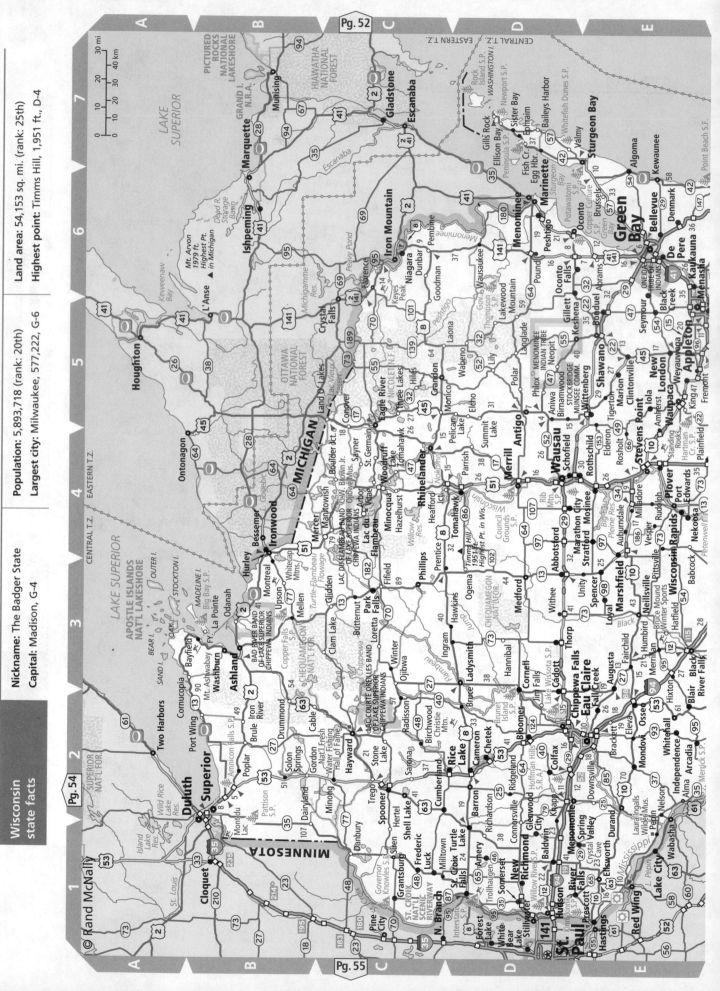

© Rand McNally

Wisconsin state facts

Nickname: The Badger State
Capital: Madison, G-4

Population: 5,893,718 (rank: 20th)
Largest city: Milwaukee, 577,222, G-6

Land area: 54,153 sq. mi. (rank: 25th)
Highest point: Timms Hill, 1,951 ft., D-4

NOTE: Maps are not always in alphabetical order.
See Page 1 for map location in this atlas.

Wisconsin   107

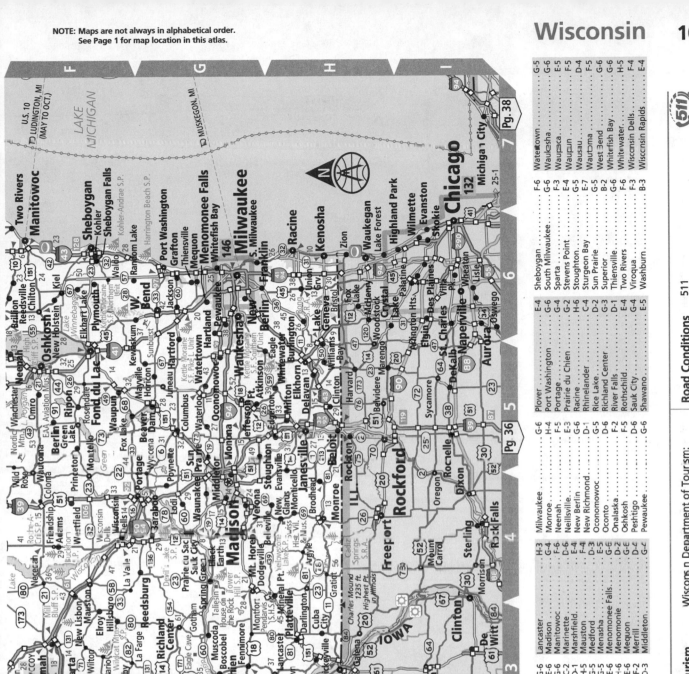

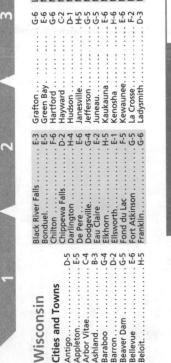

Travel planning & on-the-road resources

Tourism Information
Wisconsin Department of Tourism:
(800) 432-8747, (608) 266-2161
www.travelwisconsin.com

Road Conditions & Construction
511
(866) 511-9472
511wi.gov, wisconsindot.gov

Wyoming

Cities and Towns

Wyoming state facts

Land area: 97,063 sq. mi. (rank: 9th)

Highest point: Gannett Peak, 13,804 ft, C-3

Population: 576,851 (rank: 50th)

Largest city: Cheyenne, 65,132, F-8

Nickname: The Equality State

Capital: Cheyenne, F-8

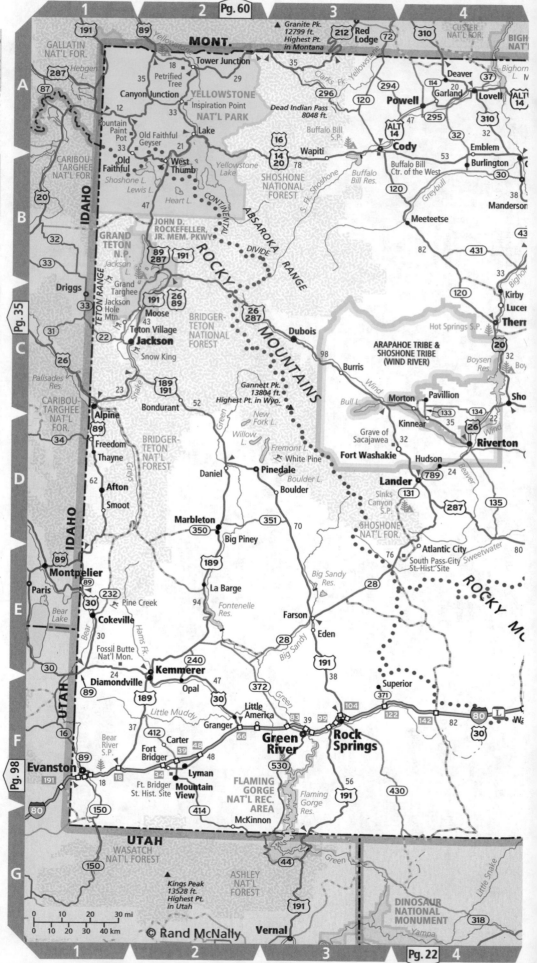

© Rand McNally

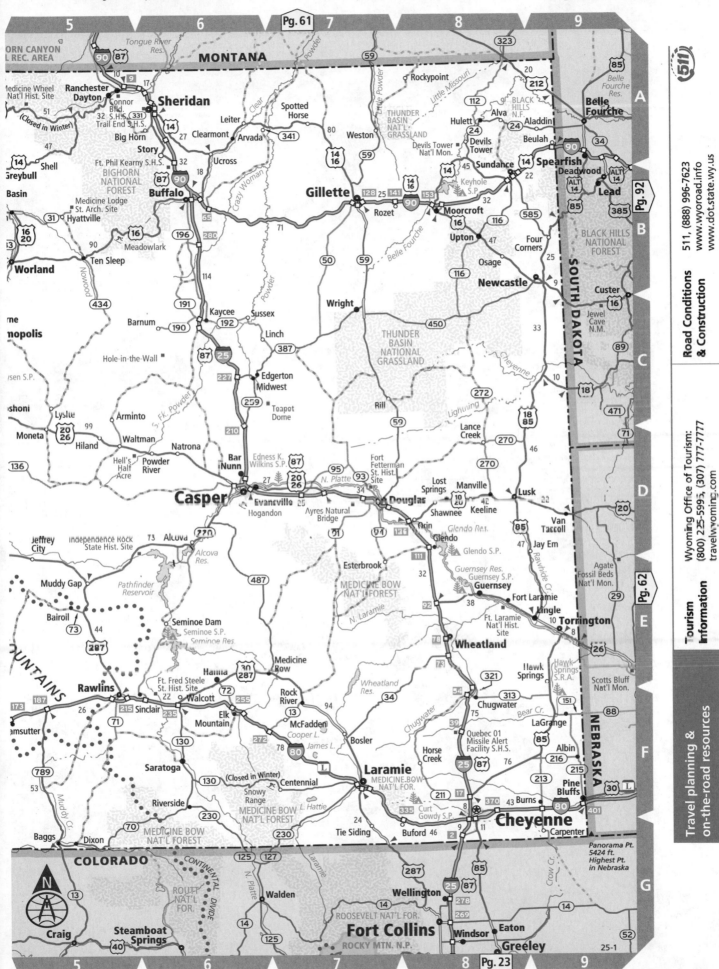

Road Conditions & Construction

511, (888) 996-7623
www.wyoroad.info
www.dot.state.wy.us

Tourism Information

Wyoming Office of Tourism:
(800) 225-5996, (307) 777-7777
travelwyoming.com

Travel planning & on-the-road resources

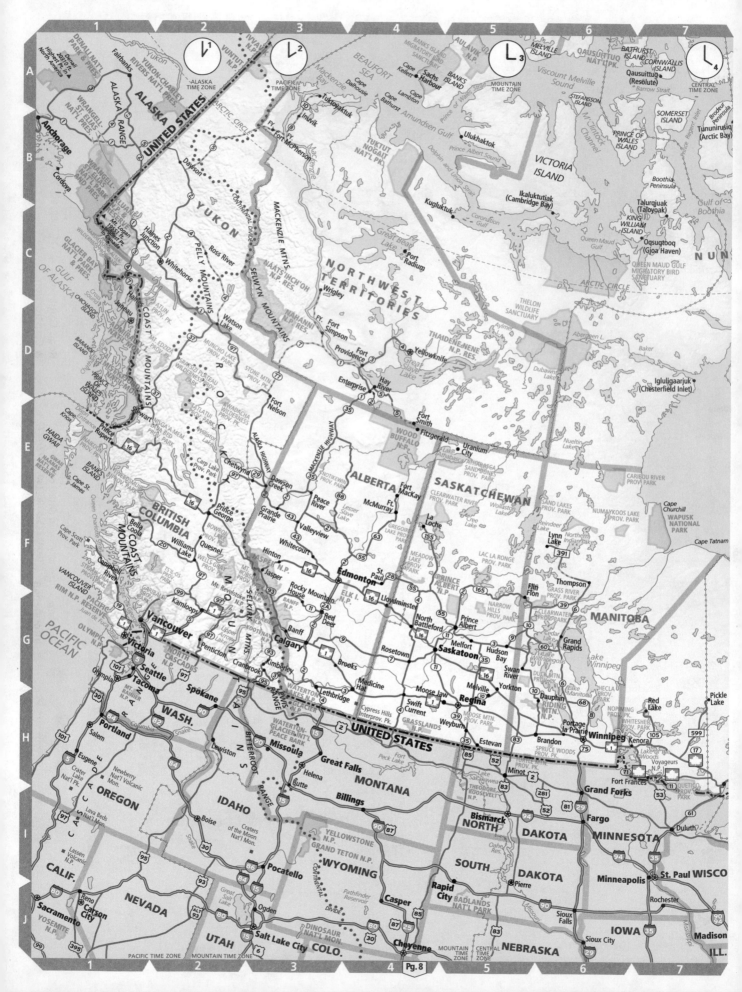

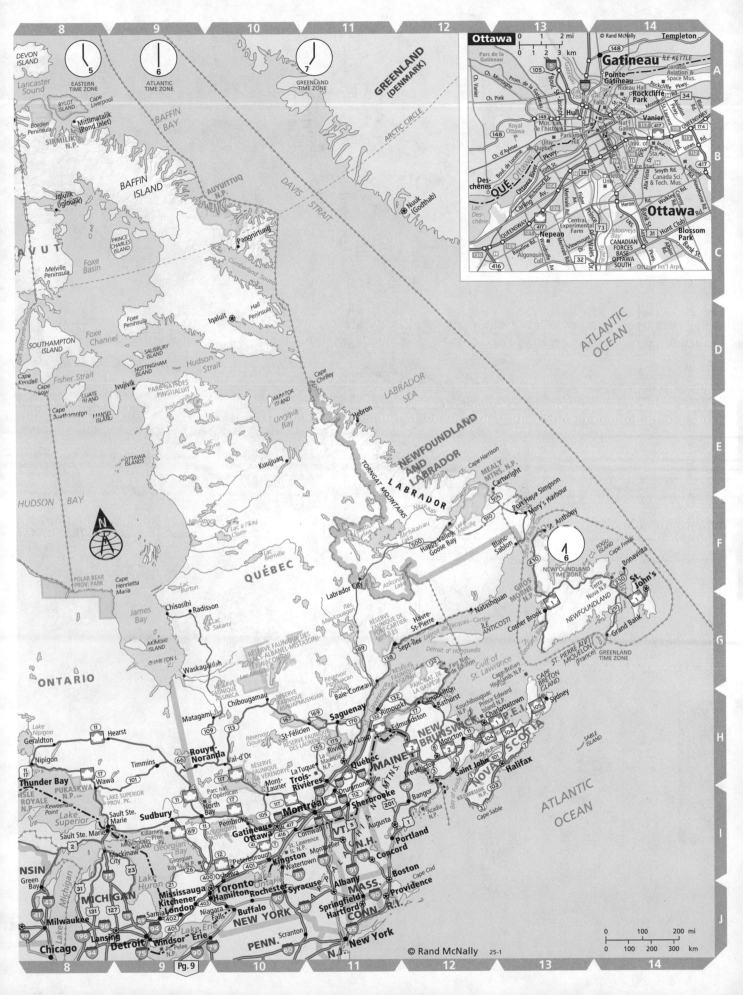

© Rand McNally 25-1

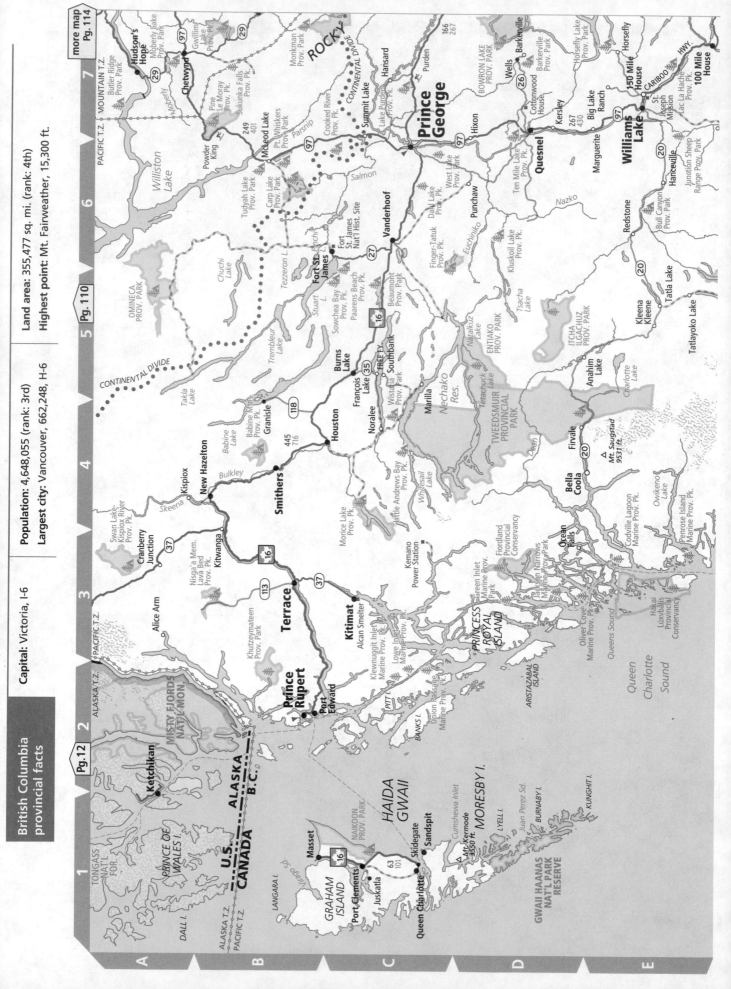

British Columbia provincial facts

Capital: Victoria, I-6

Population: 4,648,055 (rank: 3rd)
Largest city: Vancouver, 662,248, H-6

Land area: 355,477 sq. mi. (rank: 4th)
Highest point: Mt. Fairweather, 15,300 ft.

NOTE: Maps are not always in alphabetical order.
See Page 1 for map location in this atlas.

British Columbia • Alberta/Western   113

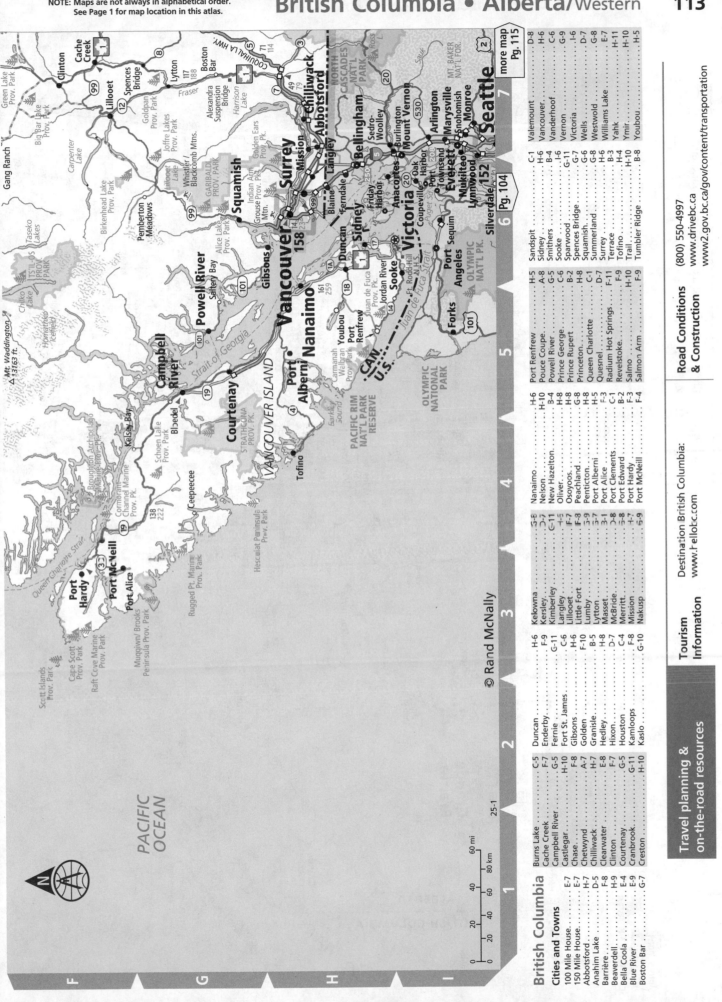

© Rand McNally

British Columbia		
Cities and Towns		
100 Mile House	E-7	
150 Mile House	E-7	
Abbotsford	H-7	
Anahim Lake	D-5	
Barrière	F-8	
Beaverdell	H-9	
Bella Coola	E-4	
Blue River	E-9	
Boston Bar	G-7	

Burns Lake	C-5
Cache Creek	F-7
Campbell River	G-5
Castlegar	H-10
Chase	F-8
Chetwynd	A-7
Chilliwack	H-7
Clearwater	E-8
Clinton	F-7
Courtenay	G-5
Cranbrook	G-11
Creston	H-10

Duncan	H-6
Enderby	F-9
Fernie	G-11
Fort St. James	C-6
Gibsons	H-6
Golden	F-10
Granisle	B-5
Hedley	H-8
Hixon	D-7
Houston	C-4
Kamloops	F-8
Kaslo	G-10

Kelowna	G-8
Kersley	D-7
Kimberley	G-11
Langley	H-6
Lillooet	F-7
Little Fort	F-8
Lumby	G-9
Lytton	G-7
Masset	F-3
McBride	D-8
Merritt	G-8
Mission	H-7
Nakusp	G-10

Nanaimo	G-6
Nelson	H-10
New Hazelton	B-4
Oliver	H-8
Osoyoos	H-8
Peachland	G-8
Penticton	H-8
Port Alberni	H-5
Port Alice	F-3
Port Clements	F-3
Port Edward	B-3
Port Hardy	F-3
Port McNeill	F-4

Port Renfrew	H-5
Pouce Coupe	A-8
Powell River	G-5
Prince George	C-6
Prince Rupert	B-2
Queen Charlotte	F-3
Quesnel	D-7
Radium Hot Springs	F-11
Revelstoke	F-9
Salmo	H-10
Salmon Arm	F-9

Sandspit	F-3
Sidney	H-6
Smithers	B-4
Sooke	H-6
Sparwood	G-11
Spences Bridge	G-7
Squamish	G-6
Summerland	G-8
Surrey	H-6
Terrace	B-3
Tofino	H-4
Trail	H-10
Tumbler Ridge	B-8

Valemount	D-8
Vancouver	H-6
Vanderhoof	C-6
Vernon	G-9
Victoria	H-6
Wells	D-7
Westwold	G-8
Williams Lake	E-7
Yahk	H-11
Ymir	H-10
Youbou	H-5

Travel planning & on-the-road resources		
Tourism Information	Destination British Columbia: www.hellobc.com	
Road Conditions & Construction	(800) 550-4997 www.drivebc.ca www2.gov.bc.ca/gov/content/transportation	

more map
Pg. 115

Pg. 104

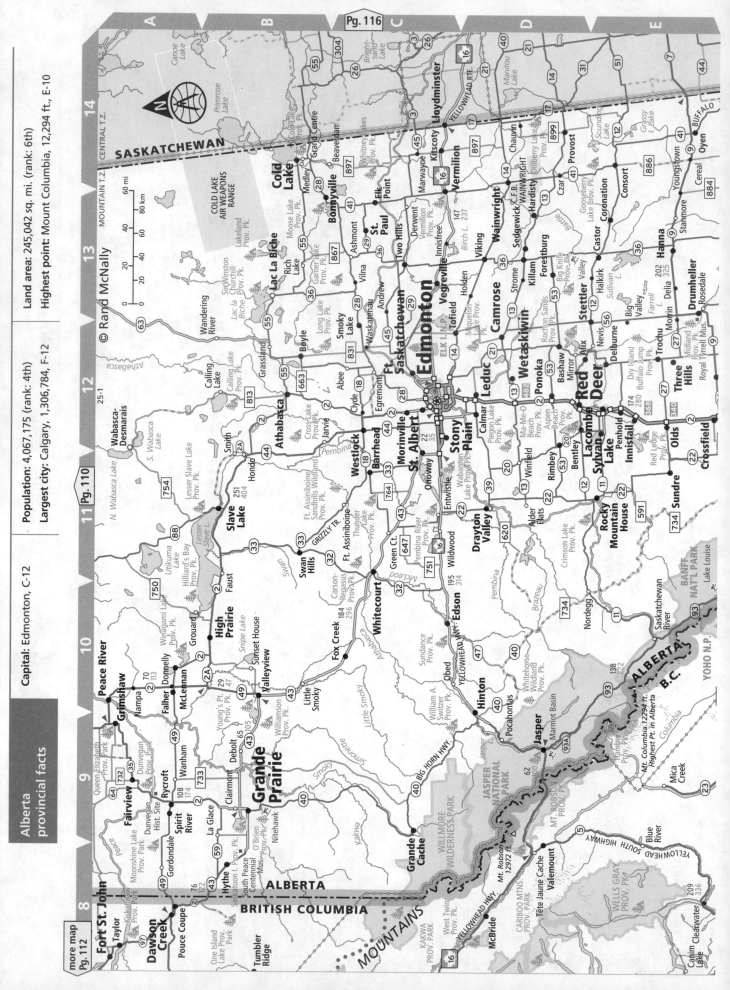

Pg. 116

Alberta provincial facts

Capital: Edmonton, C-12

Population: 4,067,175 (rank: 4th)
Largest city: Calgary, 1,306,784, F-12

Land area: 245,042 sq. mi. (rank: 6th)
Highest point: Mount Columbia, 12,294 ft., E-10

© Rand McNally

more map Pg. 112

SASKATCHEWAN

CENTRAL T.Z.
MOUNTAIN T.Z.

COLD LAKE AIR WEAPONS RANGE

ALBERTA
BRITISH COLUMBIA

BANFF NAT'L PARK

YOHO N.P.

JASPER NATIONAL PARK

WILLMORE WILDERNESS PARK

WELLS GRAY PROV. PK.

MT. ROBSON PROV. PK.

Mt. Columbia 12,294 ft. Highest Pt. in Alberta

Mt. Robson 12,972 ft.

YELLOWHEAD HWY.
YELLOWHEAD SOUTH HIGHWAY

MOUNTAINS

NOTE: Maps are not always in alphabetical order.
See Page 1 for map location in this atlas.

British Columbia • Alberta/Eastern

115

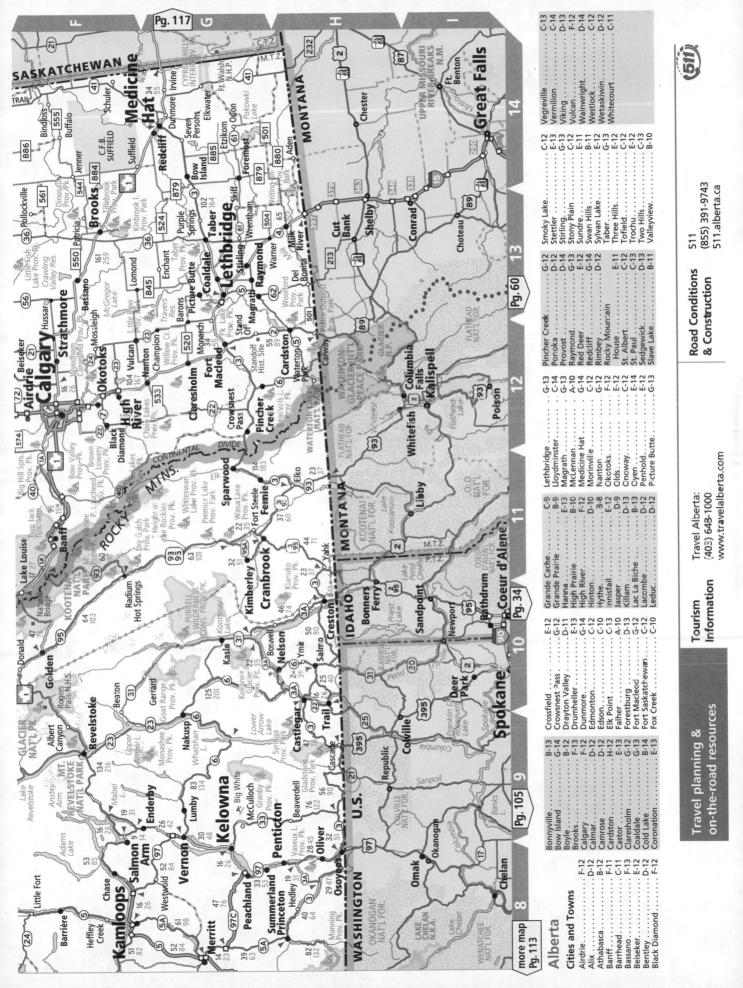

Alberta

Cities and Towns

Airdrie	F-12
Alix	D-12
Athabasca	B-12
Banff	F-11
Barrhead	C-11
Bassano	E-12
Beiseker	E-12
Bentley	D-12
Black Diamond	F-12

Bonnyville	B-13
Bow Island	G-14
Boyle	B-12
Brooks	F-13
Calgary	F-12
Calmar	D-12
Camrose	D-12
Cardston	H-12
Castor	D-13
Claresholm	F-12
Coaldale	G-13
Cold Lake	B-14
Coronation	E-13

Crossfield	E-12
Crowsnest Pass	G-12
Drayton Valley	D-11
Drumheller	E-13
Dunmore	G-14
Edmonton	C-12
Edson	D-10
Elk Point	C-13
Falher	A-10
Forestburg	D-9
Fort Macleod	B-13
Fort Saskatchewan	C-12
Fox Creek	C-10

Grande Cache	C-9
Grande Prairie	B-9
Hanna	E-13
High Prairie	B-10
High River	F-12
Hinton	D-10
Hythe	B-8
Innisfail	C-10
Jasper	C-13
Killam	D-13
Lac La Biche	B-13
Lacombe	D-12
Leduc	C-10

Lethbridge	G-12
Lloydminster	C-14
Magrath	G-12
McLennan	A-10
Medicine Hat	G-14
Morinville	C-12
Nanton	F-12
Okotoks	E-12
Olds	D-9
Onoway	C-11
Oyen	E-14
Penhold	D-12
Picture Butte	G-13

Pincher Creek	G-12
Ponoka	C-14
Provost	D-14
Raymond	A-10
Red Deer	G-14
Redcliff	C-12
Rimbey	G-12
Rocky Mountain House	F-12
St. Albert	C-12
St. Paul	E-14
Sedgewick	D-13
Slave Lake	B-11

Smoky Lake	G-12
Stettler	D-12
Stirling	G-13
Stony Plain	D-14
Sundre	E-12
Swan Hills	B-11
Sylvan Lake	G-13
Taber	E-12
Three Hills	E-11
Tofield	C-12
Trochu	E-13
Two Hills	E-12
Valleyview	B-11

Vegreville	C-13
Vermilion	C-14
Viking	D-13
Vulcan	F-12
Wainwright	E-11
Westlock	B-11
Wetaskiwin	D-12
Whitecourt	C-11

Travel planning & on-the-road resources

Tourism Information	Travel Alberta: (403) 648-1000 www.travelalberta.com
Road Conditions & Construction	511 (855) 391-9743 511.alberta.ca

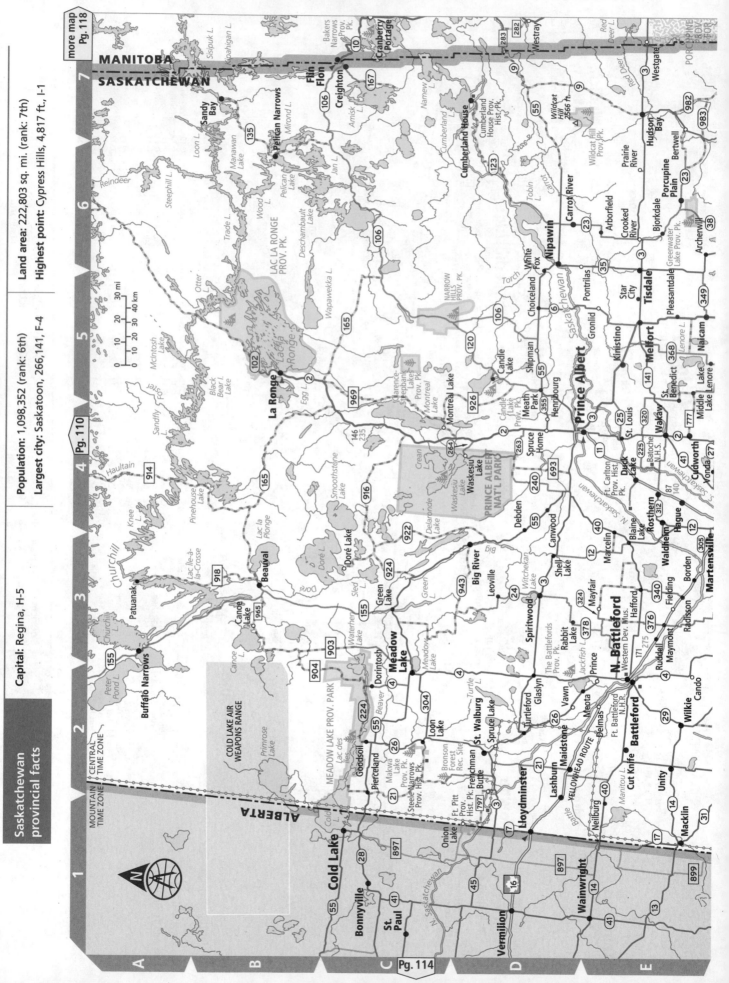

more map Pg. 118

Pg. 110

Pg. 114

Pg. 114

Saskatchewan provincial facts

Capital: Regina, H-5

Population: 1,098,352 (rank: 6th)
Largest city: Saskatoon, 266,141, F-4

Land area: 222,803 sq. mi. (rank: 7th)
Highest point: Cypress Hills, 4,817 ft., I-1

MANITOBA
SASKATCHEWAN

ALBERTA

MOUNTAIN TIME ZONE | CENTRAL TIME ZONE

NOTE: Maps are not always in alphabetical order. See Page 1 for map location in this atlas.

Saskatchewan • Manitoba/Western   117

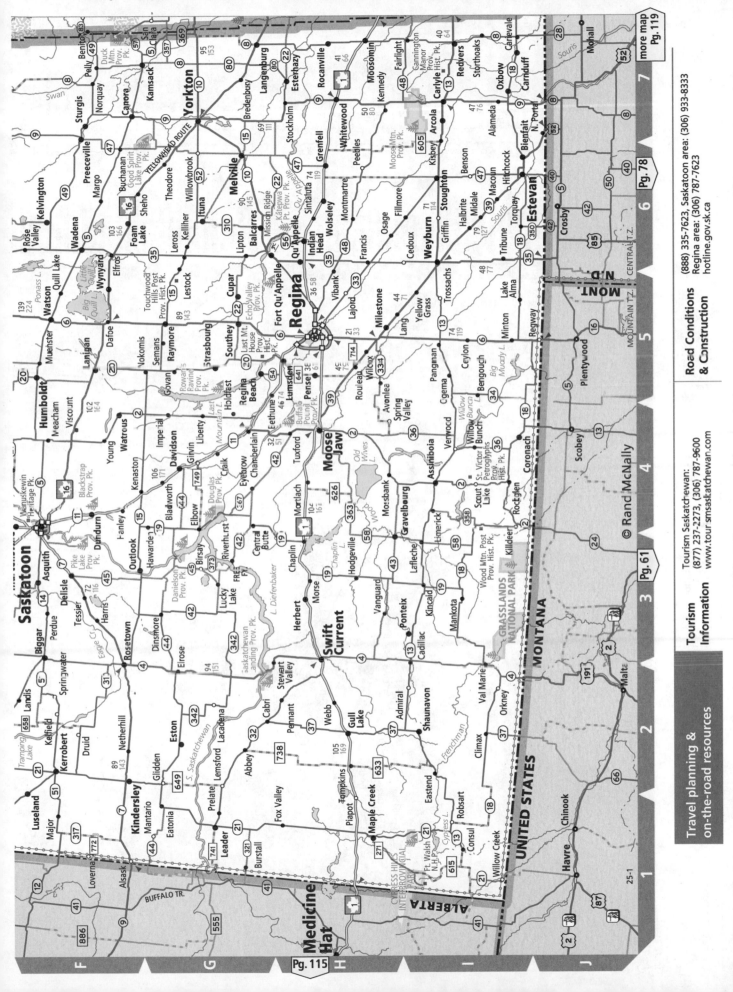

Tourism Information
Tourism Saskatchewan:
(877) 237-2273, (306) 787-9600
www.tourismsaskatchewan.com

Road Conditions & Construction
(888) 335-7623, Saskatoon area: (306) 933-8333
Regina area: (306) 787-7623
hotline.gov.sk.ca

Travel planning & on-the-road resources

© Rand McNally

Manitoba provincial facts

Capital: Winnipeg, H-11

Population: 1,278,365 (rank: 5th)

Largest city: Winnipeg, 749,607, H-11

Land area: 208,614 sq. mi. (rank: 8th)

Highest point: Baldy Mountain, 2,730 ft., G-8

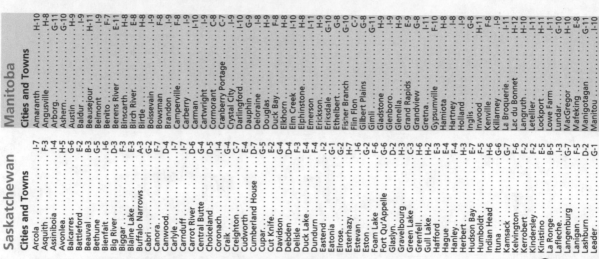

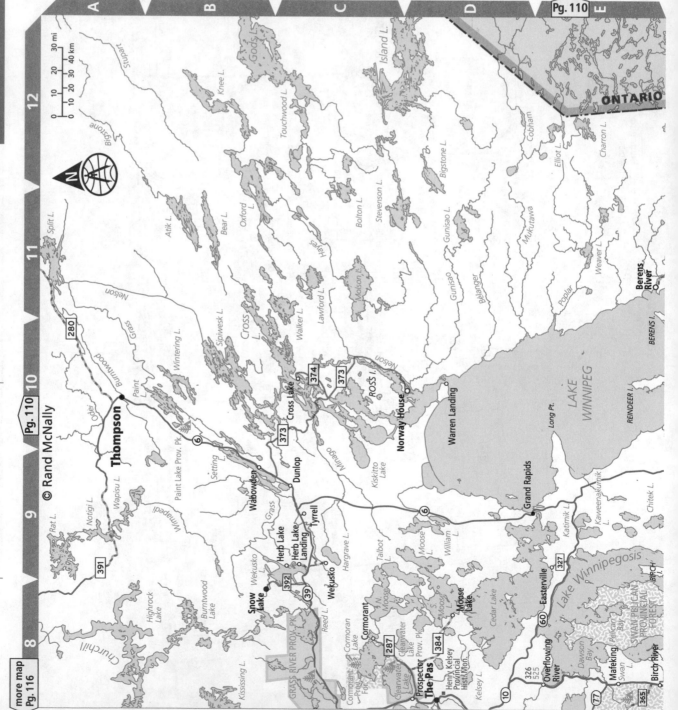

more map Pg. 116

Pg. 110

© Rand McNally

NOTE: Maps are not always in alphabetical order.
See Page 1 for map location in this atlas.

Saskatchewan • Manitoba/Eastern   119

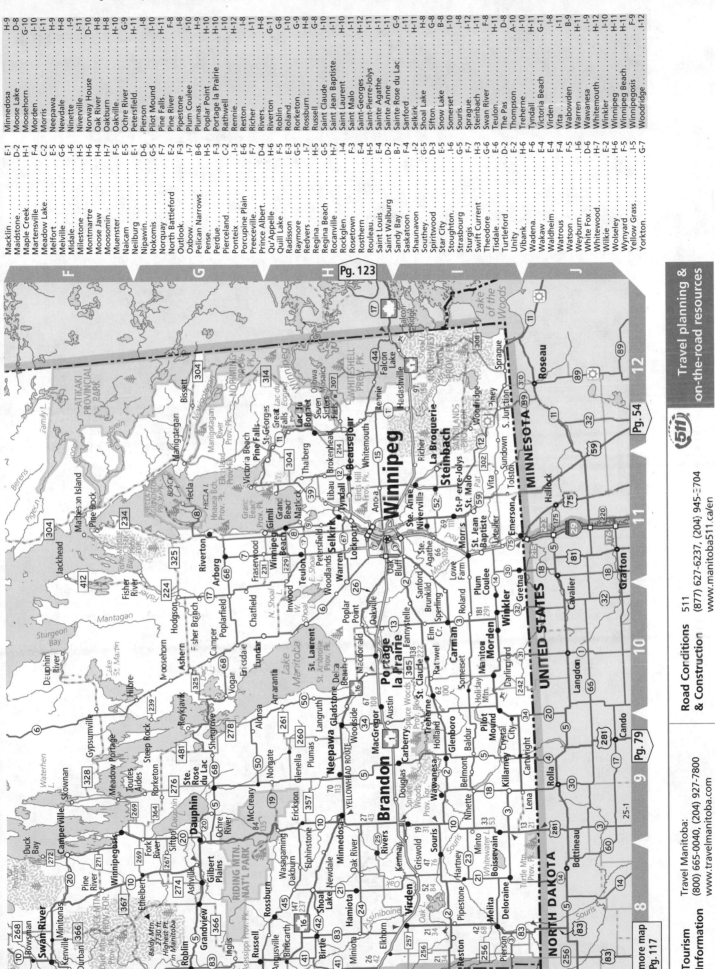

Pg. 123 · Pg. 54 · Pg. 79 · more map Pg. 117

Travel planning & on-the-road resources

511

Tourism Information — Travel Manitoba: (800) 665-0040, (204) 927-7800 www.travelmanitoba.com

Road Conditions & Construction — 511 (877) 627-6237, (204) 945-3704 www.manitoba511.ca/en

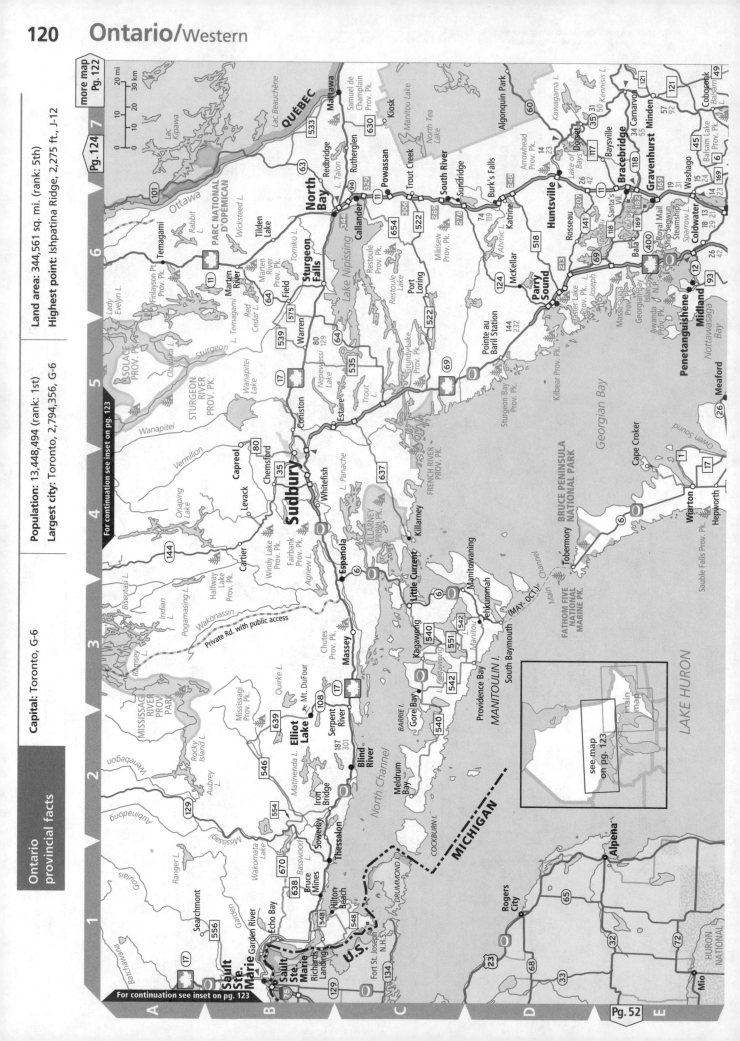

Ontario provincial facts

Capital: Toronto, G-6

Population: 13,448,494 (rank: 1st)
Largest city: Toronto, 2,794,356, G-6

Land area: 344,561 sq. mi. (rank: 5th)
Highest point: Ishpatina Ridge, 2,275 ft., J-12

For continuation see inset on pg. 123

QUÉBEC

PARC NATIONAL D'OPEMICAN

North Bay

Sudbury

Parry Sound

Huntsville

Bracebridge

Gravenhurst

Midland

Penetanguishene

Georgian Bay

BRUCE PENINSULA NATIONAL PARK

FATHOM FIVE NATIONAL MARINE PK.

LAKE HURON

MICHIGAN

Sault Ste. Marie

Elliot Lake

Blind River

Thessalon

Bruce Mines

Espanola

Massey

Little Current

MANITOULIN I.

Alpena

Rogers City

Mio

HURON NATIONAL

see map on pg. 123

main map

For continuation see inset on pg. 123

Pg. 52

A   B   C   D   E

NOTE: Maps are not always in alphabetical order.
See Page 1 for map location in this atlas.

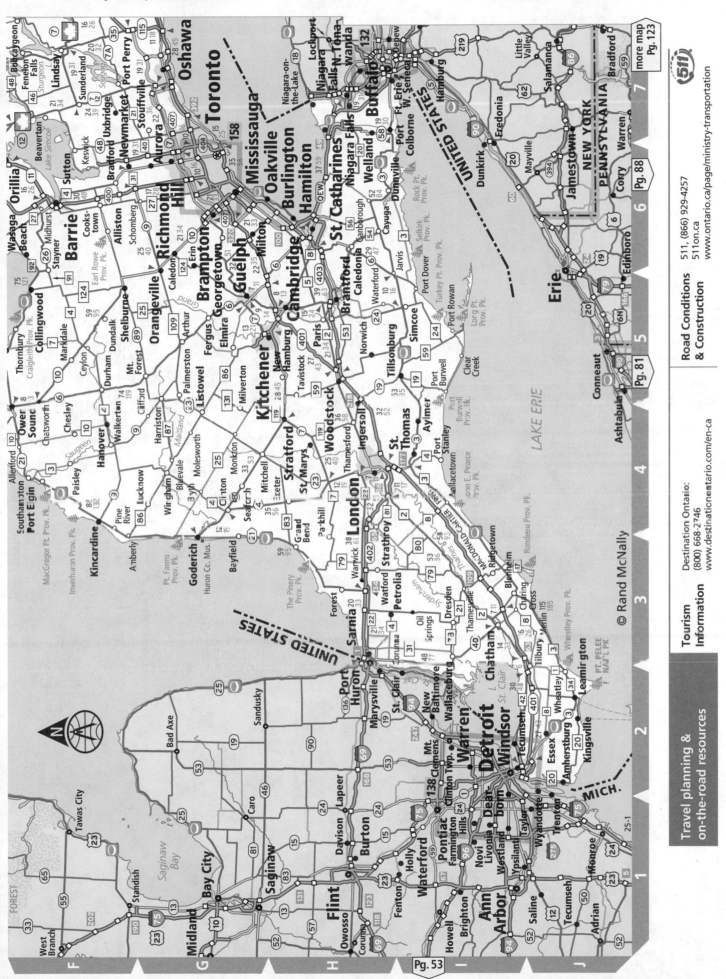

© Rand McNally

511

Road Conditions & Construction	511, (866) 929-4257 511on.ca www.ontario.ca/page/ministry-transportation
Tourism Information	Destination Ontario: (800) 668-2746 www.destinationontario.com/en-ca

Travel planning & on-the-road resources

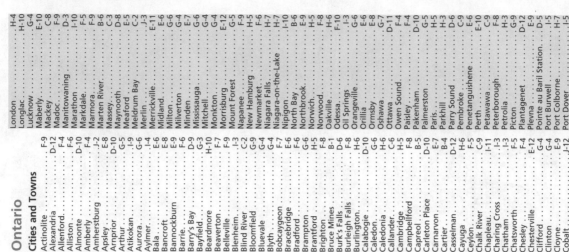

Ontario provincial facts

Capital: Toronto, G-6	**Population:** 13,448,494 (rank: 1st)	**Land area:** 344,561 sq. mi. (rank: 5th)
	Largest city: Toronto, 2,794,356, G-6	**Highest point:** Ishpatina Ridge, 2,275 ft., J-12

more map Pg. 120

Pg. 124

Pg. 72

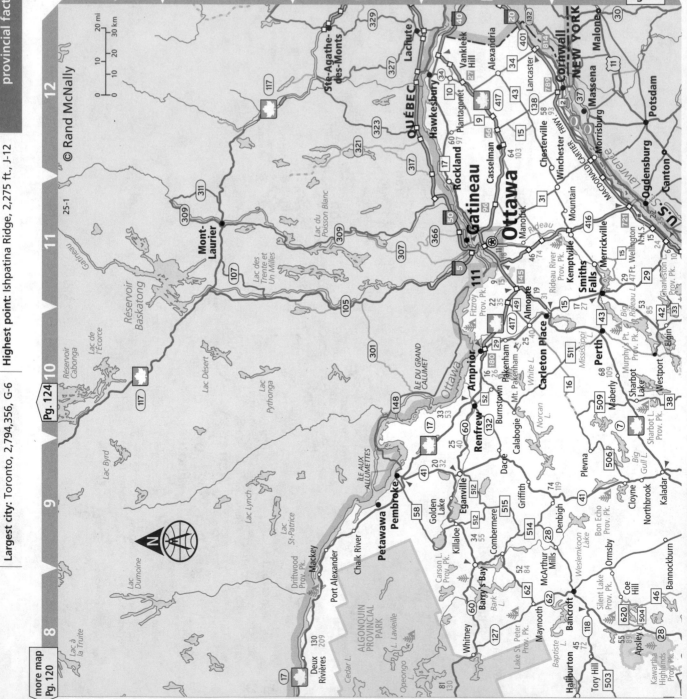

© Rand McNally

NOTE: Maps are not always in alphabetical order.
See Page 1 for map location in this atlas.

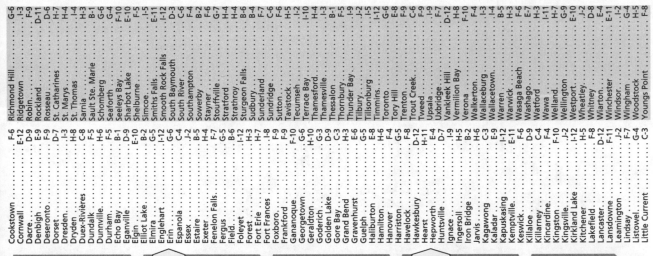

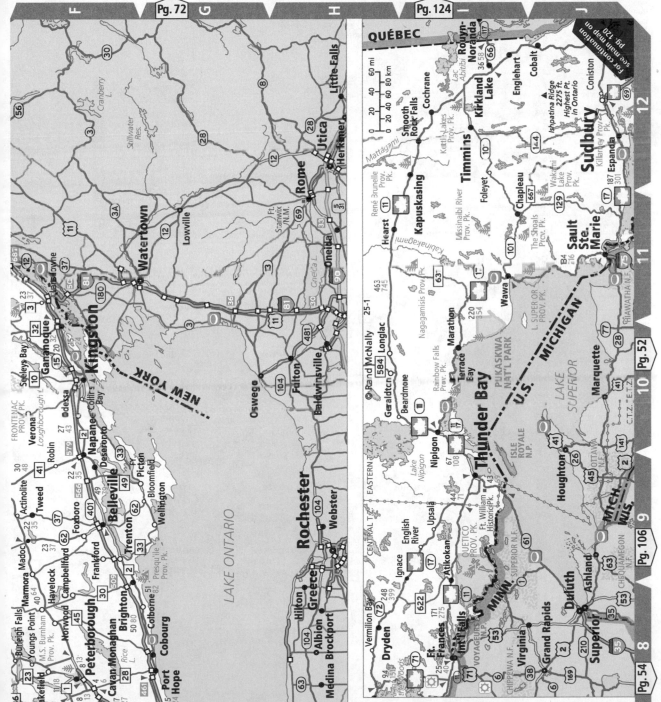

Pg. 72 · Pg. 124 · For continuation see main map on pg. 120 · Pg. 52 · Pg. 106 · Pg. 54

Travel planning & on-the-road resources

511

Tourism Information	Destination Ontario: (800) 668-2746 www.destinationontario.com/en-ca
Road Conditions & Construction	511, (866) 929-4257 511on.ca www.ontario.ca/page/ministry-transportation

Québec

Cities and Towns

Land area: 501,390 sq. mi. (rank: 2nd)
Highest point: Mont d'Iberville, 5,420 ft.
Population: 8,164,361 (rank: 2nd)
Largest city: Montréal, 1,762,949, F-3
Capital: Québec, D-6

Québec provincial facts

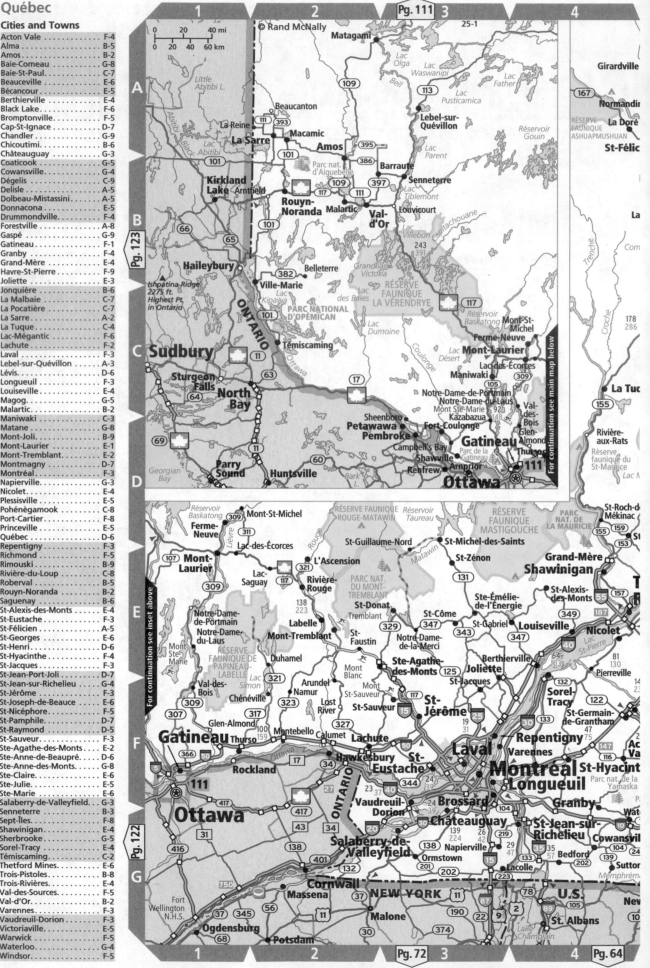

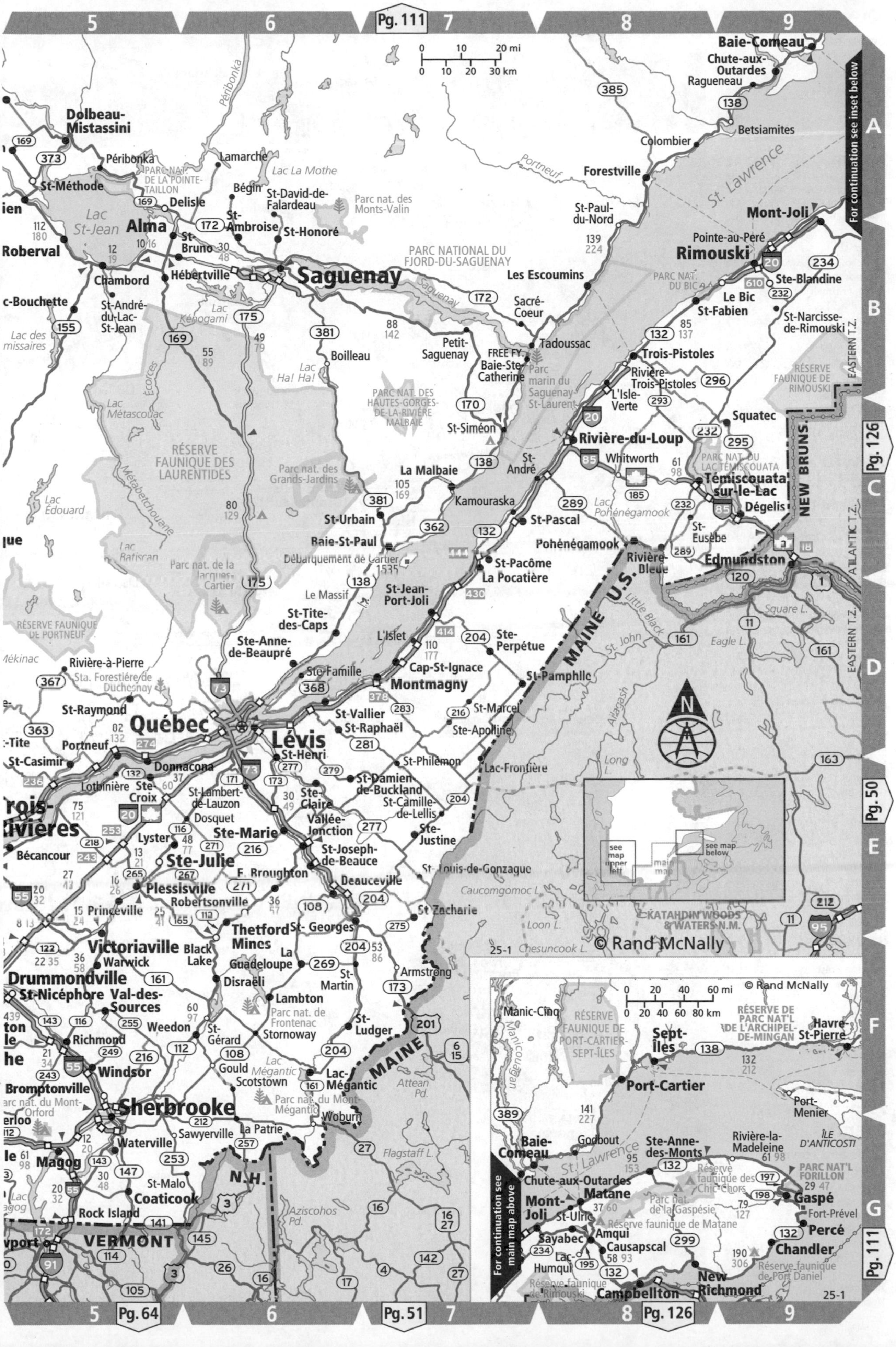

NOTE: Maps are not always in alphabetical order.
See Page 1 for map location in this atlas.

Pg. 111

0 10 20 mi
0 10 20 30 km

Road Conditions & Construction
511, (888) 355-0511
www.quebec511.info/en
www.transports.gouv.qc.ca/en

Tourism Information
Tourisme Québec:
(877) 266-5687, (514) 873-2015
www.bonjourquebec.com/en-ca

Travel planning & on-the-road resources

For continuation see inset below

Pg. 126
Pg. 50
Pg. 64
Pg. 51
Pg. 111
Pg. 126

Baie-Comeau
Chute-aux-Outardes
Ragueneau
Colombier
Betsiamites
Forestville
St-Paul-du-Nord
Mont-Joli
Pointe-au-Père
Rimouski
Ste-Blandine
Le Bic
St-Fabien
St-Narcisse-de-Rimouski
Squatec
Trois-Pistoles
Rivière-Trois-Pistoles
L'Isle-Verte
Rivière-du-Loup
Whitworth
Témiscouata-sur-le-Lac
Dégelis
St-Eusèbe
Edmundston
Les Escoumins
Sacré-Coeur
Tadoussac
Petit-Saguenay
Baie-Ste-Catherine
St-Siméon
La Malbaie
St-André
Kamouraska
St-Pascal
Pohénégamook
Rivière-Bleue

Dolbeau-Mistassini
Péribonka
Lamarche
St-Méthode
Delisle
St-David-de-Falardeau
Alma
St-Ambroise
St-Honoré
St-Bruno
Roberval
Chambord
Hébertville
Saguenay
St-André-du-Lac-St-Jean
Boilleau
Lac-Bouchette
Lac St-Jean
Lac Kénogami

PARC NATIONAL DU FJORD-DU-SAGUENAY
PARC NAT. DE LA POINTE-TAILLON
Parc nat. des Monts-Valin
PARC NAT. DES HAUTES-GORGES-DE-LA-RIVIÈRE MALBAIE
RÉSERVE FAUNIQUE DES LAURENTIDES
Parc nat. des Grands-Jardins
RÉSERVE FAUNIQUE DE PORTNEUF
Parc nat. de la Jacques-Cartier

Baie-St-Paul
Débarquement de Cartier
Le Massif
St-Urbain
St-Tite-des-Caps
Ste-Anne-de-Beaupré
Ste-Famille
St-Jean-Port-Joli
L'Islet
St-Pacôme
La Pocatière
Cap-St-Ignace
Montmagny
Ste-Perpétue
St-Pamphile

St-Raymond
Rivière-à-Pierre
Sta. Forestière de Duchesnay
Québec
Lévis
St-Henri
Portneuf
St-Casimir
Donnacona
Ste-Croix
Lotbinière
Dosquet
Lyster
Ste-Marie
Vallée-Jonction
St-Joseph-de-Beauce
St-Vallier
St-Raphaël
St-Damien-de-Buckland
St-Camille-de-Lellis
Ste-Justine
St-Marcel
Ste-Apolline
Lac-Frontière
St-Philémon
St-Louis-de-Gonzague

Trois-Rivières
Bécancour
Ste-Julie
Plessisville
Robertsonville
Princeville
Victoriaville
Warwick
Drummondville
St-Nicéphore
Val-des-Sources
Richmond
Windsor
Bromptonville
Waterloo
Sherbrooke
Waterville
Magog
Coaticook
St-Malo
Rock Island
Thetford Mines
Black Lake
La Guadeloupe
Disraëli
Lambton
Stornoway
St-Gérard
Gould
Scotstown
Lac-Mégantic
Woburn
St-Georges
Deauceville
St-Zacharie
Armstrong
St-Martin
St-Ludger
F. Broughton

Parc nat. de Frontenac
Parc nat. du Mont-Mégantic
Parc nat. du Mont-Orford
La Patrie
Sawyerville

VERMONT
N.H.
MAINE
U.S.
NEW BRUNS.
EASTERN T.Z.
ATLANTIC T.Z.

© Rand McNally

KATAHDIN WOODS & WATERS N.M.

Inset map:
© Rand McNally
0 20 40 60 mi
0 20 40 60 80 km
Manic-Cinq
RÉSERVE FAUNIQUE DE PORT-CARTIER-SEPT-ÎLES
RÉSERVE DE PARC NAT'L DE L'ARCHIPEL-DE-MINGAN
Sept-Îles
Havre-St-Pierre
Port-Cartier
Port-Menier
Baie-Comeau
Chute-aux-Outardes
Godbout
Mont-Joli
St-Ulric
Matane
Ste-Anne-des-Monts
Rivière-la-Madeleine
ÎLE D'ANTICOSTI
PARC NAT'L FORILLON
Gaspé
Fort-Prével
Percé
Chandler
New Richmond
Réserve faunique des Chic-Chocs
Parc nat. de la Gaspésie
Réserve faunique de Matane
Causapscal
Amqui
Sayabec
Humqui
Campbellton
Réserve faunique de Port Daniel
Réserve faunique de Rimouski

For continuation see main map above

25-1

Provincial facts

NEW BRUNSWICK
Population: 747,101 (rank: 8th)
Largest city: Moncton, 79,470, D-5
Land area: 27,509 sq. mi. (rank: 11th)

NEWFOUNDLAND & LABRADOR
Population: 519,716 (rank: 9th)
Largest city: St. John's, 110,525, B-9
Land area: 138,290 sq. mi. (rank: 10th)

NOVA SCOTIA
Population: 923,598 (rank: 7th)
Largest city: Halifax, 439,819, F-6
Land area: 20,396 sq. mi. (rank: 12th)

PRINCE EDWARD ISLAND
Population: 142,907 (rank: 10th)
Largest city: Charlottetown, 38,809, D-6
Land area: 2,194 sq. mi. (rank: 13th)

Pg. 111
Pg. 125
Pg. 50

NOTE: Maps are not always in alphabetical order.
See Page 1 for map location in this atlas.

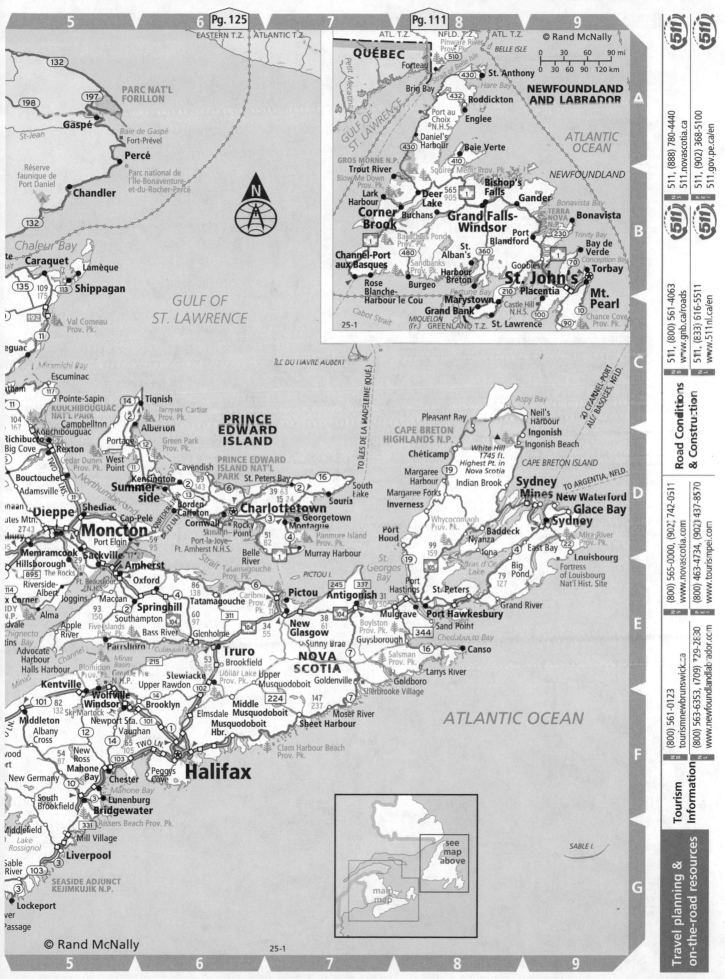

© Rand McNally

Pg. 125
Pg. 111

© Rand McNally

EASTERN T.Z.   ATLANTIC T.Z.   ATL. T.Z.   NFLD. T.Z.   ATL. T.Z.

QUÉBEC

NEWFOUNDLAND
AND LABRADOR

ATLANTIC
OCEAN

NEWFOUNDLAND

GULF OF
ST. LAWRENCE

PRINCE
EDWARD
ISLAND

CAPE BRETON
HIGHLANDS N.P.

CAPE BRETON ISLAND

NOVA
SCOTIA

ATLANTIC OCEAN

Halifax

SABLE I.

see
map
above

main
map

25-1

511 (888) 780-4440
511.novascotia.ca

511 (902) 368-5100
511.gov.pe.ca/en

511 (800) 561-4063
www.gnb.ca/roads

511 (833) 616-5511
www.511nl.ca/en

Road Conditions
& Construction

(800) 565-0000, (902) 742-0511
www.novascotia.com

(800) 463-4734, (902) 437-8570
www.tourismpei.com

Tourism
Information

(800) 561-0123
tourismnewbrunswick.ca

(800) 563-6353, (709) 729-2830
www.newfoundlandlabrador.com

Travel planning &
on-the-road resources

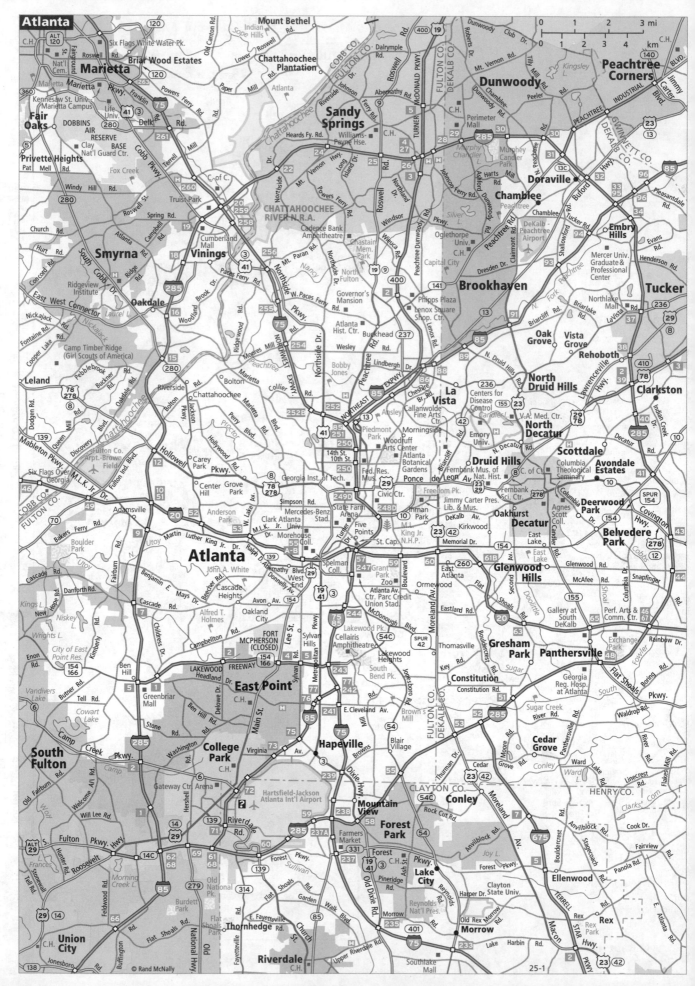

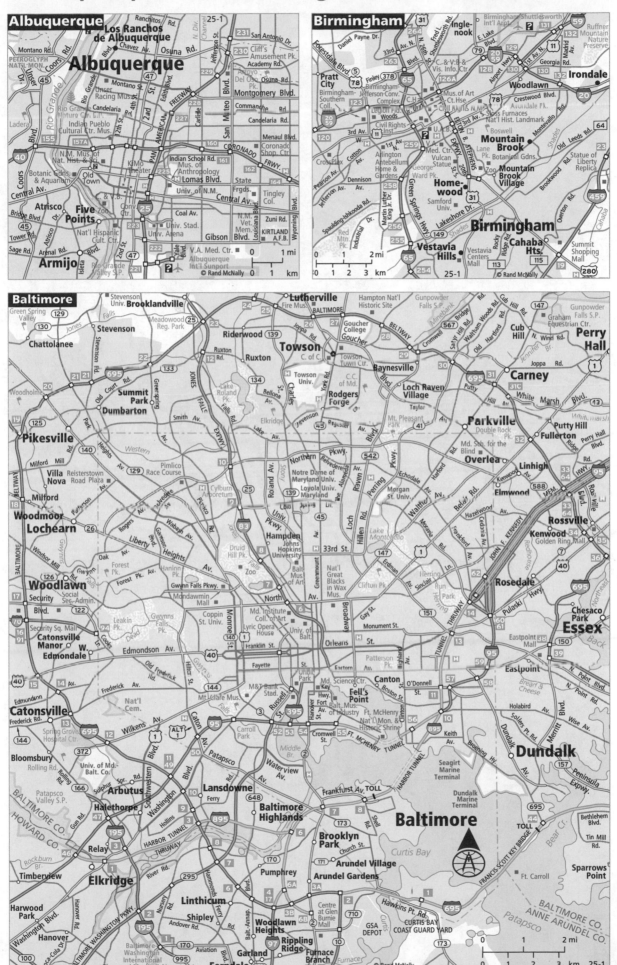

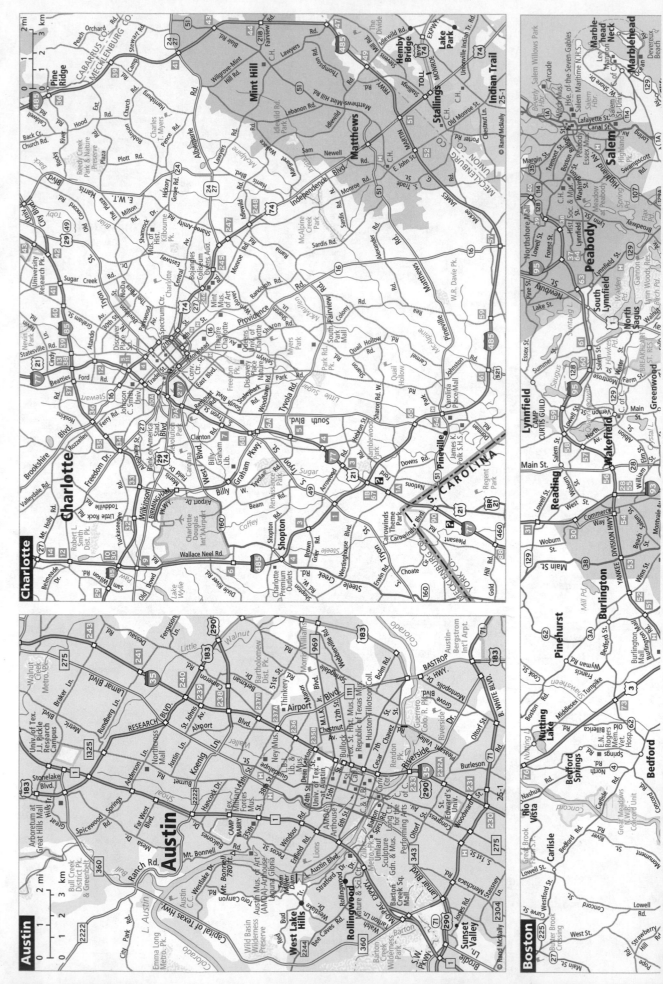

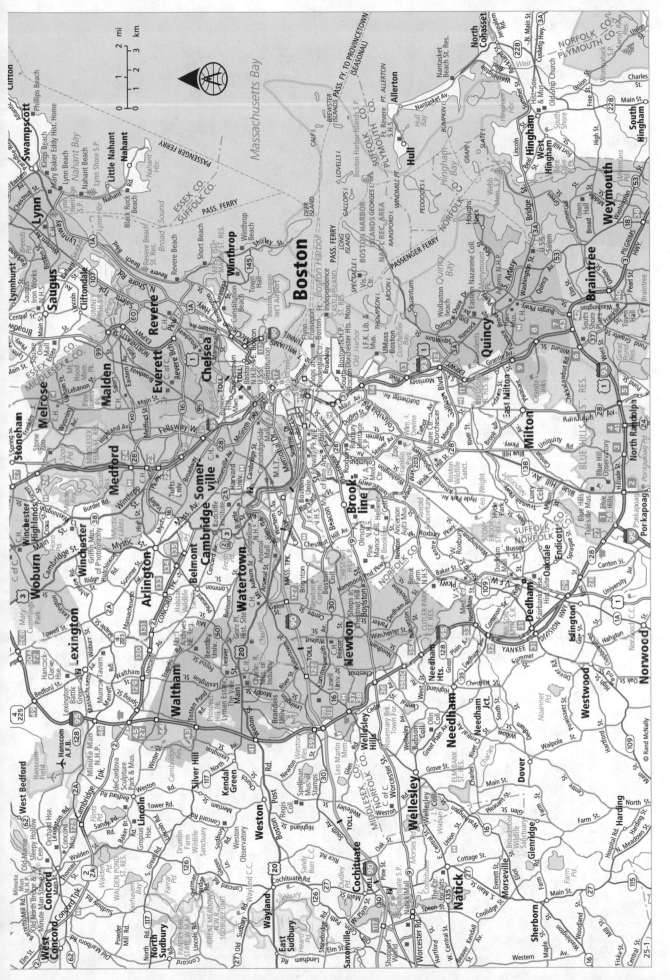

25-1

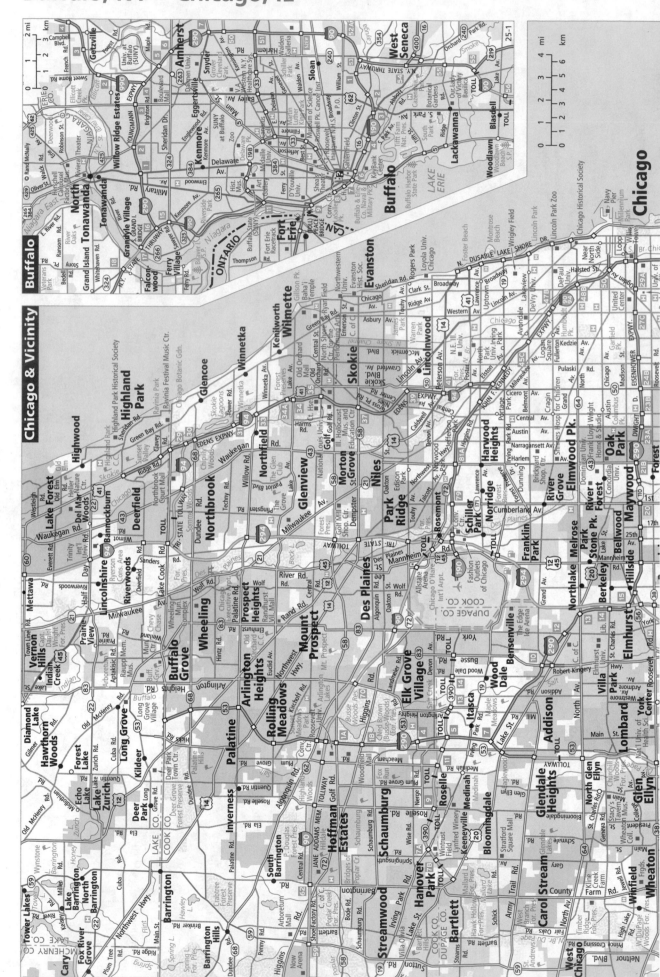

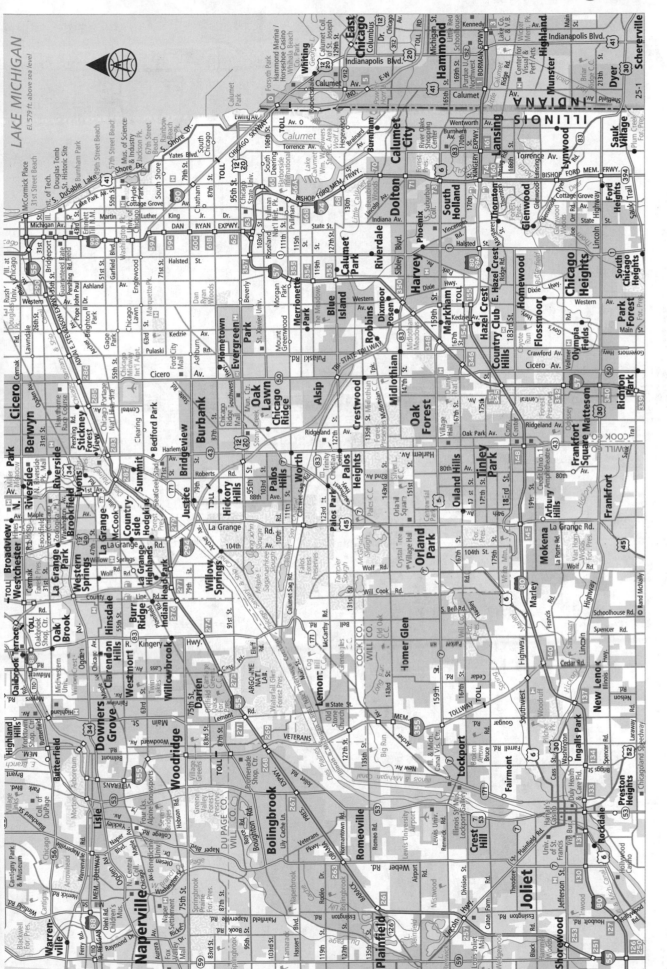

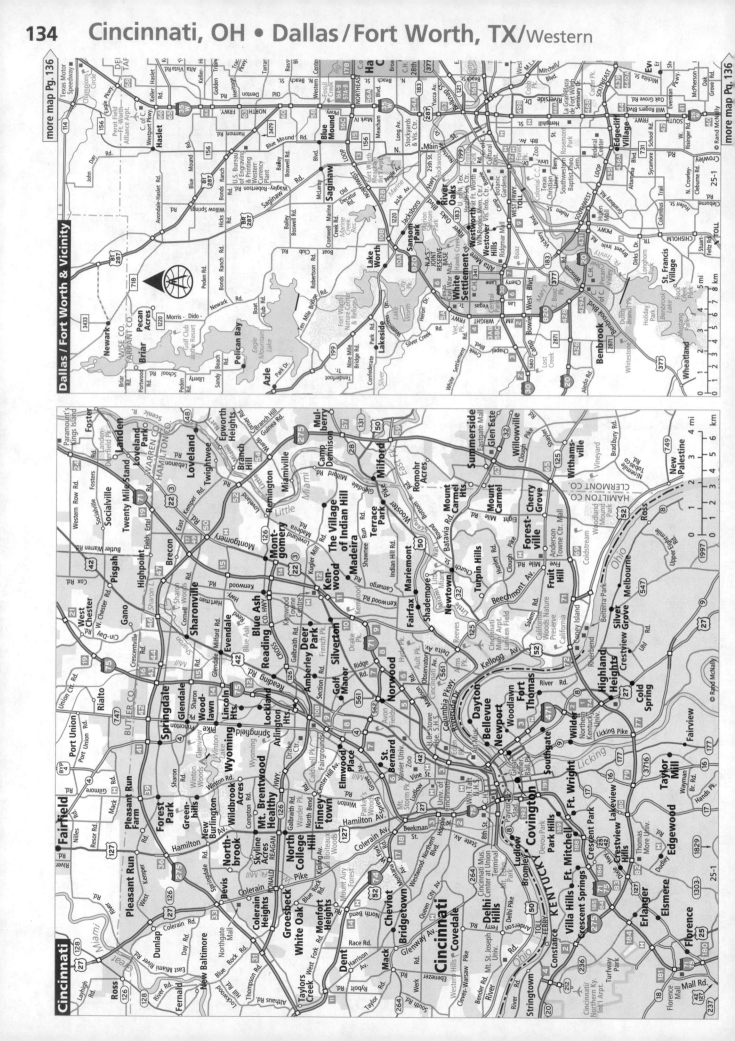

more map Pg. 136
more map Pg. 136

Dallas / Fort Worth & Vicinity

Cincinnati

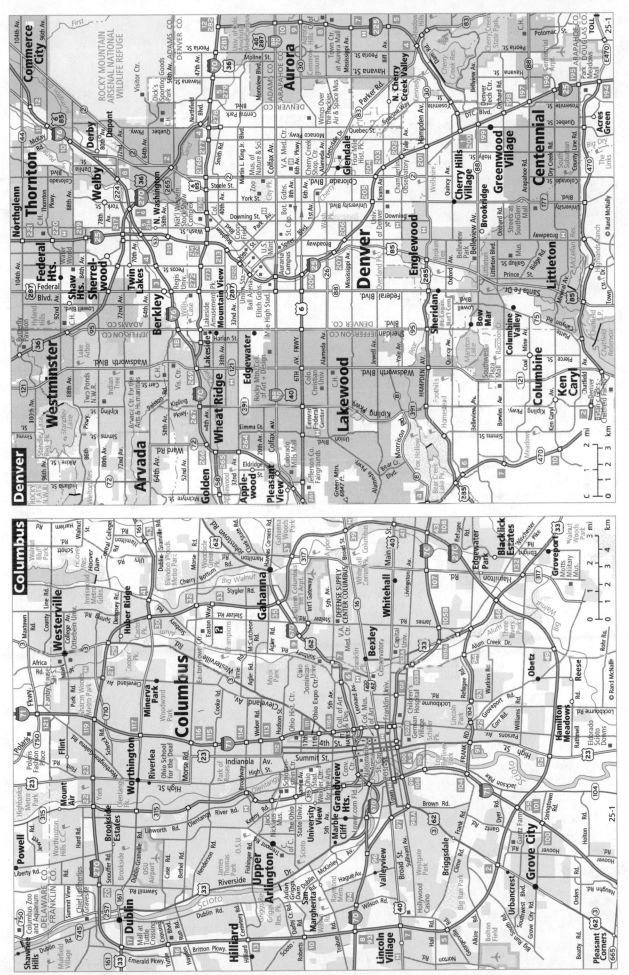

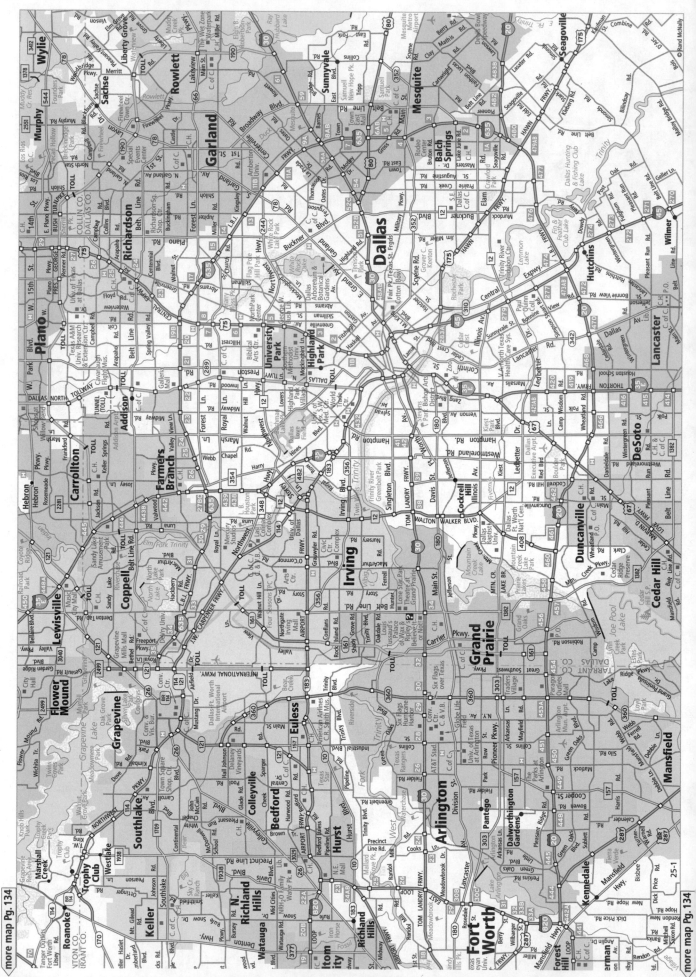

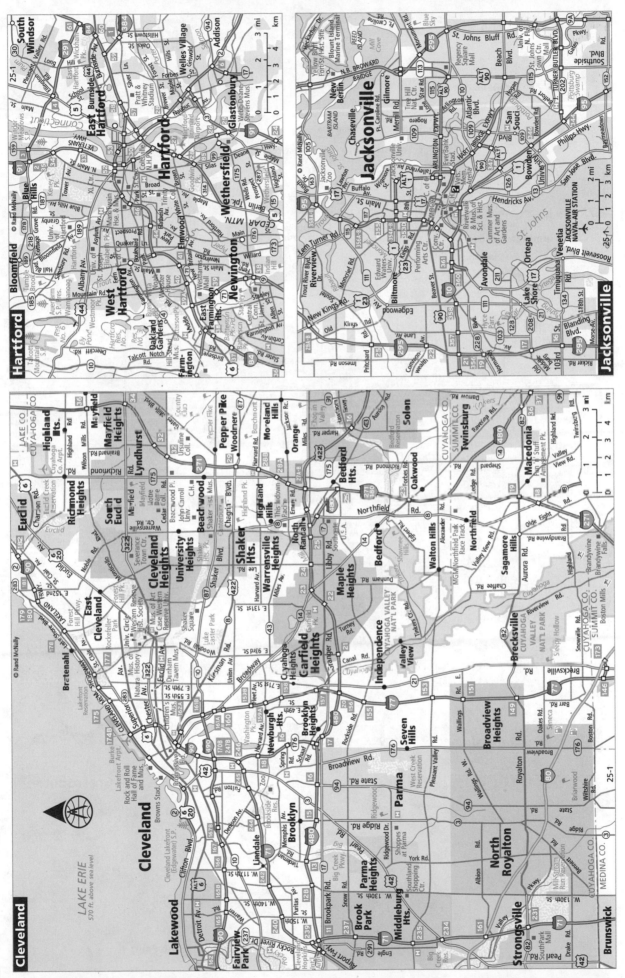

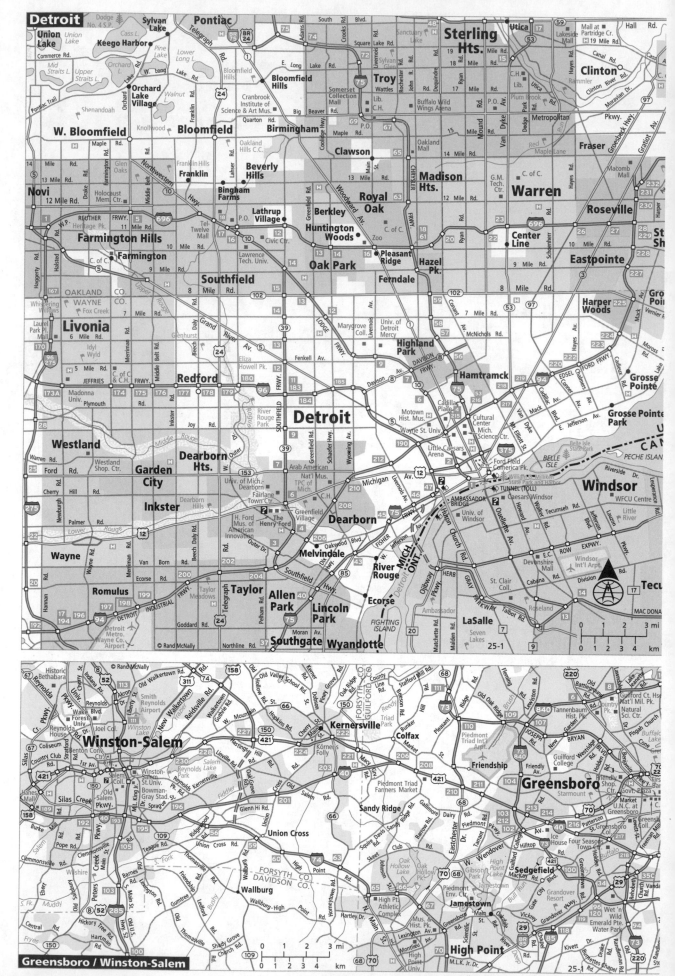

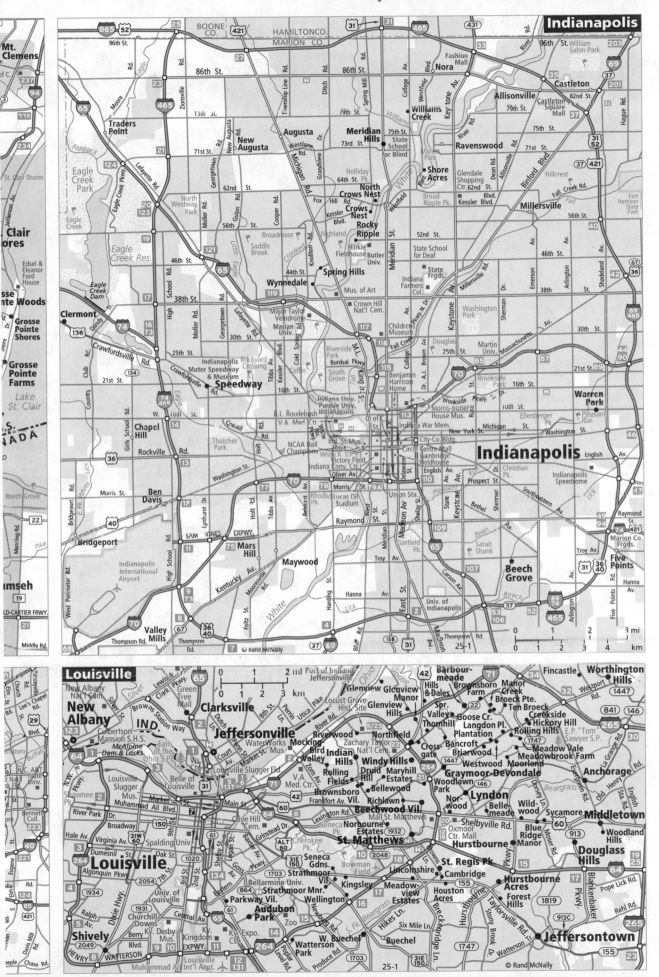

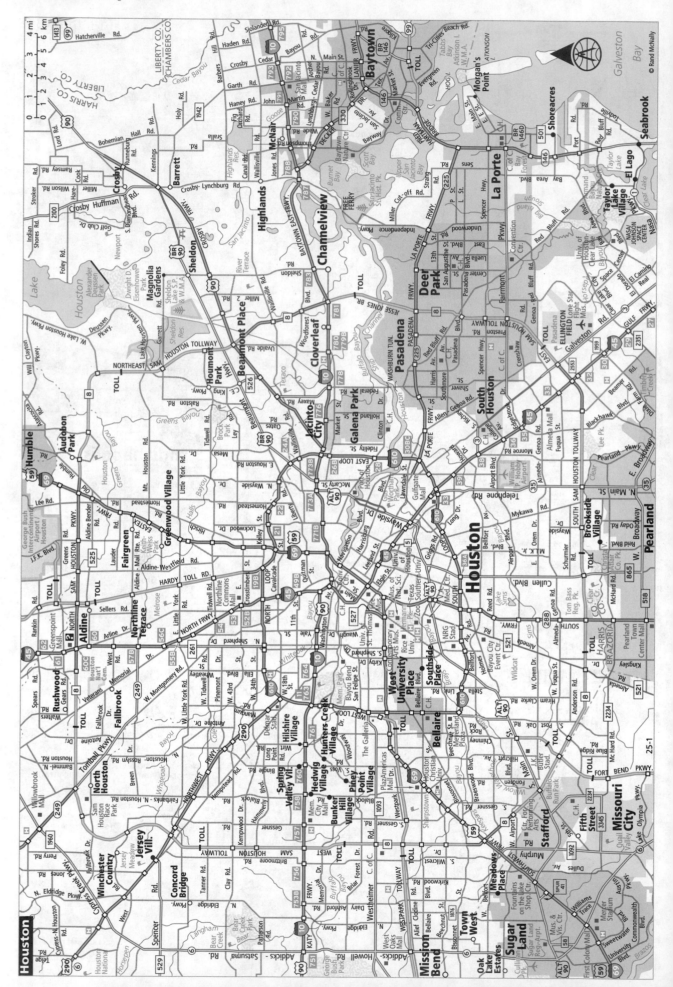

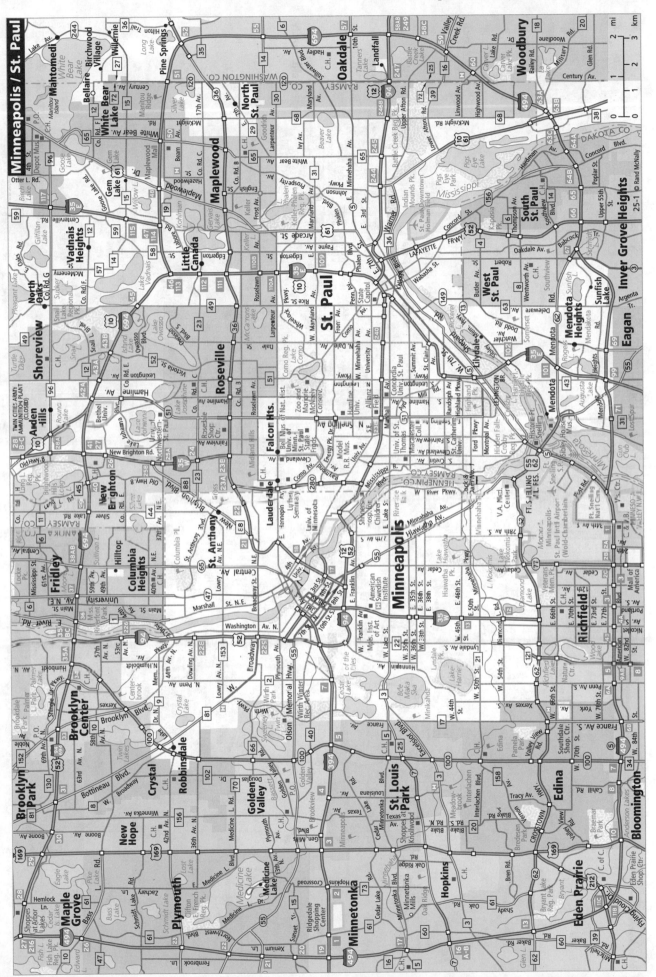

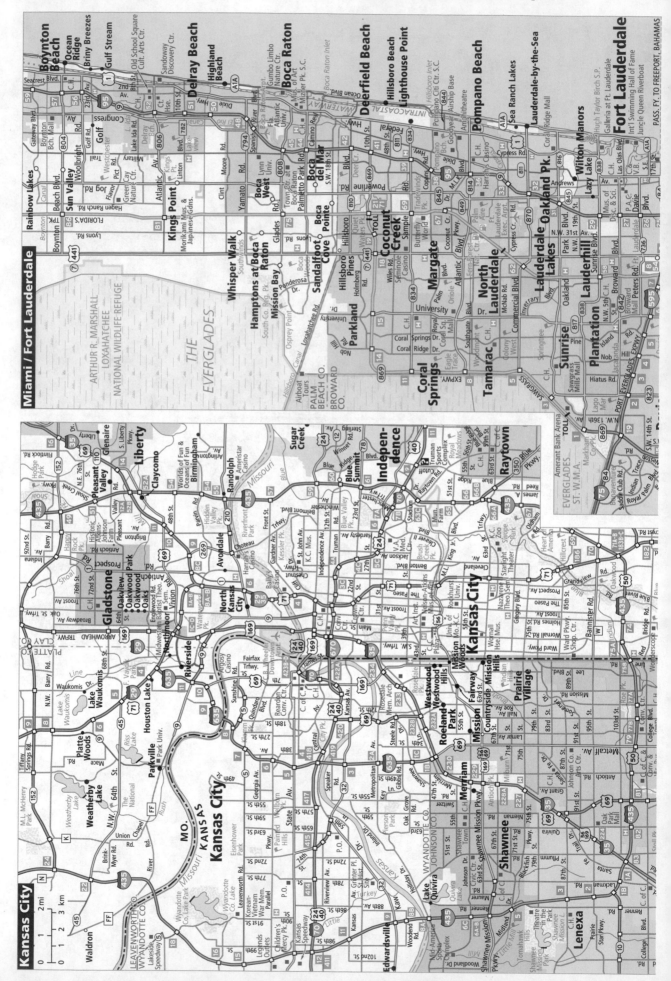

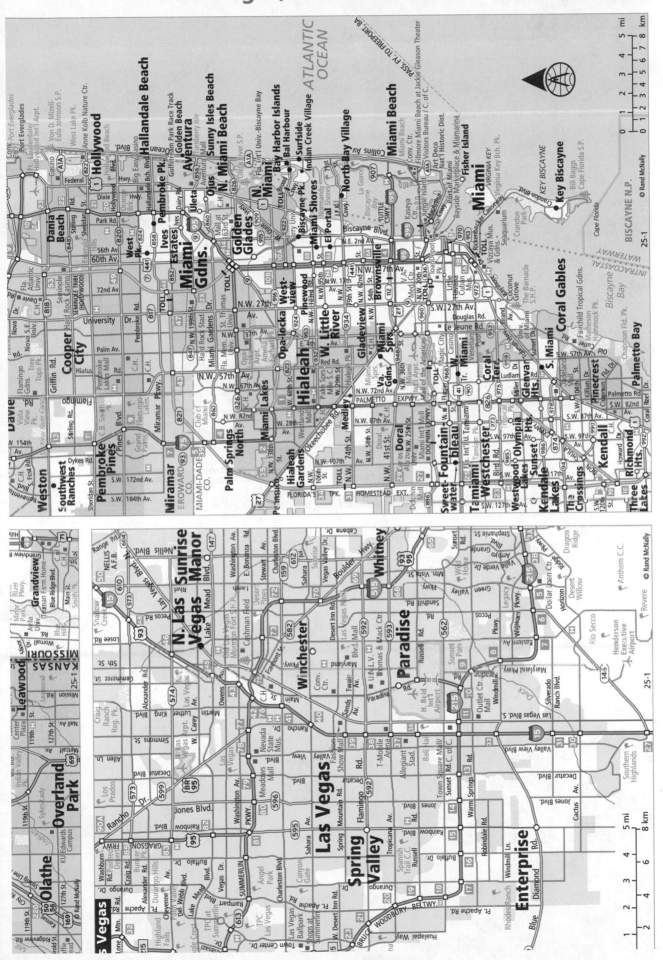

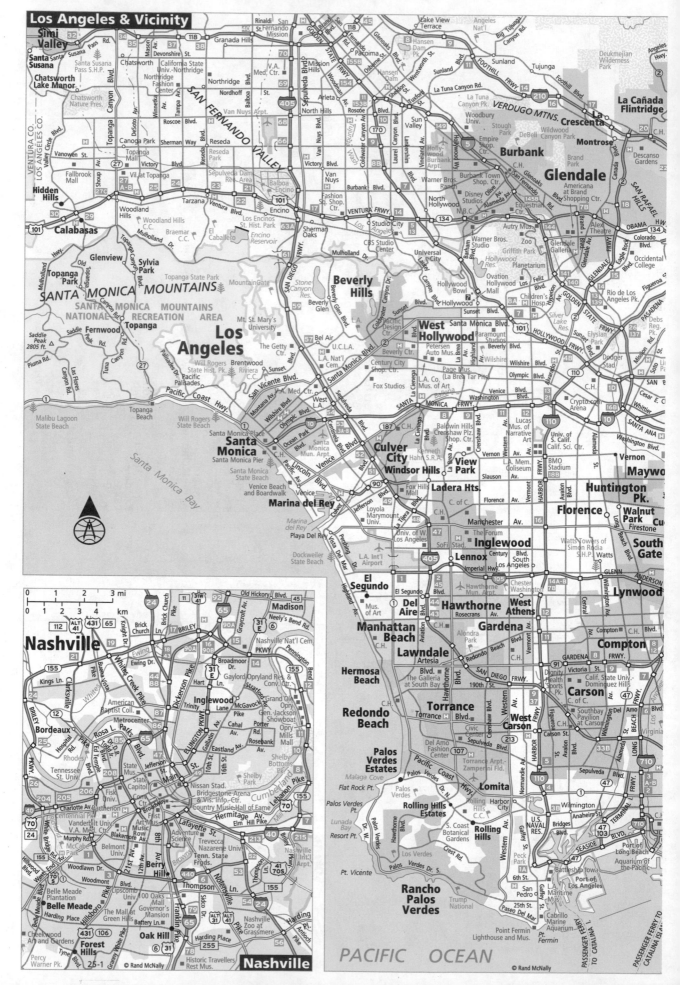

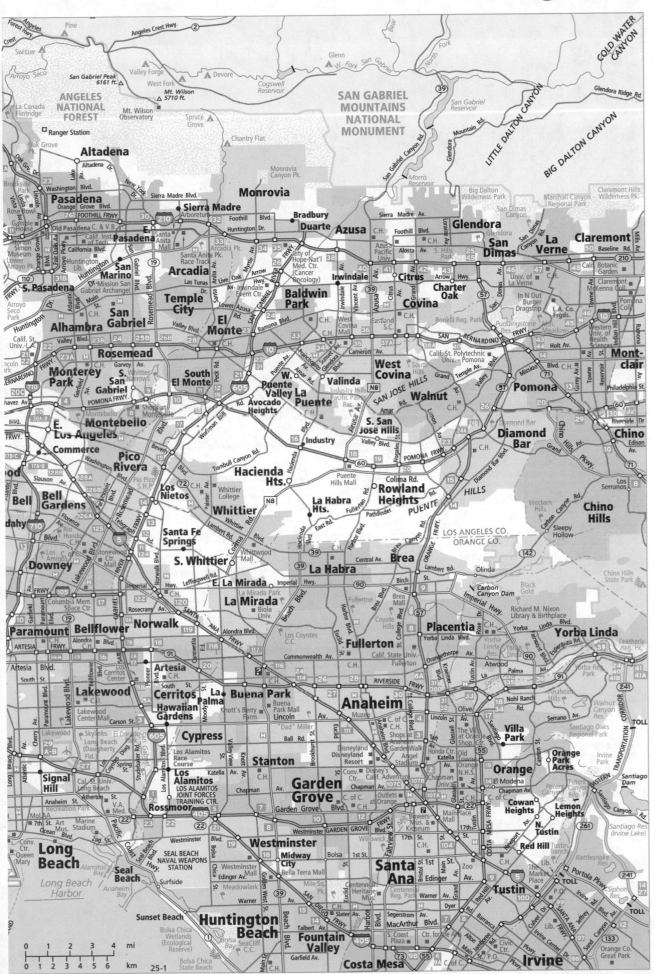

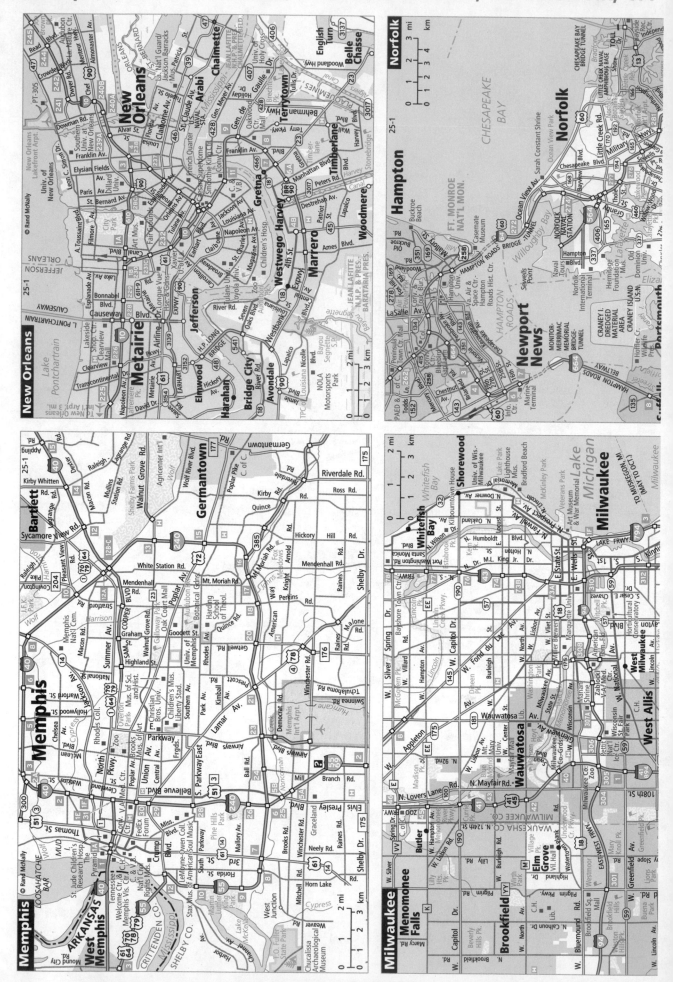

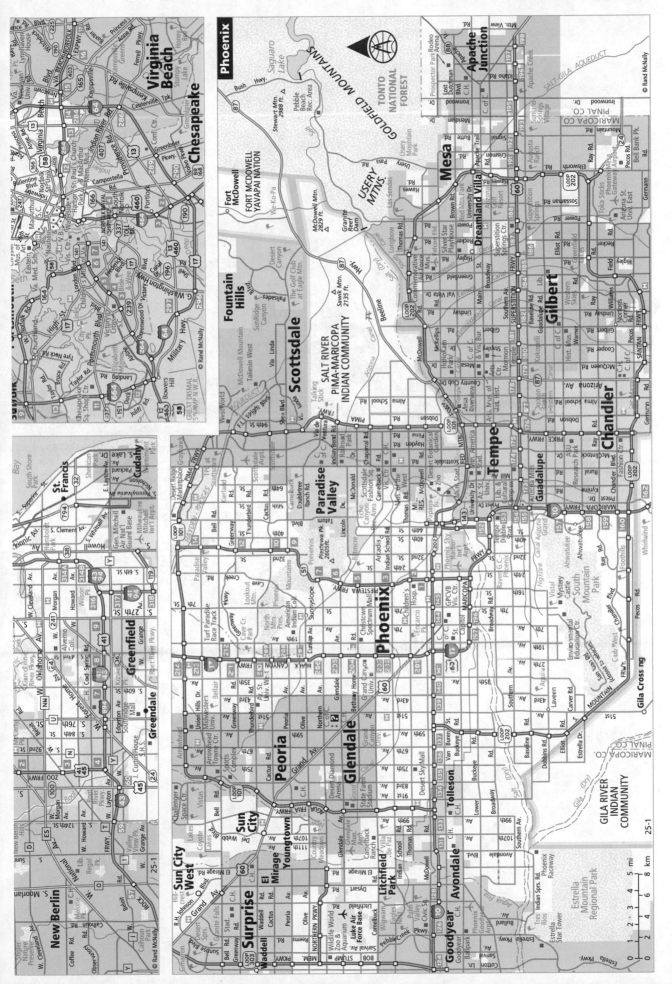

© Rand McNally

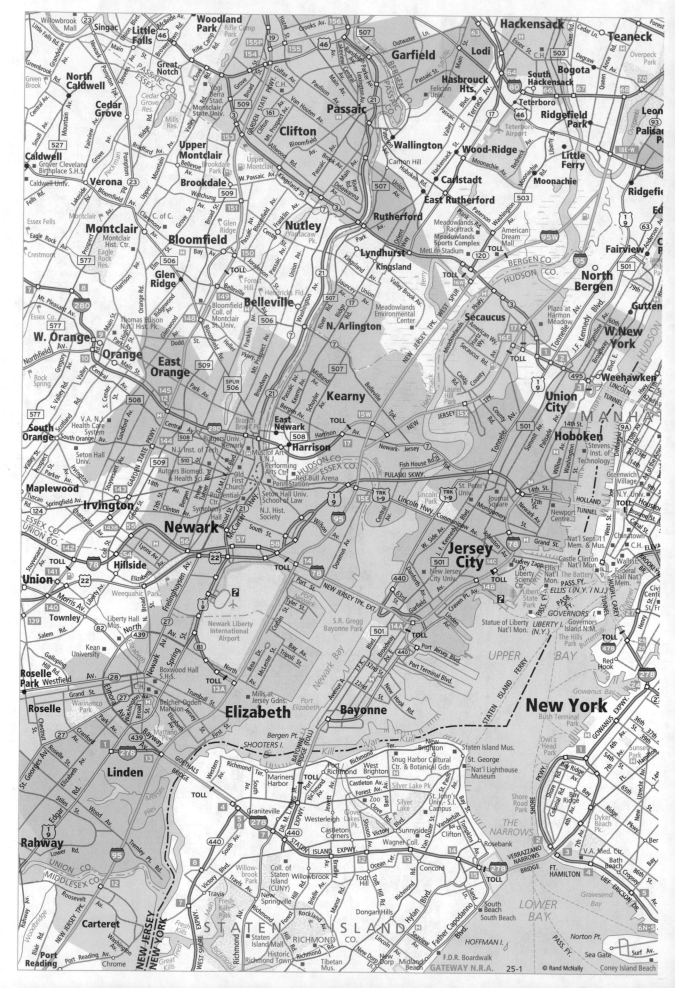

New York /
Newark
& Vicinity

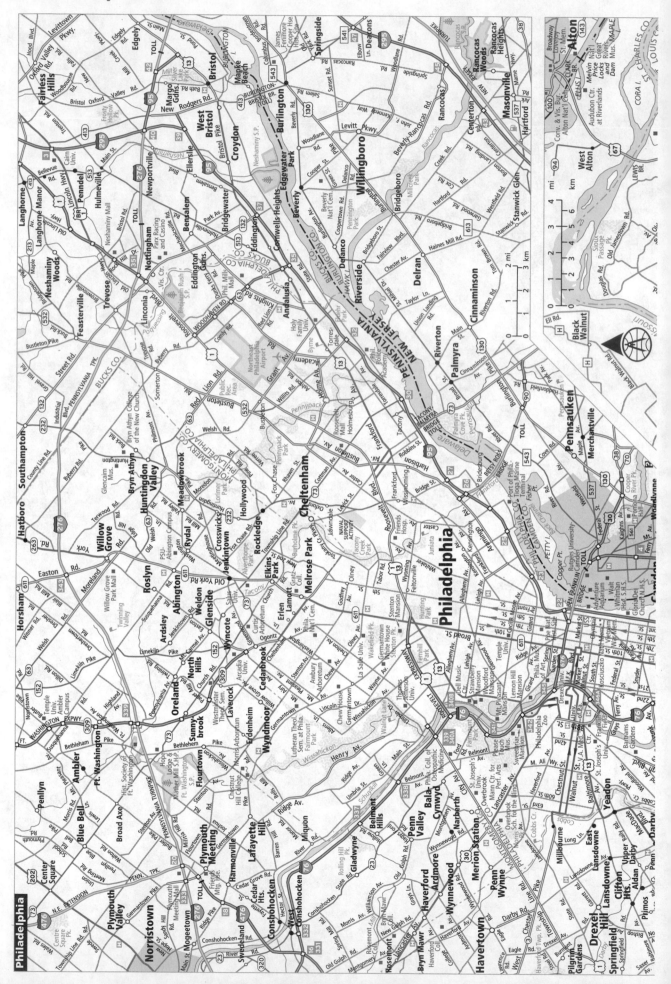

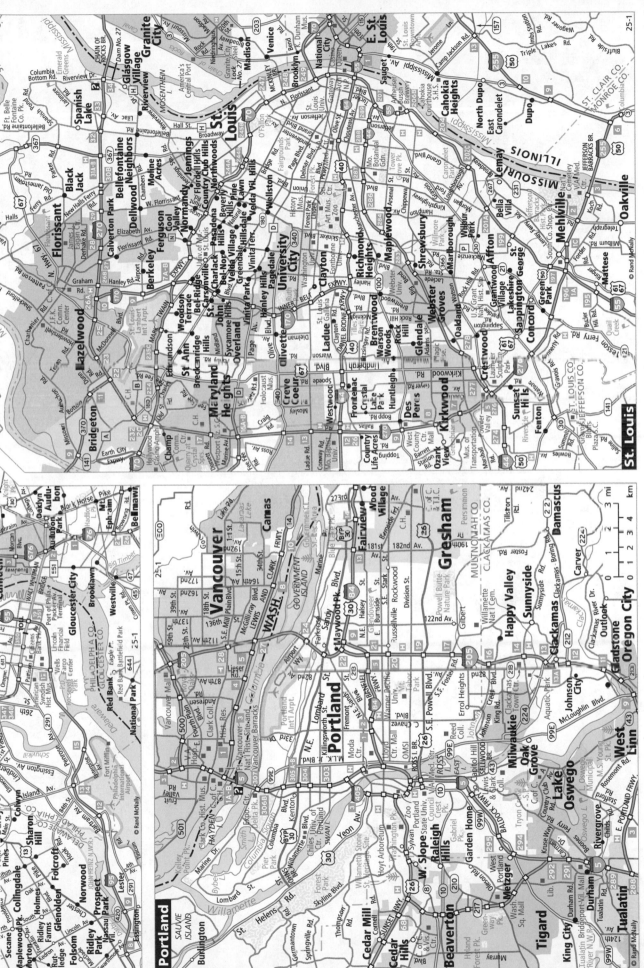

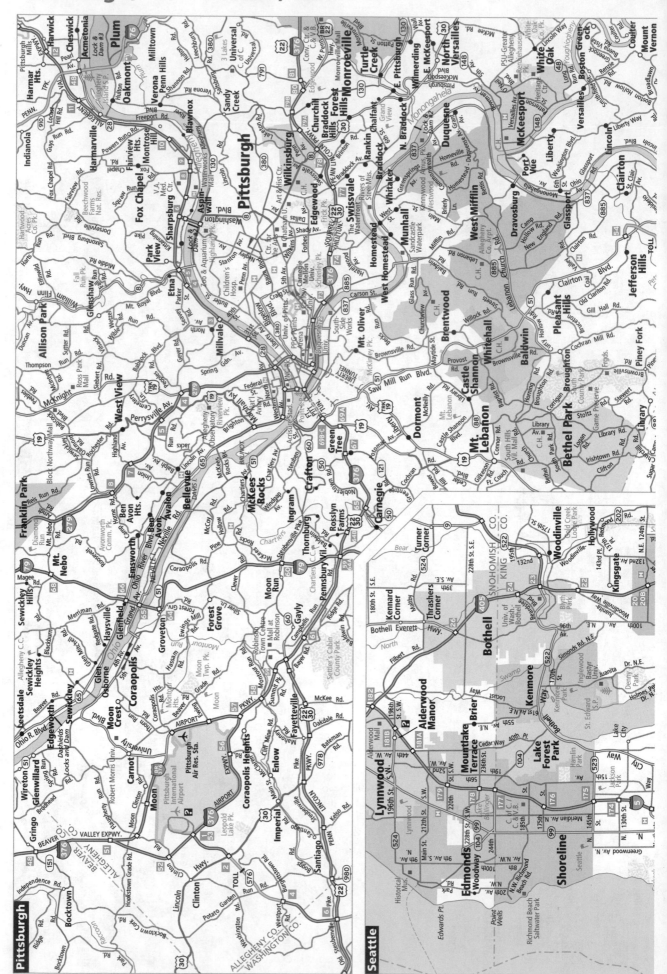

Pittsburgh

Seattle

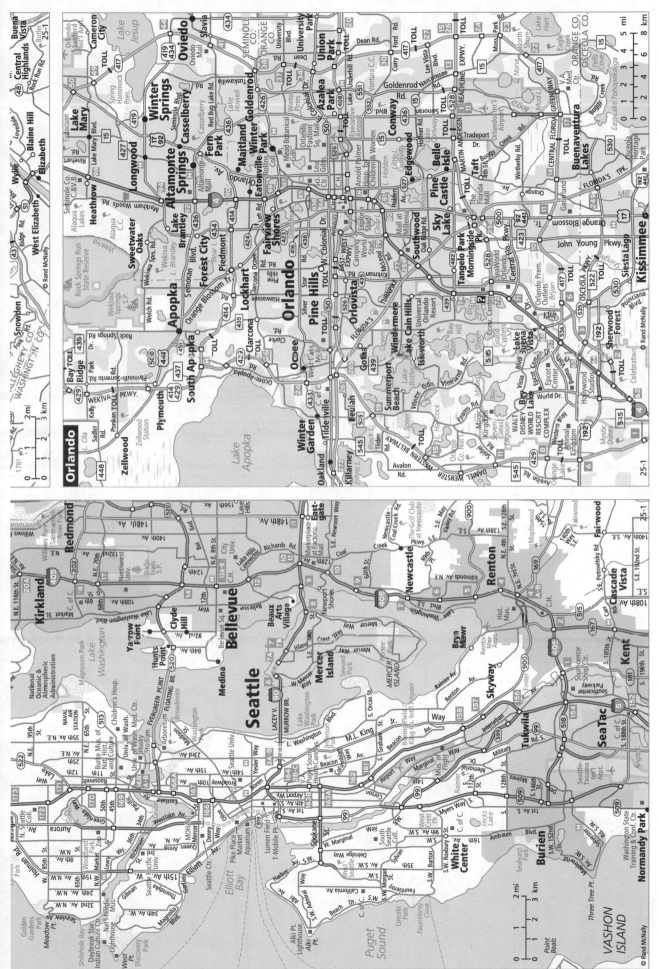

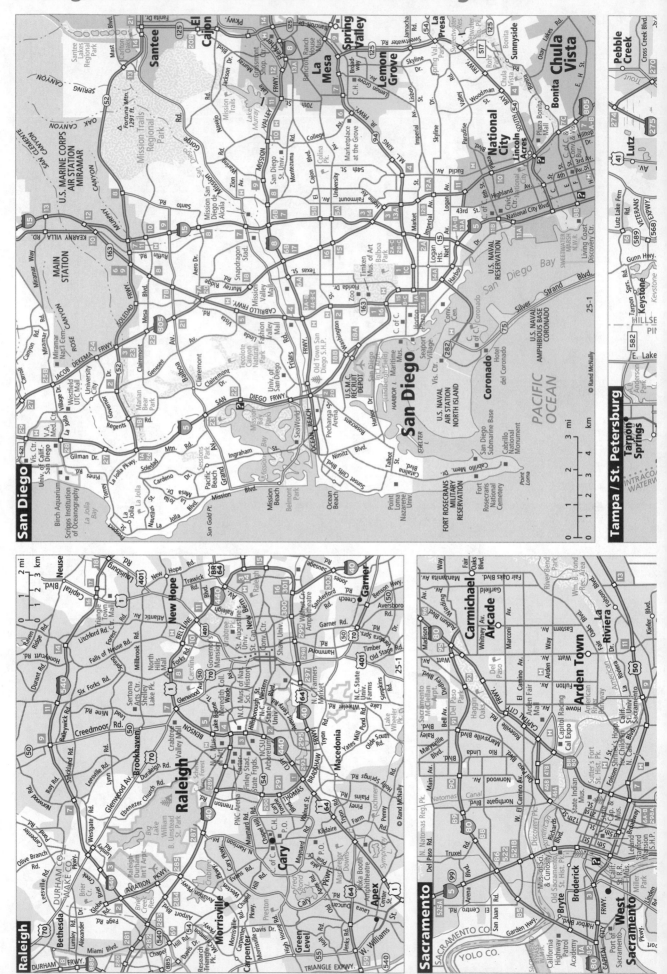

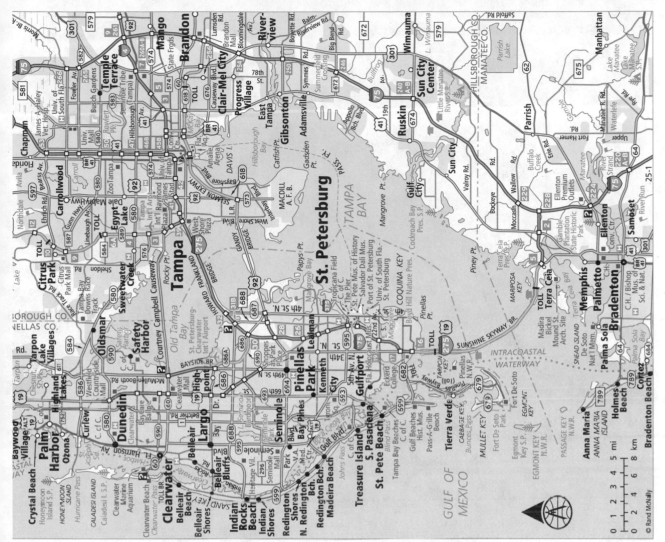

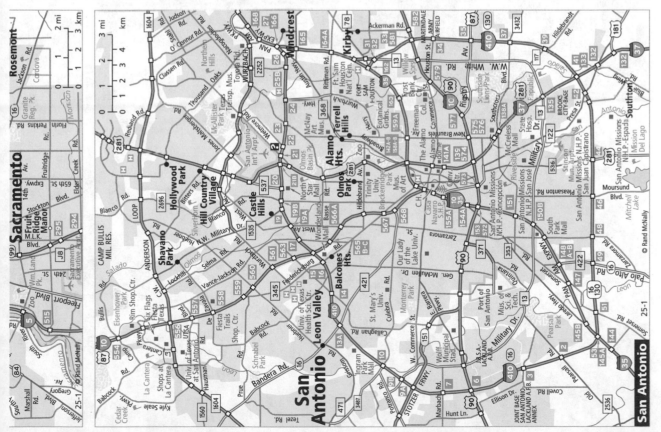

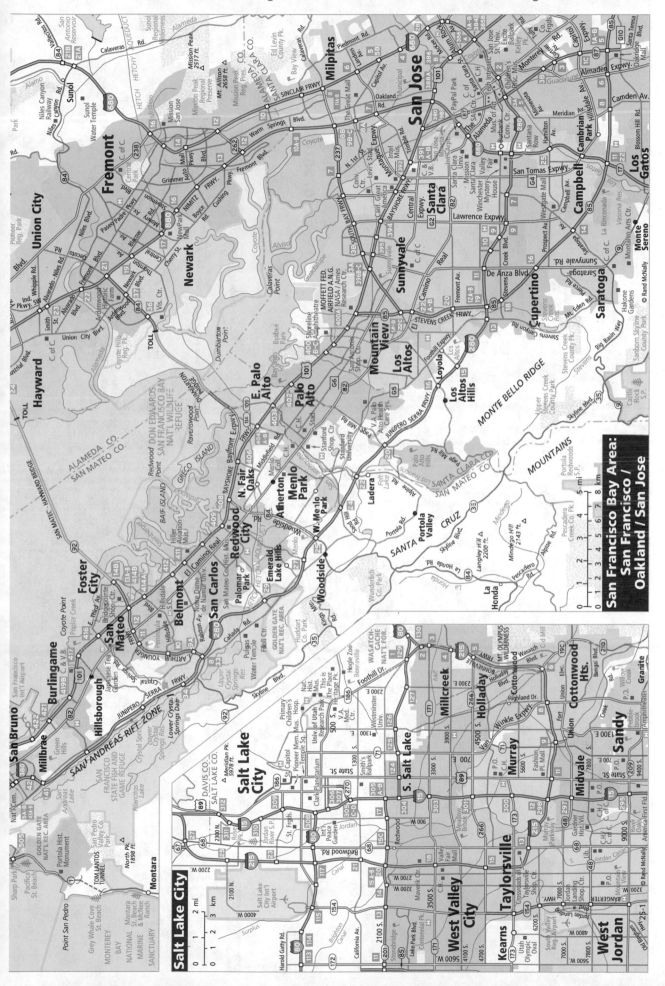

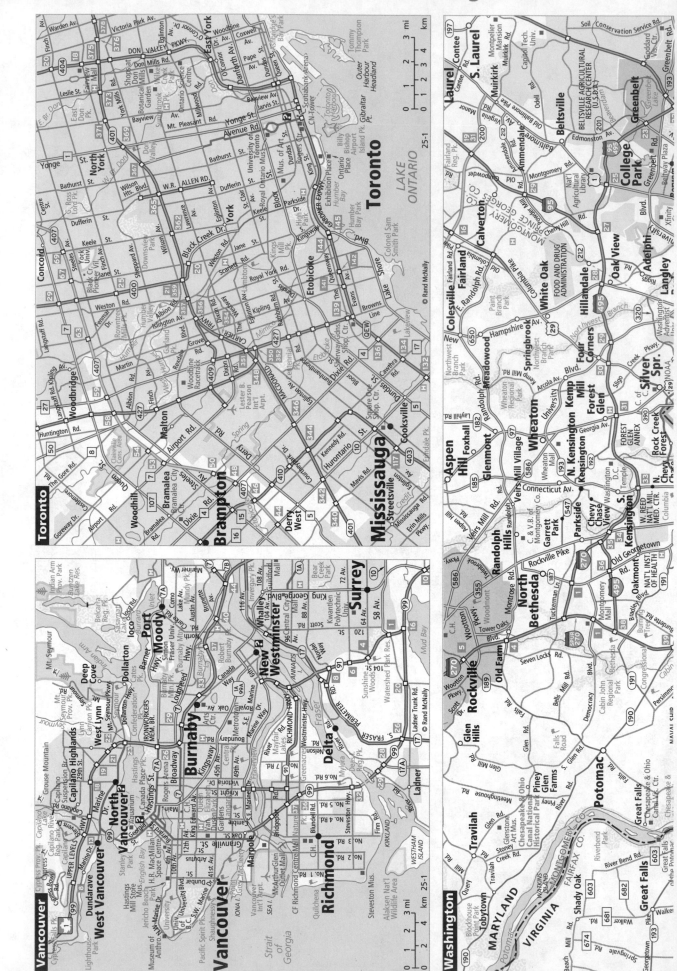

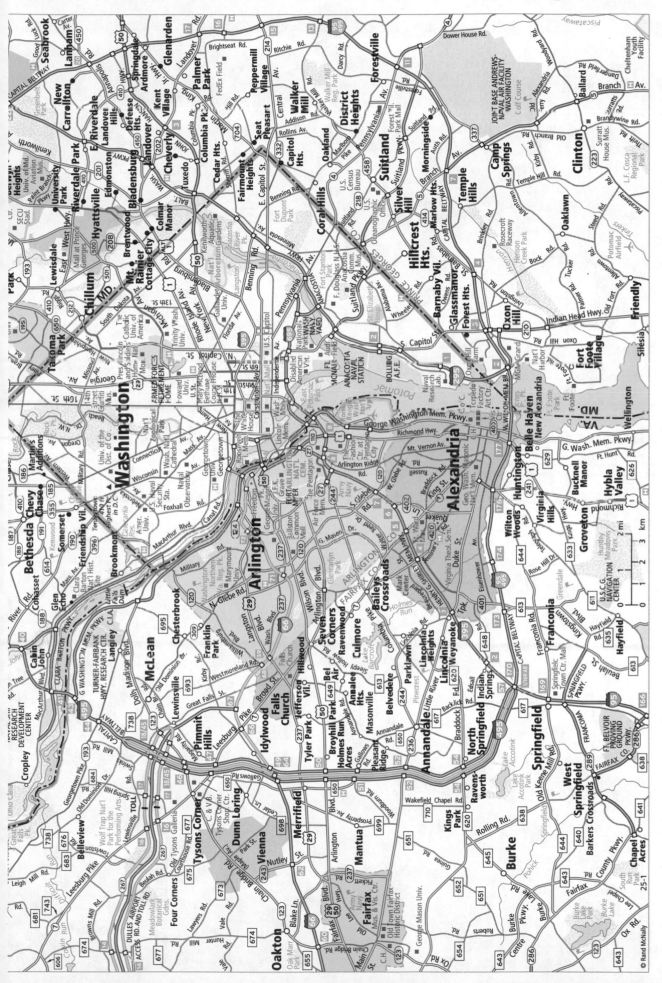

© Rand McNally